T'ang China

*Also by S.A.M. Adshead*

CHINA IN WORLD HISTORY

CENTRAL ASIA IN WORLD HISTORY

SALT AND CIVILIZATION

MATERIAL CULTURE IN EUROPE AND CHINA, 1400–1800

THE PHILOSOPHY OF RELIGION IN NINETEENTH-CENTURY ENGLAND

# T'ang China

## The Rise of the East in World History

S.A.M. Adshead

First published 2004 by
PALGRAVE MACMILLAN
Houndmills, Basingstoke, Hampshire RG21 6XS and
175 Fifth Avenue, New York, N.Y. 10010
Companies and representatives throughout the world

PALGRAVE MACMILLAN is the global academic imprint of the Palgrave Macmillan division of St. Martin's Press, LLC and of Palgrave Macmillan Ltd. Macmillan® is a registered trademark in the United States, United Kingdom and other countries. Palgrave is a registered trademark in the European Union and other countries.

ISBN 1-4039-3456-8 hardback
ISBN 1-4039-3457-6 paperback

This book is printed on paper suitable for recycling and made from fully managed and sustained forest sources.

A catalogue record for this book is available from the British Library.

Library of Congress Cataloging-in-Publication Data

Adshead, Samuel Adrian M. (Samuel Adrian Miles)
    T'ang China : The rise of the East in world history / S.A.M. Adshead.
        p.  cm.
    ISBN 1–4039–3456–8 (acid free) – ISBN 1–4039–3457–6
    (acid free : pbk.)
        1. China – History – Tang dynasty, 618–907.  2. Frank, Andre
    Gunder, 1929 – ReOrient.  3. International economic
    relations – History.  4. Capitalism – History.  5. Competition,
    International – History.  6. Economic history.  I. Title: Rise of the
    East in world history.  II. Title.

    DS749.35.A38  2004
    951'.017–dc22

                                                        2004046704

10   9   8   7   6   5   4   3   2   1
13  12  11  10  09  08  07  06  05  04

Transferred to digital printing in 2007.

To Robert Ferris

*Ferro non auro*

# Contents

# Preface

R.C. Zaehner, himself a scholar in Zoroastrianism, suspected Soviet spy, convert to Catholicism and Spalding Professor at Oxford, liked to quote the Hindu aphorism that the gods hate the obvious and love the obscure. Whatever may be thought of this dictum as divinity, its preferences are not to be recommended to authors. A book which combines polemic against a fellow academic, presentation from a comparative standpoint of a distant period of Chinese history, and prognosis about the future direction of the world order, clearly needs apology to establish its unity as an argument in the still young sub-discipline of world history. For concurrent with polemic, presentation and prognosis, this book, focused on the world around AD750, forms a prequel to my earlier forays into world history in China, Central Asia, Salt, Material Culture and Critical Theology. All its three elements are designed to contribute to the project which Joseph Fletcher called the interlocking of histories: not all histories or the whole of history, but a history and the whole in history.

First, the polemic. In 1999 I was asked by the *American Historical Review* to review Andre Gunder Frank's *Re-Orient: Global Economy in the Asian Age* published the previous year. For the reasons elaborated in Chapter 1 my overall judgement on Frank's thesis had to be negative. Yet I felt it demanded further response than was possible within the compass of a review, in the form of an alternative thesis regarding China's role in world history. I have been asked why I have chosen to append my own interpretation to what I regard as the mistaken view of Frank. My reply is that error is sometimes more fertile than truth. Errors, like truths, may be shallow or profound. The thesis advanced in Frank's book is, I believe, an error of the second character. Such books are not uncommon in history. Indeed history progresses by them. One thinks of Pirenne's *Muhammed and Charlemagne* and Tawney's *Religion and the Rise of Capitalism* or, in Chinese history, Wittfogel's *Oriental Despotism* or even Needham's *Science and Civilisation in China*. Their particular theses have had to be discarded in the light of further research, argument and reconceptualization. Nevertheless, their stimulus to the discipline has been greater than that of works which contain only shallower, less vulnerable truths. For the historian should not make Descartes' mistake of supposing that the indubitable is the true. On the contrary, the true, because of its range of assertions and denials, will always be highly dubitable, even if, despite improbability, with appropriate evidence it may still be affirmed with full conviction. The indubitable, on the other hand, is not the true, but the vacuous.

It is therefore the high quality of Frank's book which invites extended response. It is sure, moreover, to figure for many years in reading lists of courses in world history. Here it may find too uncritical reception among students still shaped by materialist reductionism, fashionable Sinophilia or anti-Occidentalism, and the outlook expressed in the Clintonian dictum of 'It's the economy, stupid'. My book aims to give students both a critique of Frank's book and a presentation of an alternative view. Like Ronald Knox in *Absolute and Abitophel*, I have no problem with puffing his sales if I may confound his views.

Second, presentation. To provide an alternative to Frank's view of the unalterable centrality of China in a world order conceived exclusively in economic terms, this book presents an account of the rise of the East, comparative to other major centres of civilization, in the T'ang period and its sixth-century antecedents. It argues that the rise was not only economic, but also political, social and intellectual, so that by the reign of emperor Hsüan-tsung (713–756), China had achieved a multiple preeminence similar to that of the United States today, though in a world order more loosely drawn than that of the present age of globalization. What is presented here is not the whole of T'ang history. It is a history of the T'ang from a comparative standpoint sufficient to show that the preeminence of China was both novel and based on a wide portfolio of performance in which the political and intellectual investments were the most profitable assets. Chinese historians have long thought that the reign of Hsüan-tsung marked one of the high points of their history, rivaled only by that of the Ch'ien-lung emperor (1735–1799) under the Ch'ing. This book provides additional justification for their enthusiasm from the new and more universal perspective of world history. T'ang history, it may be argued, should be part of everyone's history as a credit to the species and not merely to a people.

The presentation of T'ang history in the context of my debate with Frank may also serve as a prequel to my earlier work in world history. Since its inception, most notably by William H. McNeill's *The Rise of the West* (1963), now happily repristinated by the son and father team J.R. McNeill and William H. McNeill's *The Human Web: A Bird's Eye View of World History* (2003), the proper field of world history has been variously interpreted. On the one hand, it has been interpreted holistically as the quintessence of human history: for example in materialist or neo-Darwinian versions, though Teilhard de Chardin's *Phenomenon of Man* and *Man's Place in Nature* indicate that these terms are far from synonymous. On the other hand, it has been interpreted analytically as relationship between parts, for example, the study of contact between the major civilizations and the making of comparisons between them at equivalent points in their development, as has been done successfully by the Minnesota school headed by Edward L. Farmer or in recent studies of energy, consumerism and particular commodities. This approach was given a further, prospective dimension by the influential work of Samuel P. Huntington *The Clash of Civilizations and the Remaking of the World Order* (1996) whose predictions have seemingly been confirmed by subsequent events, notably Nine Eleven. That day has been seized on by commentators as marking a turning point in world history though historians will share Andrew Robert's reservation of judgement during a television panel.

Both these interpretations, the holistic and the analytic, have their legitimacy in demarcating world history from other kinds of history: national, regional, local, individual or thematic. Both may produce good work. There is true history but no absolute history. Both interpretations should be judged heuristically by their fruitfulness in promoting an effective and fully professional subdiscipline in historical science. It is with this end in view that I have proposed that the proper field of world history should be the study of world institutions. By these I understand institutions which were or are active in two or more of the world's four primary civilizations: Western Eurasia, East Asia, Black Africa and pre Columbian America. For, unlike Samuel P. Huntington, I do not think civilizations should be multiplied without necessity. Constituted only at the base by ecology, language, script and high culture, for purposes of historical analysis the fewer the better. Moreover, I do not think that a division between

Europe and Asia is a useful one for long-term historical analysis. Consequently, Nine Eleven should be seen not as a clash of civilizations, but a clash within a civilization, or, perhaps, thanks to globalization, within civilization.

If the proper field of world history is the study of world institutions, then the world order may be conceived as the aggregate of such institutions at a given moment. Its level of globalization may be gauged by, on the one hand, their degree of integration, and, on the other, by their relative dominance over other, non-global institutions. Following Joseph Fletcher, I have argued that the ongoing world institutions which constitute the modern world order came into existence in the thirteenth century in the wake of the Mongol invasions. These invasions temporarily unified large parts of East Asia and Western Eurasia and indirectly affected Black Africa and eventually pre-Columbian America. The Mongol invasions were the big bang of world history. From it emerged the three foundational world institutions: the basic information circuit in the exchange between Western Eurasia and East Asia of the elements of each other's geography and history; the microbian common market, as it was called by E. Le Roy Ladurie, in the unification of the disease patterns of East Asia and Western Eurasia; and the global arsenal in the merging of separate equestrian styles, the adoption across Eurasia of composite armies of horse, foot and artillery and the articulation of transoceanic seapower beginning with the voyages of Cheng Ho. Further world institutions appeared in early modernity: the religious internationals in the Naqshbandiyya, the Gelugspa and the Society of Jesus; the world market in bullion, commodities and capital with its successive headquarters in Seville, Amsterdam, London and New York; and the secular republic of letters and sciences, adumbrated first in the world of the Timurids. Next, three more world institutions took shape after 1800: the higher polytechnic created by successive industrial revolutions; the common political consensus in what we rather misleadingly call democracy and might better call constitutional government: and the consumerist patina, mind mattering in food, dress, shelter and leisure, late medieval in origin, but generalized by industrial technology and the rise of what Gilles Lipovetsky has called the empire of the ephemeral. Finally, in our own day, associated with the Anglophone overlay, the continuous rise since 1500 of the percentage of world population speaking English at least as a second language, there has been the convergence in communications which, by making information the ultimate resource in peace and war, has integrated the other world institutions to a new degree, and in what Philip Bobbitt has called the International super infrastructure, has laid the foundations for a global civilization, a true cosmopolis, to use Bernard Lonergan's term. Thus the world order builds itself anew on its earliest stratification, the basic information circuit.

Though ongoing world institutions, and with them world history, only began in the thirteenth century, they were preceded by temporary, non-enduring, world institutions whose coexistence created world orders, albeit more loosely textured and less dominant than that occasioned by the Mongolian explosion. One such institution was T'ang cosmopolitanism: the intense interest in things and people foreign exhibited by the court at Ch'ang-an, which, along with the attractions of China, brought an unprecedented influx of non-Chinese to the Middle Kingdom, both from other parts of East Asia and from Western Eurasia. T'ang cosmopolitanism was a distant anticipation of the consumerist patina. It was rooted in the intellectual register but it had repercussions in politics, economics and society. It was accompanied by military interventions by Chinese forces in territories beyond East Asia: in northern India, Persia, Transoxiania, the Himalayan interface, and parts of Southeast Asia still more Indianized than Sinified. Chinese consumer goods, notably ceramics, reached the eastern coast of Black Africa. Chinese accidental voyagers may have travelled along the Kurosiwo current via the Aleutians and the North Pacific drift to the pre-Columbian America, though no Chinese Columbus returned to report on the Inside Passage from Juneau to Seattle. T'ang cosmopolitanism reached out to the world to an extent only paralleled in Chinese history by what has been happening in post-Maoist China as portrayed recently by David Zweig's *Internationalizing China: Domestic Interests and Global Linkages* (2002).

T'ang cosmopolitanism coexisted with four other temporary world institutions: the Indo-European expansion, then at its greatest extent before its reflux before the counter thrusts of the Semitic and Altaic languages; the Buddhist ecumene which funnelled Chinese to Central Asia and India and Central Asians and Indians to China and supplied in Sanscrit the major learned lingua franca of the day; the Universal caliphate, which, before its disruption by the Abbasids, provided a cultural common market for the diffusion of Chinese science and technology to the West; and the Nestorian connection which, having been forced to relocate from Syria to Persia by the council of Ephesus, became the most missionary of Christianities, a vector of Iranian secular culture to the T'ang court and a source of more than one of East Asia's alphabets. In the world order created by the coexistence of these world institutions, T'ang cosmopolitanism acted as the keystone in the arch because of the preeminence of China in so many fields: political, economic, social and intellectual. This situation, it may be thought, has some analogy with the world order as it currently exists at the beginning of the twenty-first century. To borrow a phrase from Barbara W. Tuchman, the eighth century was a distant mirror of our own time.

Such unicentric world orders may be termed hegemonic in contrast with other, multicentric situations where preeminence in politics, economics, society and the intellect might lie in different locations. Thus in the mid-Victorian era, while political and economic paramountcy might belong to industrial Britain, meritocratic France might lay claim to greatest social progress, and Germany with its many universities be accorded intellectual priority. Hegemonic moments in the history of the world order, that is the aggregate of world institutions, have been rare. They are not to be confused with the political preponderancies which may or may not accompany them. Thus while T'ang diplomacy embraced the basileus, the Shah, the Caliph, Turkish *khagans* and various maharajahs, and T'ang armies were deployed beyond the confines of East Asia, there was no *Pax Sinica* in the eighth century comparable to the *Pax Americana* of the twenty-first. Conversely, political preponderances, even if global in scope, need not be associated with hegemony in the world order. Thus the *pax Hispanica*, the planetary empire of Philip II, though like the T'ang, international in its personnel as has been recently demonstrated by Henry Kamen, could at most claim preeminence for its politics at Madrid and society at Valladolid, while economic preeminence rested with Antwerp or Genoa, and intellectual preeminence in spirituality, science, art and music focused on Rome. So hegemony and preponderance are things dissociable. If hegemonic world orders are rare, hegemonic world orders combined with political preponderance are even rarer. Indeed, it may be regarded as one of the novelties of our time so there must be raised the question whether this unique conjuncture, whose origins remain to be explored, can continue.

Third, prognosis, prompted both by this current singularity and by Frank's prediction of a remanifestation of Sinocentrism both in the world order, and, it would seem, in political predominance. Prognosis does not come naturally to historians. They are too aware of the contingency, indeterminism, whylessness and insufficiency of reason of the course of events to suppose the past offers much guidance to the future. Historians must follow Popper in rejecting historicism, whether scientific or romantic. Nevertheless, a historian may imitate the historicist if only to show that there are plausible alternatives to his prognoses, so that the future is at least open. For Frank, on the other hand, the future is not open. Where the economy goes, indeed where bullion goes, everything goes: politics, society and intellect. Moreover political predominance must follow from world-order hegemony. The balance of all kinds of power will shift to China, if indeed it has ever really left it.

The alternative scenario outlined in the last section of this book is that, if the level of globalization (in the sense of the degree of integration of world institutions and of their impact on other institutions) continues to rise, then the national or regional shifts in where the centre of the world order lies may become anachronistic. If information becomes both the first and final resource, then the centre will simply be where the maximum of information is temporarily mobilized: a moment in time rather than a point in space, a when without a where. In such a despatialized world order the centre will be everywhere and nowhere in what J.R. McNeill has named a state of complex sameness. The internet heaven requires no temple. Consequently it will make no sense to ask whether it is in Washington, Moscow, Beijing or São Paulo. The world order will be an Indra's net of mutually reflecting faceted jewels: what the Avatamsaka philosophy of T'ang China called the Tower of Maitreya and characterized as *shih-shih wu-ai*, the non-obstruction of relations between realities. Similarly, if political predominance, as Philip Bobbitt has predicted, becomes a function of the world order and access to its information, then it too will lose its spatial identity and become a series of *ad hoc* alliances of the willing. Such an outcome, the product of the current simultaneous hegemony and preponderance of the United States, might be regarded less as the supersession of the West than its universalization. For a global scenario where sight rather than might is right, could hardly subsist without the political institutions of the common consensus of Western constitutional government. The T'ang period is a distant mirror of our current selves: it too was threatened by overextension abroad and antiglobalization at home: but it does not have to be an image of our future.

Whatever may be thought of these speculations, it will be sufficient if prognosis reinforces polemic and presentation in underlining our contention that China's relative position in the world order has not been constant, as Frank would have us believe. It has changed as the world order has changed and as China itself has changed. Five emperors in Chinese history consciously addressed the problem, or opportunity, of China's relationship with the wider world, but they conceived it in quite different terms. Han Wu-ti (140–87BC), aware of China's provinciality, reached out to the more developed West through embassies, road-building and the export of silk. T'ang Hsüan-tsung (713–756) could be confident of China's centrality and hegemony, but nevertheless welcomed the outside world, enlisted its élites as De La Vaissière (2002) has shown, and used what it had to offer to embellish the Middle Kingdom. Khubilai of the Yüan (1260–1294), Marco Polo's 'the mightiest man from Adam our first parent down to the present moment', saw his two Chinas, Cathay and Manzi, as the storehouse of a Eurasian Chinggisid consortium. The Yung-lo emperor of the Ming (1402–1424), inspired by a desire to emulate Khubilai and by Manichaean ecumenism inherited from his dynasty's sectarian origins, pursued an active *Weltpolitik* of diplomatic accommodation with Timurid Central Asia by land and naval initiative to outflank it by sea, in the Muslim moment of Chinese history. Ch'ien-lung of the Ch'ing (1735–1799), alternately confident and anxious, always conscious that his power within the wall depended on his power beyond it, opted eventually not for a *Weltpolitik*, but for an East Asian empire of the five scripts, *wu-wen* – Manchu, Mongolian, Tibetan, Chinese and Arabic – as the best means to minimize enemies and maximize friends. All these rulers in their different contexts witness to the theme of this book, the creativity of China, which never manifested itself more brightly than in its period, the rise of the East.

Many people have contributed to this book directly and indirectly. Every author must echo Henry Ford in ascribing any achievement to others. Here I will only single out Professor Michael Lee for recommending me for a research fellowship at the University of Reading, for whose library services I am especially grateful. Special thanks are also due to Simon and Carol Sizer without whom this book would not have seen the light of day. It is dedicated, however, with gratitude and affection, to the person who first brought us to the village.

S.A.M. ADSHEAD

*Mortimer Common*
*All Saints 2003*

# 1
# Polemic: Before the Rise of the East

The argument is about changes in preeminence between the main centres of civilization and the reasons for them. What is argued for is an acceptance of both systemic and singular reasons for such changes and a recognition of their interdependence. Although the book opens with a polemic and concludes with a prognosis, the argument is pursued in a period: the rise of the East between 500 and 1000AD, in particular the reign in China of the T'ang emperor Hsüan-tsung 713–756. The T'ang period should be recognized as a significant part of everyone's history, for it provided not only one of the most illustrious epochs of Chinese and East Asian history – one of Hsüan-tsung's epithets was Ming Huang, the brilliant emperor – but it also supplied material for later borrowing by the West, which, more than renaissances of its own classical past, eventually restored it to global ascendancy. Under the T'ang, China, partly from foreign, even global, resources, notably Buddhist, remade itself and made possible the remaking of the West. Bacon's three Chinese contributions to civilization: print, gunpowder and magnetic navigation, all originated in late antiquity. So too did other significant physical technologies: successive basin solar evaporation for salt, co-fusion steel, proto-porcelain, chemical therapies and clockwork; paralleled in social technology by civil service examinations, fiscality based on indirect taxation, medical colleges and official pharmacopeias. China in the reign of Hsüan-tsung held a preeminence similar to that of the United States today. His capital Ch'ang-an, of which Sian is a shrunken remnant, was a Washington and a New York rolled into one, with a dash of West Coast too. It was a magnet alike for poli-

1

tics, economy, society and intellect. It was the centre of the world order.

The preeminence of China under the T'ang raises questions as to how it arose and whether it will return. Here the polemic and the prognosis are engaged. The polemic, hopefully respectful and certainly admiring, is directed against part of Andre Gunder Frank's *Re-Orient: Global Economy in the Asian Age* (University of California, Berkeley, 1998). Frank would not accept a rise of the East in the period 500–1000, because he believes that the East, China in particular, was always central to the world order, at least since 3000BC. Consequently, it could not rise. Moreover, he believes that centrality can be explained purely in systemic terms without regard to singularity, that is localized conditions, what he calls exceptionality. My polemic therefore contends that in AD500, the East was in some senses inferior to the West and that its subsequent rise requires singular as well as systemic factors for its explanation. My middle chapters will then explore the rise and its reasons in politics, economy, society and intellect, placing the emphasis on the first and the last in the causal network. Finally, following a survey of the return to the West after AD1000, the prognosis, from the standpoint of the analysis of the preceding rise, concurs with the opinion of another eminent authority, Chris Patten, in his *East and West: The last Governor of Hong Kong on Power, Freedom and the Future* (Macmillan, London, 1998). Patten argues that in the short and middle term, it is unlikely that the East, China in particular, will replace the West as the centre of civilization. His reasons are systemic rather than singular, which is appropriate since globalization is now more intense than it was in the world of late antiquity. He deflates Asian values, downplays the uniqueness of China, and emphasizes universal factors, such as plural politics, market economics and the rule of law, which, while they may have found their first expressions in the West, are not neccessarily alien to the East, as Amartya Sen has also suggested. Indeed these factors are the basis of the embryonic world system of today. Nevertheless, even in the future, idiosyncrasy, exceptionalisms and the unique parameter will have their part to play in a world order which must always comprise both system and singularity. Such a duality, indeed, is a condition of the openness of the future, as it has been of the contingency of the past. Hilaire Belloc's Byzantine official who, at the beginning of the seventh century, weighed every factor but was unaware of the imminent maturity of Muhammed, remains to mock our systemic calculations in prognosis.

The present chapter falls into three sections: first, an exposition of Frank's concept of the world order; second, a critique of that conception; third, from the standpoint of that critique, an account of the preponderance of the West in the prior half of the first Christian millennium. This forms the preamble to the examination of the rise of the East after AD500 in the subsequent chapters.

## Frank's concept of the world order

Although Frank does not do this, it will be convenient in what follows to distinguish world order, world interconnections, world institutions, world network, and world system. World order is least precise and most inclusive. It denotes any set of global contacts, however tenuous, whether arising from geology, climate, genetics or human activity. Thus conceived, it exists, like God in Anselm's onto-logical argument, almost necessarily. It is at least a reasonable assumption if there is a world at all. World interconnections are less presumptive and more specific. They refer to the minimum con-stituents of a world order, as, for example, the genetic unity of humankind, dating back to 100,000BC, described recently by Luigi Luca Cavalli-Sforza.[1] World institutions are more specific again and less abstract. In two earlier books I have described their emergence since the thirteenth century and given them functional names: the basic information circuit, the microbian common market, the global arsenal, the republic of letters, the religious international, the world market, the higher polytechnic and the common consensus. To these might be added an Anglophone overlay and further superor-dinates await identification by experts in sport, youth culture and consumerism. Other world institutions existed once but no longer: the Indo-European expansion, the Zoroastrian revelation, the Achaemenid and Macedonian world empire, the Buddhist ecumene, T'ang cosmopolitanism, the Universal Caliphate and the Nestorian connection; though the Buddhist ecumene may only be in eclipse. A world network is the coexistence of several world institutions and, depending on their strength, some interaction between them. Finally, a world system is a full panoply of strong world institutions integrated to greater or less extent to produce further convergence and coalescence, even though such globalization need not be regarded as all-powerful or irreversible. If a world order may be presumed, it is not clear that a world system in this strong sense – as opposed to interconnections, institutions, network – does yet exist. With these distinctions in mind, we may now approach Frank's concept of the world order. It may be summarized in six propositions:

*First*, using the above distinctions, for Frank, the world order is systemic. It is more than interconnections or a network. Both now and far into the past, it is a system in a strong sense: integrated, autonomous, not depending on anything outside itself, almost an absolute. Though a product of human activity, it has escaped the control of its creators. Nothing falls outside it, nothing falls through its mesh, so that at times its author seem less Frank than Frankenstein!

*Second*, the system is holistic. Frank is insistent on this. He refers to 'the canon of holism', for the principle is both methodological and thematic.[2] Thus in his introduction he writes:

> To find the really germane factors in economic, social, and cultural 'development', we must look holistically at the whole global sociocultural, ecological-economic, and cultural system, which itself both offers and limits the 'possibilities' of all of us. Since the whole is more than the sum of its parts and itself shapes its constituent parts, no amount of study and/or assemblage of the parts can ever lay bare the structure, functioning and transformation of the whole world economy/system.[3]

By holistic is meant that the system is not only all-encompassing, but is the universal cause of everything else. Unlike other world-order theorists, such as Fernand Braudel and Immanuel Wallerstein for whom the world order is one agent among many, and not necessarily the most commanding, for Frank it is the sole agent. Consider the following passage from the Introduction where the brackets are Frank's: 'There is no way we can understand and account for what happened in Europe or the Americas without taking account of what happened in Asia and Africa – and vice versa – nor what happened anywhere without identifying the structure and dynamic of the whole world (system) itself.'[4] Subsequently, in an account of global trade from 1400 to 1800, he insists: 'As cannot be repeated often enough, it is the whole (which is more than the sum of its parts) that more than anything else determines the "internal" nature of its parts and their "external" relations with each other.'[5] Finally, he writes: 'For only the study of the continuing structure of the one and only world (system) can illuminate the hows, whys and wherefores of the "development", "rise" or "fall" of any part of the world (system), be it in Europe, America, Africa, Asia, Oceania, and/or any part thereof.'[6]

Holism, as method and thesis, is important to Frank because it enables him to deny singularity or exceptionalism. European exceptionalism in the first place, the attempt to find special features in European history which might explain Europe's apparent dominance, but logically, any exceptionalism – Chinese, Asian, Islamic or African. Frank argues:

> There is no way to see what happens at a distance anywhere else in – let alone in all – the world by using a European or Chinese or any other microscopic perspective. On the contrary, any of these views is possible only with a telescopic perspective capable of encompassing the whole world and all its parts, even if the details of the latter may remain unclear from afar. Not only are all perspectives in terms of European or any other 'exceptionalism' doomed to blindness. So are those using the perspective of a European-based world-economy/system (or any Sino-, Islamic-, or Afrocentric analogues thereof) . . . In conclusion, what we need is a much more global, holistic world economic/ systemic perspective and theory.[7]

*Third*, the holism is economic, mercantilist and bullionist. For Frank the world system is virtually synonymous with the global economy. It is a case Frank does not so much argue as assume. Not that he is a Marxist. He dismisses modes of production, in particular the Asiatic mode of production, as vigorously as Eurocentric exceptionalism, and for the same reason: both offer internal particular, not external universal explanations. Rather, he might be called a post-Marxist. His prejudice is materialist, his mindset reductionist. He does not consider whether the world system, even if its overarching holism is admitted, might not operate through a reticulation of causes set in different registers – biological, environmental, political, intellectual and so on. For him, reality is unproblematic. It is basically economic. Moreover, it is economic of a limited kind. While Frank is sometimes attracted to the demographic and agricultural theories associated with Jack A. Goldstein, generally he rejects physiocracy for mercantilism.[8] His emphasis is on trade and, in particular, the flows of precious metals generated by trade: 'These significant increases in world population growth were supported by concomitant increases in production, which were fuelled by increases in the world supply and distribution of money.'[9] Again, though Frank pays lipservice to the monetary component of these flows, particularly important in China, as has been shown by Richard von Glahn (1996), it is the commercial component which most interests him.[10] Commercial bullion constituted the world economy. Frank writes: 'For, contrary to Wallerstein, the world-wide flood of money to Asia and Russia is evidence precisely that they were parts of the same world economy as Europe and the Americas.'[11] Frank boldly entitles his chapter 'Money went round the world and made the world go round.'

*Fourth*, the world system is centred. Under the umbrella of its economic holism, it is layered, structured, and orbital. Here, it would seem, Frank has been influenced by Immanuel Wallerstein with his theory of core, semi-periphery and periphery in an evolving world-system.[12] Where Frank differs from Wallerstein is that whereas for Wallerstein the core successively creates itself, its semi-periphery and periphery before extending its system to zones external to it, which may have constituted worlds of their own, for Frank the roles are distributed by the system itself, which is always global, in accordance with the canon of holism and the absence of exceptionalism. Regional differences exist in Frank's system, sharp ones even, as between Europe and Asia for most of history, but they are properties of the system rather than contributions by its components. The actors do not improvise their roles, they are assigned them by the play which demands central and supporting characters. Nevertheless, performatively, Frank's centre is the functional equivalent of Wallerstein's core in providing the final pull and push, though it is defined in more mercantilist and bullionist terms as the ultimate depository of precious metals. His concept of the world system gives it a comet-like appearance: a rarefied tail, where precious metals are produced and exported; a more solid body through which they pass, where precious metals are both imported and exported; and a concentrated head which imports but does not export, where precious metals come to rest or, more accurately, to circulate and fructify. For, using the Keynesian identification of saving and investment, Frank rejects the notion of thesaurization as the Achilles heel of such economic centres. Bullion inflow will automatically increase population, production and productivity and production will lead to more inflow and set the rhythm of the system. In this way, as a sort of vortex, the sump is central.

*Fifth*, the system is China-centred. Through an analysis of bullion flows in the period 1400 to 1800, when silver was the principal international currency, Frank identifies China as the centre of the world system, though with India as a subsidiary centre for gold. China's centrality was based on its preeminence in the export of goods and services and in the import of silver both commercially, in the balance of payments, and as a monetary resource. China seized the silver string of the world and wound it into a ball. With respect to global trade 1400–1800, paradigmatic for a longer period, Frank writes:

> Two related factors, already mentioned in the discussion of the trade patterns above, were perhaps of the greatest significance for the world economy. One was China's world economic preeminence in production and export. China was unrivaled in porcelain ceramics and had few rivals in silk, which was China's largest export product mainly to other Asian buyers and secondarily for the Manila-Americas trade. The other important factor . . . was China's position and function as the final 'sink' for the world's production of silver. Of course, the two were related in that China's perennial export surplus (until the mid-nineteenth century) was settled primarily through foreigners' payment in silver. However, the Chinese magnet for silver also had another source: the Ming, abandoned the previous Yuan and even earlier Song dynasties' partial reliance on paper money . . . The Chinese public demand for silver and the large size and

productivity of the Chinese economy and its consequent export surplus generated a huge demand for and increase in the price of, silver worldwide.[13]

If China dominated as the sump of silver, India held similar if lesser magnetism in gold. What China drew from Mexico, Peru and Japan, India, especially Dravidian India, drew from Minas Gerais, the realm of the Monomotapa, Sumatra, Tibet, even Siberia and West Africa. In early modernity, Frank observes:

> As has been the case for millennia, gold predominantly moved through central Asia and to and around South Asia from east to west, in the direction opposite to that of silver, which moved from west to east. On the Indian subcontinent, gold moved to the south and silver to the north. Both were exchanged not only for each other but of course also for other commodities, as well as for local and especially imported foreign coins and other forms of currency.[14]

Frank elaborated: 'The British EIC also brought gold from the east to India and paid for it with silver. Gold also flowed into India, especially the south of the subcontinent, both from West Asia and from Japan and China in East Asia and especially from southeast Asia. However, India was only the penultimate "sink" for the world's silver, since India itself had to re-export some silver further eastward to remit it especially to China'.[15] India's magnetism therefore was less than China's. Frank concludes: 'the entire world economic order was – literally – sinocentric'.[16] Between 1400 and 1800,

> The two major regions that were most 'central' to the world economy were India and China ... The other, and even more 'central' economy was China. Its even greater centrality was based on its greater absolute and relative productivity in industry, agriculture, [water] transport, and trade, China's even greater, indeed and the world economy's greatest, productivity. Competitiveness, and centrality were reflected in its most favourable balance of trade. This was based primarily on its world economic export leadership in silks and ceramics and its exports also of gold, copper-cash, and later of tea. These exports in turn made China the

'ultimate sink' of the world's silver, which flowed there to balance China's almost perpetual export surplus.[17]

China's centrality was also indicated by the fact that its economy did not suffer from either inflation through too much money chasing too few goods, or deflation through hoarding. On inflation in the early modern period, Frank argues that 'throughout most of Asia the increased arrival of money from the Americas and Japan did not substantially raise prices, as it did in Europe. In Asia instead, the infusion of additional new money generated increased production and transactions, as well as raising the velocity of money circulation through more extensive commercialization of the economy.'[18] Again: 'In summary, the evidence suggests that the growing supply of new money especially from the Americas and Japan stimulated production and supported population growth in many parts of Asia.'[19] On deflation, Frank argues there was none. He refers to 'the Eurocentric myth that Asians just hoarded the money they received. On the contrary, Asians *earned* this money first because they were *more* industrious and productive to begin with; the additional money then generated still more Asian demand and production.'[20] The result was a China-centred world system: 'If the world economy had any regional and commercial basis at all, that was in Asia and it was centered if at all in China. Europe was to all intents and purposes entirely marginal.'[21]

*Sixth*, the world system is cyclical. Frank traces the system back to 3000BC: the beginning of the Bronze age which provided the initial materials on which the monetary functions of store of wealth, measure of value and means of exchange were based. Since then, though its scale in terms of what is produced and for how many has increased, its essential character has remained unchanged. Because the system is holistic, and anything can only be explained in terms of everything, change can only be endogenetic, not exogenetic, Frank writes: 'By and large however, the pattern of world trade and division of labour remained remarkably stable and displayed a substantially continuous, albeit cyclical, development over the centuries if not millennia.'[22] Subsequently, in a discussion of Hamashita Takeshi's theory of Chinese tribute trade, he remarks: 'Moreover, the Chinese "tribute trade network" in East and Southeast Asia was – and for two millennia already had been – an integral part of this wider

Afro-Eurasian world economic network. What the Europeans did was to plug the Americas into it as well.'[23] Continuity is the hallmark of the system: 'Once we look upon the whole world more holistically, historical continuity looms much larger than discontinuity, especially in Asia. Indeed as suggested in the preceding chapters, the very "Rise of the West" and the renewed "Rise of the East" then appear derived from this global historical continuity.'[24] Consequently the only change within the system is cyclical: 'The findings about parallel horizontal simultaneities and our review of the early modern world economy imply and suggest that we would do well, however, to return to a more cyclical perspective of early modern economic history and probably of all history.'[25]

Cycles have long been a staple of economic history, and Frank gives them greater length in line with the theories of the Russian economist Nicolai Dimitrievitch Kondratieff (1892–1935). Indeed, he believes not only in 50-year Kondratieff cycles, but also in 500-year super Kondratieffs, each with an ascendant, expansionist phase A and a descendant, recessionary phase B. Frank is cautious:

> any and all observed fluctuations and pulsations are not necessarily cyclical . . . To have more – indeed, any – confidence that a pulsation is truly cyclical, it is necessary to demonstrate why, or at least that, the upper and lower turning points of inflection of the curve that maps these pulsations are endogenous and not only exogenous to the system. That is, not only must what goes up come down and vice versa; but the going up itself must generate the subsequent downturn and the going down the subsequent upturn.[26]

Nevertheless, Frank is convinced that this can be done and the point is important because it allows him to portray the temporary and in part illusory rise of the West between 1800 and 2000 as a consequence of the phase B of a super Kondratieff going back to 1500 or even earlier, and centred like all the previous ones on Asia and particularly China. The underlying structure has not been changed by the European mobilization of the Americas. The twenty-first century and its next two successors will belong to Asia and preeminently to China. By 2025, according to some estimates, China will again possess a third of the world's wealth as it did in 1800, and per capita preeminence will follow in due course in accordance with a world order which remains systemic, holistic, economic, centred, sinocentric and cyclical.[27]

## A critique of Frank's concept of the world order

Frank's synthesis is radical, extreme and comprehensive. It calls for a thoroughgoing displacement of historical perspective and methods; it is a bold intellectual programme, a true *scienza nuova* like that of Vico. What follows is qualification rather than total rejection. Yet, in this case, because of the thoroughgoing character of the proposal, qualification is tantamount to rejection. Frank is right about many things, but wrong about everything. This may be seen if his six assertions are taken in order.

*First*, the world order is systemic. What is at issue here is the degree of unity of the world order. It may be conceded that there have always been points of contact between the components of what Teilhard de Chardin called the Human Phenomenon, but whether those contacts are best described as system, rather than interconnections, institutions or a network is more open to question. Frank's world system is both universal and ancient. In the first place it differs from Braudel's *économies-mondes* which are island universes in a global archipelago. Secondly, it differs from Wallerstein's view which puts the origin of the modern world system in the sixteenth century. To sustain both universality, true globality, and antiquity back to 3000BC, Frank needs to admit a degree of unity in the world order which is less than systemic in the ordinary sense of the word.

Interconnections, one may agree, are both old and wide. Initially there was the genetic connection. Although the new alliance between genetics and history is in its infancy, it has already established that, at least since *sapiens* replaced Neanderthal, *habilis* and *erectus*, there have been no true human races. The human genome is unitary and the genetic differences within it are not large. Cavalli-Sforza states: 'According to that first estimate, the woman from whom all modern human mitochondria descend lived about 190,000 years ago', adding 'this first attempt was not so bad'.[28] Subsequently, Bryan Sykes of the Oxford Institute of Molecular Medicine has concluded that 'almost all native Europeans belong to one of seven distinct clans each with a founding mother . . . But there is virtually no consistent pattern to the way the clans are distributed in modern Europe: in the thousands of years of European history they have become thoroughly mixed.'[29] Since Europe was originally populated from Asia, and to a lesser degree from Africa, similar continuities are likely to be traceable there. As Teilhard de Chardin saw, the absence of human branching is striking. The continued convergence rather than divergence is not easily explained by the first three principles of evolution – mutation, natural selection and drift – but only by the fourth, flow, especially the mobility of women, which in turn implies contact between groups.[30] Next, there was the linguistic connection. No truly primitive languages, in the sense of possessing only a rudimentary capacity to express a gamut of meaning, exist today. All existing languages appear to follow a similar deep structure. All are put into families which are then traced to super families (Austric, Eurasiatic, Nostratic, etc.), which will one day, no doubt, be ascribed to a single, aboriginal family. Yet it is unlikely that human language began as single and indivisible and only subsequently diverged and ramified, it is more likely that it began as multiple and divided and that prehistoric, probably middle-Palaeolithic, convergence through contact and imitation preceded further historic divergence. That contact again implies connection. Finally, there was the dress connection. Clothes, no less unique to humanity than developed language, have received less attention from prehistory than food, partly because the evidence has survived less well, and partly because it has been insufficiently recognized that since nature is lavish in providing nutriment especially in the form of fish, though outside Africa she is parsimonious in providing warmth, thermoregulation has been a greater problem for humans than nutrition. Professor Steven Mithin of the University of Reading has argued that dress, outside Africa, was an invention of the late Palaeolithic, a response in part no doubt to the last ice age, but one with profound psychological and social consequences which were eventually generalized everywhere. Such generalization, a first instance of the force of fashion, again implies contact at least to the level of peer polity and personal emulation.

Yet impressive as these connections are as founding human unity before the Neolithic Revolution modulated it through diversity of crops and domestic animals, it may be doubted whether they amounted to a systemic world order. Even in the period of the rise of the East, AD500–1000, when true world institutions had appeared, what they constituted might be more than a co-presence, but it was less than a network, much less than a system. Indeed, in the strong sense in which Frank intends it, it is not certain that there is a world system today.

*Second*, the world system is holistic. Here the issue is not the unity of the world order, but its power, in the sense of causal determination of its components. Holism is not an implication of system. One may believe in a world system, perhaps from some determinate date, 1250, 1500, 1800, 2000 and so on, and deny its holistic character: that anything can only be explained by everything. System does not exclude exceptionalism; indeed, exceptionalism or singularity can be envisaged as the mode of the system, for it is a poor way to praise the whole by denigrating the parts. In itself exceptionalism is only a recognition of Leibniz's principle of the identity of indiscernibles: that everything is itself and not another thing. Whether the system is in fact all-determining, as Frank supposes, or whether the relation between whole and parts is a more reciprocal one, can only be settled by causal analysis at particular times and places. Frank's demand for a global perspective need not have the consequence he thinks it has in the canon of holism.

Holism is Frank's weapon against exceptionalism, for, unlike system, holism does exclude exceptionalism. One reason why Frank affirms holism and denies exceptionalism is that his history is insufficiently grounded in geography. Apart from time, space is the most basic factor in singularity. Frank lacks Braudel's marvelous sense of place. In his system, as in Gertrude Stein's suburbia, there is no there there. He takes too much for granted the conventional list of continents as constituting genuine historical realities. Asia is particularly unsatisfactory in this respect and Europe is not much better. Asia covers too much that is culturally disparate while Europe covers too little that is culturally distinctive. A better schema, because emphasizing culture rather than nature, is to regard the world before the covergence of histories, when its order was only a set of interconnections, as consisting of four primary civilizations: pre-Columbian America, Black Africa, Western Eurasia and East Asia. This schema has been criticized as Sinocentric, as leaving Western Eurasia too disparate, and as implicitly racist. But some Sinocentrism is necessary to counterbalance the Europocentrism of much Western historiography, a point which may elicit Frank's support. Whatever the subsequent originality of the civilizations of Christendom, Islam and India, Western Eurasia as a primary civilization does have a degree of unity in language, culture, institutions and shared history; and the primary civilizations are post-genetic, cultural entities, so that coincidence with skin pigmentation, if that is what is meant by race, is accidental as well as partial. A division into primary civilizations is, of course, only a beginning of legitimate exceptionalism in human historical geography. A full panoply of Braudelian structures needs to be deployed: peninsulas, highlands, lowlands, islands large and small; and further structures appropriate beyond the Mediterranean, such as have been outlined by Pierre Chaunu and Frederic Mauro for the Iberian Atlantic, by Anthony Reid for Southeast Asia, and Robert Delort for the Baltic.[31] It is on such specifications in space and time that the analysis of the independent actions of the parts in relation to the whole are based. They both permit it and demand it. In them are rooted the exceptionalisms, the historic personalities and singularities, which a radical global perspective, a horizontal integration of histories, has no reason to reject, and many reasons to expect and identify. The world order should be understood not as the whole of history but as the whole in history. Whole and parts stand not in holistic but reciprocal relations. Holism, as either whole to parts, or inversely from parts to whole, should be discarded.

*Third*, the holism is economic, mercantilist and bullionist. Economics is the most successful of the social sciences, more esteemed than sociology or anthropology. Even in non-Marxian Paris, *Économies*, especially in the form of *ports, routes et traffiques* long took precedence over *sociétés* and *civilizations*, while *mentalités* made only a tardy appearance. It is natural that Frank should privilege economics. Yet any reductionism is unfortunate and unified field theories have a long record of only temporary success. Unity is nearly always undermined by further unsuspected multiplicity. In particular, economics, the effort to wring a living from the environment by making an ecology, has always been only one strand in human activity. Consider the three basic Palaeolithic interconnections noted above: genetics, language and dress. All may have possessed economic or ecological facets, but all had or developed other facets. A world order need not be mainly economic. Its different registers, political, economic, social, intellectual and so on cannot be privileged *a priori*. In the case of the period AD500–1000, the intellectual register of the world order, specifically its religious institutions, was more significant than its economic. If, for a later period, Frank would admit that the global economy is *part* of the world system, we would have no quarrel with him, just as we do not question the relevance of the whole to the parts, so long as it does not exclude the relevance of the parts to the whole. Reductionism below should be discarded along with holism above.

If Frank's option for economics as the prime constituent in the world system may be considered natural, his choice of a mercantilist and bullionist version of economics is more surprising. Economics has fluctuated between regarding money as everything (mercantilism), nothing (Classical) or something (Keynesianism, Monetarism, post-Monetarism). Keynes' rehabilitation of mercantilism in the *General Theory* was little more than a *jeu d'esprit*, and while the *Treatise on Money* is more monetarist and has accordingly been upgraded by neo-Keynsians such as Robert Skidelsky (1992), neither offers much support for Frank. As so often, Frank spoils a good case by exaggeration. In traditional as in modern economics, bullion flow, both commercial and monetary, was both an indicator and an activator, but so too were propensity to consume, the sectoral directions of consumption, liquidity preference, the proportion of public to private expenditure, the level of enterprise culture and the conditions of territory, technology and taste. Frank's reluctance to allow causal efficacy to any but his chosen parameter again leads him into unnecessary extremism and implausibility. His bullionism rests on too restricted a view of what constitutes money. He undervalues cartalism, the ability of the state to designate money through its particular tax requirements, and he undervalues tokenism, the ability of either the state or society to designate non-metallic monies. Thus in the first half of the T'ang period, the state's tax requirements in effect made silk the principal currency of China, while under the Sung the use of paper currency expelled silver, so that the Islamic world, long subject to silver famine, was able to resume coinage.[32] In these circumstances bullionism of the kind Frank assumes could not prevail. Even where bullion prevailed, more attention needs to be paid to private paper, instruments of credit, and personalized rates of interest – all things characteristic of China. As economics is general, so bullionist mercantilism in particular is not enough.

*Fourth*, the world system is centred. Here again there are objections of both principle and practice to Frank's concept. First, systems do not necessarily have centres. It is possible to conceive of a-centric economic or other systems. For example, Philip Huang so characterizes the so-called Kiangnan model of late imperial and early republican China in the Yangtze delta, whose origins in T'ang times will concern us later.[33] Similarly, Janet Abu Lughod characterizes the world system of the Islamic commonwealth, which preceded those of the Mongols and Europeans, as non-hegemonic – polycentric certainly, a-centric possibly.[34] Frank himself allows degrees of centrality to both China and India. Second, the term centre as applied to systems, economic and otherwise, is metaphoric. It may be used to denote a number of different realities, of which four in the economic sphere are of most relevance to Frank's argument.

First it may denote the zone of maximum wealth regardless of the size of the population who share it. Thus countries or areas may be arranged in order of gross domestic product at various dates, and the richest regarded as central. Second, it may be used to denote the zone of maximum per capita wealth. Here city states, tax havens and oil sheikhdoms may outpace territorial countries in this kind of centrality. Third, it may be used to denote the zone whose initiatives have the greatest impact economically on other zones, possibly richer, either per capita or absolutely. It was this kind of centrality that Chaunu attributed to Seville in the days of the Iberian Atlantic/Pacific world market: Seville set the rhythm. Finally, and this is where Frank lays most emphasis, centre may be used to denote the ultimate depository, or sink, of precious metals. Now it is not clear that all these four senses necessarily coincide. They may do with respect to the United States today and possibly did so with respect to China under the T'ang, as we shall argue. Frank considers that all four coincided in China as late as 1800. His assessment is open to question, but even if accepted the coincidence should not be regarded as necessary. One kind of centrality cannot be inferred from another. In particular, bullion flows, quite apart from thesaurization do not guarantee centrality in the other senses. Bullion catchment is a phenomenon of commercial balance and monetary requirement, it has no necessary connections with a large percentage of global wealth, high per capita income, or powerful external effects. Bullion flows do not automatically produce growth, larger production and heightened productivity, but only in appropriate, possibly exceptionalist, circumstances. If a system is centred in all four senses, that centrality will not be an inherent property of the system, but in part the product of contingencies. Frank's concept of centrality is not sufficiently thought through. The metaphor never quite becomes a message.

*Fifth*, the system is China-centred, However centre is defined and whatever the facts may have been, this assertion has the effect of reducing, part at any rate, of Chinese history back to the changeless *ewige stillstand*, from which generations of Sinologists have sought to release it. If China was placed at the centre of the global economy by grace of the world system, then it was not there by merit of the Chinese. In particular, if centre be defined as sink of precious metals, this approach obscures precisely the monetary history of China now beginning to emerge from darkness. Recent work by von Glahn (1996) and others has shown that both before and after its unification in 221BC, China practised a succession of monetary systems: archaic, antique, late antique, medieval, late imperial and republican. These covered a wide spectrum: on one axis cartalist to catallacticist, state fiat to market acceptance; on the other axis, bullionism to tokenism, precious metals to no metals at all. It is difficult to see these successive choices as imposed on China exogenetically by the world system. Though China is not rich naturally in either precious or base monetary metals (hence the precocious experimentation in tokenist paper money), external factors cannot be the complete explanation of phase transitions. For this one must look into China's internal contexts: the degree of monetarization, the components of the demand for money, the particular kinds of liquidity preference. Frank's canon of holism makes this difficult to do since it would smack of exceptionalism. For even the centre of a holistic world system cannot exercise initiative of its own. Thus Chinese history evaporates at the moment it is most needed. When at last, like a tributary emissary from the periphery, we reach the central country, see the Son of Heaven and prostrate ourselves before him, he turns out to be a *roi fainéant*, a Taoist impotentate confined to non-action.

Frank's approach obscures not only Chinese history, but also Chinese geography. In particular, it obscures shifts in China's centre of gravity, indeed in the application of the term China. No one would regard Europe as an unchanging, unambiguous monolith. Shifts from the eastern Mediterranean to the western, from the Mediterranean to the North, from the Continent to the Islands and back again, are the commonplaces of its history. Its successive post-Roman, political ascendancies – Frankish, Papal, Spanish, Swedish, French, English and German – are not regarded as dynastic cycles, repetitions of the same, even if, in global perspective, imposed from without by greater Kondratieff cycles. In reality, China too has never been an unchanging, unambiguous monolith. Its meaning has varied as much as Europe's. It has been many as well as one. Periods of interdynastic disorder – only a derogatory term for multistate order – have been long and creative. Even under the single form of the imperial state – China's most prominent, superficial historical feature – there was variety in structure, function, range of power horizontal and vertical. Centres of gravity – political, economic, social and intellectual – frequently non-coincident, have circulated through macroregions and provinces. Thus between 1920 and 1950, China was divided four ways: Kuomintang, Communists, Warlords, Japanese Satellites. Nanking and Chungking were political capitals, Shanghai was the economic capital, Peking the intellectual capital, while Yenan functioned as counter-capital in one direction, Mukden in another, not to speak of other cities serving as local capitals or warlord headquarters. An extreme example no doubt, but such assignments and circulations, each with its singularities and exceptionalisms, are the tone and colour of Chinese history. They are obscured and not illuminated by the concept of an ongoing, perennial centre of a global economy, constituted as such by being a universal monetary sink. China was the central country in more than this sense, indeed sometimes not in any sense.

*Sixth*, the world system is cyclical. Business cycles have long been a staple of economic history and entrepreneurial experience. In 1620 a correspondent of the Privy Council complained that trade, like the moon, was on the wane. A more recent example would be the underwriting profit cycle which was held to characterize Lloyds insurance market. What is at issue here is whether the concept of an endogenous cycle has proper application over longer terms and more widely based fluctuations. Frank insists that the 50 and 500-year fluctuations with which he is concerned, and which he uses to explain such phenomena as the apparent rise of the West, are true endogenous cycles and not just exogenous pulsations and waves. Here, it may be observed that Frank goes beyond the views of Kondratieff himself who, it seems, regarded his long waves or conjunctures as exogenous rather than endogenous, the product of external factors such as technological development or political promotion. It was Joseph Schumpeter who first interpreted Kondratieff's long waves in endogenous cyclical terms.[35] It is easy to see why Frank was attracted to this interpretation of Kondratieff; anything else would mean the abandonment both of the canon of holism and of economic reductionism. Frank cannot allow anything to be outside his system, so that its fluctuations must be endogenous and must be cyclical if they are not to be random. However, if the canon of holism and the ultimacy of economics are dropped, then long-term, exogenous, interfactorial conjunctures become possible. Their existence in fact is then a question of enquiry and judgement. Some long waves may be regarded as cyclical, others as not. If the world order in a particular period were less than systematic, only a network or co-presence of institutions, then such waves might be more likely to be exogenous or generated by shifts between registers. Even a highly integrated system, however, might not proceed cyclically, as its complexity and multifactorial character could give rise to more contingency and manifest phenomena of indeterminist chaos, for, as Robert Musil (1979) observed, history has to accept a principle of insufficient reason: the ultimate spontaneity of singularities. In the world order, cyclicity, if it exists at all, may be a phenomenon of the middle passage: after the world order was too weak for necessity, before the world order was too strong for necessity.

*   *   *

To conclude. Frank's concept of the world order cannot be accepted as it stands. System, holism, economic reductionism, centrality, sinocentrality and cycles, its six main elements, are all open to question. Nevertheless, it remains a brilliant synthesis, a superb theory in Roger Penrose's sense, as the most radical interpretation of Joseph Fletcher's demand for horizontally integrated macrohistory.[36] As such, critique lays an obligation to do better. In particular, it calls the historian to investigate how the global and the exceptional have cooperated to produce long-term shifts in the balance of civilization. This will now be attempted for the Rise of the East which occurred in the second half of the first Christian millenium: a dark age for Western Europe, but light ages for Byzantium, Islamdom and India, and high-noon meridian for China. The first step must be to assess the state of civilizations before the Rise of the East, and where any balance of advantage between them might lie.

## The preponderance of the West

Civilizations are multifunctional; they require analysis at different levels, of which political, economic, social and intellectual are only the most obvious. Comparison between them, where it is possible and incommensurables are not involved, may give different results at these various levels. Superiority at one level does not guarantee superiority at all. Similarly, shifts in superiority and inferiority at one level may be accompanied by countercurrents at others, which may in the long run reverse the major tendency. Nevertheless, these caveats admitted, a convergence of evidence indicates that in the first half of the first Christian millennium, and specifically around the year AD 400, the balance of advantage lay with the West rather than China. This may be shown by a comparison between the Roman and Han-Chin empires.

### Similarities

At the political level, the Roman and Han–Chin empires were at least comparable. Both covered similar areas: Rome, under Hadrian, slightly larger at 1,800,000 square miles, the Eastern Han, at the end of the second century AD, slightly smaller at 1,500,000 square miles. Both operated through privileged bureaucracies composed, on the one hand, of the slaves and freedmen of Caesar's household, and on the other of the 'guests' *k'o* and protégés of great aristocratic families the Tou, the Pan, the Wang and the Ssu-ma. Both maintained large armies of infantry on closed, but porous, frontiers whose protection required *limes*: walls, watchtowers and security zones. Both empires began effectively in the second century BC. Both in their origins owed something to the example of the Achaemenid empire, the world's first imperial state, as reconstructed by Macedon. Both started from the western peripheries of their respective civilizations before moving east to take over older economic and cultural cores. Both then returned west to incorporate barbarians previously outside civilization. Subsequently, trajectories were similar: a lesser, political crisis around the beginning of the Christian era which saw a transition from republic to principate and from meritocratic Western Han, to aristocratic Eastern Han; a greater political crisis in the third century AD which led to a recasting of empire with new capitals, Trier and Constantinople in the West, and a new dynasty, the Chin, in China. Finally, both empires experienced disruption: earlier in China, on the lines of north and south, the first divided, the second united, later in the West, on the lines of west and east, the first divided the second united. In both areas of division, barbarian aristocracies, originally leaders of mercenary armies in search of employer states, were added to existing ruling classes.

At the economic level, both the Roman West and the Chinese East had advanced agricultural foundations, based in the first on wheat and barley, and in the second on millet and wheat. In both cases, irrigation, by aqueducts and water wheels in the West, by canals and water wheels in the East, played a part in raising per areal yields to support an urban superstructure. In both, too, arable farming was supplemented by pastoral, though at this time to a greater extent in the East where great aristocrats doubled as runholders in the Sino-Mongolian borderlands. Parallel to both kinds of agriculture, West and East both possessed basic techniques of metal winning and metal working in copper, tin, lead, iron and zinc and in their alloys of bronze and brass. In textiles, wool principally in the West, hemp principally in the East, both shared a similar technology of spinning, weaving, plain or twill, application of vegetable dyes, tailoring and sewing. Both shared a preference in dress for loose civilized draping rather than tight barbarian shaping, though in both, trousers and the battle dress of the *limes* were making progress. Styles of building did differ, the East preferring wood, the West preferring stone, but overall the level of shelter provided for the generality did not contrast significantly. Both civilizations deployed an economic infrastructure which provided 50 million people with standards of living higher than those of Black Africa and pre-Columbian America, higher too than those of the surrounding barbarians, on whom consequently they exerted a powerful magnetism to install themselves within the *limes*, whether as mercenaries, economic migrants or asylum-seekers. At the social level, both the Roman West and the Han–Chin East were urbanized societies which culminated in splendid capital cities: Rome, Constantinople, Trier and Milan in the West, Ch'ang-an, Lo-yang and Nanking in the East. Both, at the apex, were dominated by political and military aristocracies: in the Roman empire, the old senatorial aristocracy plus the new aristocracy of the *virtus Illyrica*; in the Han empire, the *hao-tsu*, the grand clans, the old families who had restored the Han after the usurpation of Wang Mang, the newer *wai-ch'i* or consort families, with whom subsequent emperors had tried to control them. These aristocracies owed their social leverage less to land, though latifundia existed as basic investments in both East and West, than to portfolios of office, command, *clientelae*, cultural advantage, genealogy and marriage prestige, whose periodic readjustment ensured long-term survival despite accidents of politics and war. At the base of society in both East and West were the cultivators, esteemed in theory if often despised in practice. Their condition was diverse, more by terrain and crops than by status or class, but characteristically they were not a downtrodden peasantry or plantation peons. In China, in the central provinces of Honan, Shansi and Shensi, the smallholders were the basis of the tax registers and muster rolls and when they declined so did the dynasty. Szechwan by contrast, as indicated by the *Hua-yang kuo-chih*, the earliest Chinese local gazetteer, was a land of gentry villas which allied irrigated wheat and the production of well salt with fishponds, tea gardens, forestry and copper mines, but there too it seems farm servants and tenants shared in the prosperity. In the West, Tchalenko's thriving olive oil producing villages of the Antioch hinterland, Bagnall's prosperous grain-producing Coptic villages of the Egyptian chora and Wacher's comfortable co-resident farm workers on the 1,000 villas of lowland Britain have qualified Rostovtzeff's picture of a 'dark people' cut off from classical culture.[37] Rural alienation existed, but in both China and the West the threat to classical stability came less from such peasantry, but from soldiers, sectaries, barbarians and a potentially radical interface. For, at both ends of the Eurasian continent, between the urbanized apex and the rural base came a third layer, the *liu-min*, the people of the routes, positioned less in consumption or production than in distribution: carters, coolies, cameleers, travelling merchants, boat people, entertainers, vagrants, camp followers, quacks, pilgrims, students and emissaries, all who must resort to mobility. At the top of this third layer was an intelligentsia, not rich but educated and potentially powerful if given aristocratic protection, in a world where intelligence was at a premium.

At the intellectual level, both the Roman and the Han–Chin empires were culture states, kingdoms of the written word. Herein they differed from their common ancestor the Achaemenid empire which rested on a dynasty, an ethno-class and a common protection of cults, with Zoroastrianism only the house religion of the ruling family. In Rome and China, the word which provided the cement of empire was the word of a *paideia*: the paradigms, manners and protocols of a curriculum. More a medium than a message, this word was rooted in bodies of literature, both prose and poetry, propagated through their memorization in the classroom, and acclimatized as the communications code of a male ruling class, though in both civilizations eminent bluestockings from Sappho to Pan Chao to Hypatia were active participants. *Ching* – classics, warp, mainstream – did not exclude *wei* – apocrypha, weft, undercurrents in astrology, numerology, magic and theurgy. *Ching* could also accommodate *chiao*, sectarian religion, whether native or imported: the revealed Word of scripture and *sutra* which in both civilizations was playing an increasing role from the middle of the second century AD. For paganism, the cultic component of the *paideia*, was less a religion than a ritual, piety rather than position. Neither St Augustine (d 430) nor Hui-yüan (d 417) felt excluded from the *paideia* though both claimed to transcend it.

## Dissimilarities

At the political level, there was a difference in topography. Rome was both a land and a sea power, Han China, except episodically, only a land power. The Chinese world turned its back on the sea, because, till the third century AD, its local seas led nowhere. River power was significant in the regional wars of the *San-kuo* period (221–280), but the significance was limited in that the Huang-ho, the principal river of China down to AD 500, with its shifting bed and rapid rises and falls, was more suited to irrigation than navigation. The Roman world, on the other hand, was built round the amphitheatre of the Mediterranean, an extended version of Plato's frogs round a pond. If warfare deserted the Mediterranean after Actium, sea power was still required to safeguard the grain fleets from Africa and Egypt from piracy. When Caesar and the Julio-Claudians incorporated the man-power of the Celtic world, military sea power had a role in the narrow seas of the Circumterranean *limes* and its admirals played a part in the regional wars of the third century AD. In AD 400, the emperor of the West Honorius had his capital in Ravenna, primarily a naval base, while his brother of the East Arcadius sat at the juncture of two seas.

On land, the Chinese, like the Romans, built roads of standardized design, but they built fewer of them: 22,000 miles, an average of 14 miles per 1,000 square miles of territory, compared to the Roman 48,000 miles, an average of 28 miles per 1,000 square miles of territory. Topography again was a factor. The Chinese built most of their roads radially out from the imperial capitals of Ch'ang-an and Lo-yang into the loess-lands of Shensi and Shansi, a much dissected plateau of deep valleys, terminal ravines and sudden dead-ends, inimical to intercommunication. The Romans, on the other hand, could begin with the coastal plains of Latium, Campania, Apulia and Emilia, and once free of the Appenines and the Alps had only the plain of Celtic Europe and its forest cover to contend with.

The advantage of a double communication system and the greater facility it afforded to mobilize resources and information affected the agenda of the Roman state and its agents. It enabled it to undertake welfare functions such as the *annona*: the free distribution to citizens not only of bread but also of olive oil, salt, pork and wine, along with free entry to the baths and games. Caesar's munificence set the tone for his patricians: the euergetist mode of distribution which pro-vided, at private cost but to public benefit, so many provincial cities with their amenities – baths and their fuel, amphitheatres and their animals, theatres and their actors, basilicas and their orators. Jean Durliat may have exaggerated the dependence of the ancient macro-city on the *annona*, but *panem et circenses* became a defining charac-teristic of urban *Romanitas* and a source of its greater magnificence and fragility in comparison to the polity of Han–Chin China.[38]

At the economic level, however, China enjoyed the advantage in the basic technologies of agriculture and metallurgy. An obstacle to road-making, the loess soil of interior China was an asset in arable farming. Its porosity enabled it to replenish itself by absorption of both sub-surface and atmospheric nitrogen. More continuous cultivation and less frequent fallowing were thus possible. Chinese farming therefore showed higher average yields per area over time than those of the West. Moreover, its characteristic cereal, millet, produced both higher yields per unit sown and per area than did its rival in the West, wheat. Further, though needing it less, the Chinese manured more via stye-reared pigs and the use of human nightsoil. Thanks to the Kuan-hsien barrage and the Wei valley scheme a higher percentage of Chinese farmland was irrigated in comparison with the West, which in those areas will have led to another doubling of areal yields. In addition, the Chinese farmer had better tools than his Western counterpart. Since as far back as 500BC, the Chinese had been able to cast and not merely to work iron. Cast iron is more brittle than wrought iron, but it is less likely to bend and can be sharpened to greater acuity. Consequently, the Chinese farmers employed superior hoes, ploughshares, sickles, axes, knives and spades. Similarly, the Chinese infantryman had the edge over the Roman legionary in the sharpness of his sword, spear and arrow heads, and it put him into a better position to defend his *limes* against barbarians. Possession of high-carbon cast iron as well as low-carbon wrought iron allowed Chinese metalllurgists, by a process akin to the Bessemer method, to make an intermediate product: steel, the Seric iron so much admired by Pliny, which escaped both brittleness and bending and could be sharpened to an even higher degree. This metallurgical precocity had deep roots. It went back to the ability, already displayed in the Shang and Chou bronzes, to raise higher temperatures through stronger bellows. This greater mastery over fire may have derived from the fact that in East Asia, ceramics, possibly first produced in Japan, came before agriculture rather than the other way round as in Western Eurasia.

Nevertheless, the Chinese economy was not without its bottlenecks, particularly in the field of energy. Never well timbered, a land of copses rather than forests, Interior China suffered both from the Chinese preference for building in wood rather than stone and from the superiority of the Chinese axe. Even the seemingly limitless timber resources of sub-Himalayan Szechwan were beginning to fail under the Han, where Rome and Constantinople with good local supplies and the Hyrcanian forest to command had no such problems.

Timber was the major source of energy in antiquity. Whatever the use of stone, bronze and iron, all ages before the Industrial Revolution were timber ages. Despite its inferiority in basic technology, the Roman world probably consumed more energy per capita and in total than the Chinese world. Whether it consumed it more efficiently and effectively is open to question, but it may be guessed that its ecological lavishness did provide its society with higher standards of living, at least in the things of culture. China might be better at production, but the Roman world with its superior communications was better at distribution and consumption.

At the social level, while at the apex both Rome and China were urbanized societies, there were more cities in the Roman World and a higher percentage of the population lived in them. One reason was again the greater mileage of communication in the West which allowed more cities to be supplied by roads and sealanes. Another was that while the Greeks, Macedonians and Romans multiplied cities; the Chinese empire, as evidenced by archaeology, reduced them. In China cities were primarily places of government. When government became united and centralized after 221BC, there was less need for provincial capitals and no need for rival places of courtly glamour. Many former capitals therefore atrophied. In the West, cities were primarily places of enjoyment and civic life: *apolausis* and *civilitas*. The Roman empire, a welfare state, had to provide these things either directly or through the liturgies of local oligarchies. Cities therefore were maintained, extended or created. Under the Antonines the Roman empire became a federation of cities where the Han empire remained a territorial state with a primate capital. At the base, however, Chinese producers, the *nung* and the *kung* better endowed by technology in agriculture and metallurgy and less oppressed by their urban superstructure, probably enjoyed higher status than their counterparts in the West. As the Han period advanced and became first the *San-kuo*, the Three Kingdoms, and then the Chin, the imperial tax registers and muster calls shrank as farmers and artisans commended themselves as *k'o*, 'guests', that is tenants and retainers, to great aristocratic *clientelae*. Although the shift from smallholders to dependents was deplored by political theorists committed to the imperial state, it is not clear that the change represented a deterioration of social conditions: possibly an improvement, since the *clientelae* were vehicles of social mobility for their *k'o*.

Between the apex and the base, thanks to the greater availability of routes by both land and water, the third layer was thicker in the West than in China, particularly in regard to business. Ssu-ma Ch'ien has a chapter in the *shih-chi* on millionaires in the Western Han, but they were transitional figures like the Russian oligarchs of the Yeltsin era and were not characteristic of the long aristocratic age which followed. Business in Han China did not match the sophistication of the Greco-Syrian connection in the West: the Antiochene inheritors of Athenian proto capitalism, whose activities extended from Britain to India, diffusing Christianity to Lyon and Bath in one direction and to Muziris and Mylapore in another.[39] Even subsequently, the new commercialism of salt, fish and overseas voyages associated in the *San-kuo* period with Sun Ch'üan and the kingdom of Wu at Nanking did not reach the level of Antioch and its more étatiste competitor, Alexandria.

At the intellectual level, though both the Roman and Chinese empires were culture states, their cultures differed in the spectrums they covered. Intellectual activity may be plotted against a grid formed by two axes: a horizontal axis of meaning, according to which thought is either paradigmatic or syntagmatic, that is, rhetorical or realist; a vertical axis of intention according to which thought is either categorical or critical, that is, directed to objects or to its own processes. This grid, itself a piece of low-level critical thinking, provides a fourfold spectrum: paradigmatic and categorical, categorical and sytagmatic, syntagmatic and critical, critical and paradigmatic. In terms of this spectrum, the bodies of thought most characteristic of Han China, and transmitted to the *San-kuo* and Chin, were concentrated in the two paradigmatic quadrants. China was strong in literature, poetry especially, and in literary criticism. It was less strong in the categorical and syntagmatic quadrant especially in metaphysics and cosmology, though in historical scholarship, Ssu-ma Ch'ien may be accorded second place above Herodotus but below Thucydides. Categorical realism was inhibited by the shift within the Confucian tradition from the *hsin-wen chia*, the New Text school, to the *ku-wen chia*, the Old Text school, which occurred during the usurpation of Wang Mang between the two Han dynasties. This shift represented a move away from the sygmaticism exemplified in the correlative cosmology of Tung Chung-shu, and before him of Tsou Yen, back to the literary paradigms of the classics themselves.

Empirical theories, for example in medicine, were resignified as *a priori* categories. Han thought was weakest in the syntagmatic and critical quadrant, but there, until the late middle ages, the West was not much stronger. Prescinding for the moment from religion, because in AD 400 Christianity had conquered in the West while Buddhism and Taoism had not yet done so in China, the West's intellectual preeminence lay in its competing cosmologies: the rival syntheses of Heraclitus, Parmenides, Plato, Aristotle, Plotinus and the Atomists as transmitted to the Roman world by Lucretius. These represented a decisive extension of thought from the paradigmatic to the syntagmatic. Without such an extension, thought remained confined in mythology in Lévi-Strauss' sense of mental exercises and preparatory categorization. Chinese myth might be aniconic or historicized, rather than rooted in epic as in the Mediterranean or India, but myth it remained.

If the West covered a wider intellectual spectrum in Antiquity than China, it also did so in a greater range of languages and scripts. Translation, it has been claimed, was the great discovery of the Hellenistic world. Though Greek and Latin were initially the only classical languages, by the end of Antiquity their number had been extended to include Syriac, Coptic, Armenian, Georgian and Ethiopian, sometimes with new scripts. Meanwhile, the Chinese *paideia* remained monoglot and monographic though the Chinese language itself was being enriched by Iranian loan words to do with wheeled transport, medicine and magic through contacts with a wider world in Central Asia.[40]

China did not yet possess a Sinosphere or effective institutions of translation. It remained shut up within its own script and texts separated by mental and physical barriers from the rest of civilization. It was the resulting sense of isolation and provinciality which had driven emperor Han Wu-ti to send his emissaries to the West and from the middle of the third century AD sent Chinese Buddhist pilgrims in the same direction. It was a state of affairs which the next half millennium was to reverse radically.

Civilizations are seldom superior or inferior to each other in all respects. They are not blocs, but aggregates and distinctions between levels and within levels must be drawn. That said, if an overall judgement has to be made, and Frank's argument compels us to make one, it is difficult not to conclude that around AD 400 the Roman world was more advanced than the Chinese world. China might have the better economic infrastructure, on which a great future was going to be built, but in terms of superstructure – political, social and intellectual – Rome held centre-stage. It is the rise of a new Chinese centrality that we must now examine. The Rise of the East was a genuine novelty and not just the reaffirmation of an existing reality through a fresh super-Kondratieff.

# 2
# Politics: The Genius of T'ang

The Rise of the East was basically a matter of politics. Between AD500 and 1000, the Chinese political system, and by derivation China's position in the world order, was transformed by successive changes which may be called the Sui-T'ang refoundation, the silver T'ang restoration, and the Sung counter-revolution. By contrast, in Western Eurasia, that is in India, Islamdom, the Byzantine empire and Latin Christendom, there was either less progress, negative progress, no progress, or progress deferred which only gave results in the long run. China's progress, however, gave results both immediately and in the long run. Immediately, between 500 and 1000, China became the best ordered state in the world, with all the economic, social and intellectual side benefits which went with good government. In the long run, that period established what has been China's most conspicuous political characteristic ever since: the continuity of the form of ideologically-inspired bureaucratic empire. Before the period under review, during which China emerged from three centuries of disunity, continuity of political form was no more characteristic of China than it was of the West. After it, such continuity became the norm to the extent that it masked radical discontinuities in other aspects of Chinese history and gave outsiders at least the illusion of a succession of essentially similar dynasties governed by cyclical process. To see Chinese history and its place in world history more fairly, it is necessary to grasp the magnitude of China's political achievement between 500 and 1000. Just as the subsequent ascendancy of the West was to be primarily political, so China's antecedent ascendancy was also primarily political.

## The Sui-T'ang refoundation

Of the three periods of change, this was the most radical. As it was the first, however, some of its features were modified or overlaid by subsequent changes, so that later Chinese imperial states reflected these rather than the originals. Indeed, in some ways, modern Japan is a more direct heir of the Sui-T'ang refoundation than modern China, and Kyoto projects a better image of Hsüan-tsung's Ch'ang-an than Sian. The Sui-T'ang refoundation was the work essentially of six reigns: a run of good rulers and successful politics comparable to that of the Antonines. The six rulers were the two Sui emperors, Sui Wen-ti (589–605) and Sui Yang-ti (605–618), whose radicalism provoked the fall of their dynasty, and the four T'ang sovereigns who built on their foundations: Kao-tsu (618–626), T'ai-tsung (626–649). Empress Wu (655–705) and Hsüan-tsung (713–756) in whose reign the refoundation reached a climax. Almost immediately, however, overextension in several directions plunged it into the severe, multiple crisis represented by the rebellion of An Lu-shan. Nevertheless, from the standpoint of his reign, one can see what the refoundation had accomplished: a provincial, unicultural, faction-ridden aristocratic state had been transformed into a cosmopolitan, multicultural, orderly and partly meritocratic state, no longer peripheral in a minimum world order, but central in a world network created by itself. It was as if a cramped Jacobean manor house in deep woods had been converted into a spacious Palladian residence set in Capability Brown parkland.

It must first be appreciated how the old building had become so dilapidated as to compel renewal. The process began in the second century AD. When the Eastern Han was restored in AD25, it was in an environment more aristocratic and less socially mobile than the opportunity state celebrated by Ssu-ma Ch'ien. The rise of the aristocracy had begun indeed as far back as the reign of Han Wu-ti (140–87). The failure of Wang Mang's attempt to curb aristocratic dominance by land nationalization and intellectualizing government only confirmed it. Against Wang Mang's meritocracy, and the lower gentry Red Eyebrows who opposed him, the Han were restored as the champions of the aristocracy. Kuang-wu-ti (25–58) was a great landowner from Nan-yang in southern Honan and Lo-yang was selected as capital in preference to the Western Han's Ch'ang-an because it was more open to aristocratic pressure. In the reign of Kuang-wu-ti's successor Ming-ti (58–76), the emperor's hereditary allies and agnatic relatives came to dominate the court through the great offices of state. To avoid being stifled by overmighty subjects, subsequent emperors turned for a counterweight to their uterine relatives, the families of their mothers or wives. These consort families, *wai-ch'i*, external relatives, became increasingly important in Han politics. Often the consort families did not belong to the old aristocracy. They were selected because they stood outside its ramifications. But this meant that they were rapacious, determined to get rich quick, since their power hung by the gossamer thread of an empress's life. The consort families lowered the tone of court life and intensified its factionalism. Furthermore, they did not make the emperor genuinely independent. They simply added a new stratum to the aristocracy. To check the consort families, the emperors turned to their court eunuchs, originally harem domestics, but, because the emperor was isolated in the palace and constrained by protocol, often his real friends and confidential advisers. Eunuchs came from the middle classes. They had links to trade, technology and the third layer. They brought a new parameter into politics. Unfortunately, they too were rapacious and made hay while the sun shone. They did not have children, but they had brothers and sisters and there was nothing to stop them adopting heirs. So the eunuchs too acquired titles, land, clients and retainers and added another stratum to the aristocracy. Finally, at the end of the second century, when massive rebellions led by dissident intellectuals and lower gentry necessitated the employment of non-Chinese auxiliaries to suppress them, a fourth aristocratic stratum was added: the barbarian generals, who entered the *limes* with their armies, and joined the old families, the *wai-ch'i* and the eunuchs.

The thickening web of rival aristocracies weakened the Han state by depriving it of taxpayers and conscripts, who passed into patrician control as tenants and retainers. Following suppression of the mobile Yellow Turbans rebellion in Western Shantung and Eastern Honan and accommodation with the static Five Pecks of Rice movement in Central Szechwan, the Han empire broke into three pieces. Each was under different aristocratic leadership: the heirs of the eunuchs and the barbarian generals in Wei in the north under Ts'ao Ts'ao; the old Han agnatic families in Shu in Szechwan under Liu Pei;

and the new consort families in Wu in the Yangtze delta under Sun Ch'üan. These three striking figures, the *dramatis personae* of the fourteenth-century Chinese novel the *San-kuo chih yen-i*, the Romance of the Three Kingdoms, though unsuccessful in the short run, began the refoundation of Chinese political institutions. Liu Pei, the peerless cavalier of the novel, was the most conservative. A scion of the Han, the legitimist candidate, Liu stood for the development of what China already had: the intensive rice culture of the Upper Min and T'o interior delta, with its associated silk, salt, tea and timber, the original supply base of the Han dynasty. Yet other characteristics looked forward. Shu was a centralized military state, directed, as prime minister, by the diplomat master-strategist Chu-ko Liang, while partnership with the therapeutic communities of the *T'ien-shih*, Heavenly Masters, school of religious Taoism, secured civilian support. Sun Ch'üan was more innovative. Looking more like a business tycoon than a son of heaven, he built a society as much as a state. Wu stood for the extension and diversification of China in a colonial *Drang nach Suden* from the exterior delta of the Yangtze into Kiang-nan, the land south of the river and in maritime activity in the Nan-yang, the South Seas. Ts'ao Ts'ao, the villain of the novel, 'a vile bandit in time of peace, a heroic leader in an age of confusion', was the most radical. A poet and a patron of intellectuals as well as a general, Ts'ao Ts'ao was both Machiavellian and mystic, activist and quietist, outside the world to act more effectively within it. His programme was to strengthen the state by making it more intelligent and independent through a bureaucracy again made a meritocracy and through a yeoman army based on *t'un-t'ien*, military agricultural colonies up on the frontier. The programme did not live up to expectations. Wei became the strongest of the *San-kuo*, but not strong enough to conquer Shu and Wu. At home, Ts'ao Ts'ao's brainstrust underestimated the inertial resistance of aristocratic society. The people appointed to select the new meritocrats were themselves aristocrats, and naturally chose their friends, relations and protégés. On the frontier, the *t'un-t'ien*, far from checking the barbarian generals, simply fell under their influence. By the middle of the third century, the Wei were as hamstrung as the Han had been.

In 265 one of the great clans, the Ssu-ma, took the throne in Wei with much lower ambitions. Because there was no longer much difference between the aristocracies in the various regions, they were able to restore the unity of the empire in the Western Chin dynasty (265–311). Ts'ao Ts'ao had gone against the aristocratic tide and had been overwhelmed by it. Ssu-ma I, the founder of the Chin, went with it, but did not do much better. More revenue and rights of appointment were alienated, the *t'un-t'ien* were suppressed. Following the death of the founder in 290, there was first a takeover by a new consort family and then a prolonged civil war among Ssu-ma princes. In 304, Szechwan became independent again under a Tibetan dynasty, the Ch'eng-Han, while in Shansi Hsiung-nu generals established the state of Chao. In 311 the Hsiung-nu generals occupied Lo-yang and in 316 Ch'ang-an. The Ssu-ma retreated to Nanking, where they continued as the Eastern Chin till 420, but they left North China to its longest period of division since the foundation of the empire in 221BC. Yet the Western Chin was not all failure and their initiatives, too, prepared the way for the Sui-T'ang refoundation. First, they reasserted Chinese preeminence in Central Asia which had been lost under the *San-kuo*. This facilitated the influx of Buddhism, whose patronage became one of the core elements of Sui-T'ang policy. The Chin looked outward rather than inwards and in this anticipated T'ang cosmopolitanism. Second, the Chin made a hopeful, if not very effective, start on the land question. Like Wang Mang, they proposed legal limits to the amount of land members of the aristocracy could hold. Like Ts'ao Ts'ao, they made assignments of land, not only to soldier settlers, but to civilian taxpayers or potential taxpayers. The Chin grasped the problem of great estates, tax lists and muster rolls which had brought down the Han by making them poorer and weaker than their overmighty subjects. The Chin were no mightier, as they lacked an extra-aristocratic base from which to manage the aristocracy, but such land assignment was to be one of the secrets of T'ang success. For all their weakness and brevity, the Chin were a significant link between the old empire and the new. By 300 the imperial state had collapsed again, but if the fragments had not been recombined in an old unstable synthesis by the Chin, they might never have been recombined in a new, permanent synthesis by the Sui and T'ang.

The period between the fall of Lo-yang in 311 and the reconstitution of imperial unity by the Sui in 589 is known as the Nan-pei ch'ao, the northern and southern courts. In the south, however, it is sometimes called the Six Dynasties because, following the suppression of the state of Wu by the Western Chin, five further short-lived dynasties followed each other at Nanking: the Eastern Chin (317–420), the Liu Sung (420–479), the Ch'i (479–502), the Liang (502–557) and the Ch'en (557–589). The most notable of their rulers was Liang Wu-ti (502–549) under whom the social development initiated by Sun Ch'üan reached a first high point. Between 300 and 600 there had developed in the south a richer, more united, more civilian society, whose diversity insensibly relativized and reduced the role of the aristocracy, both the former consort aristocracy of Wu and the latter immigrant aristocracy which accompanied the Eastern Chin. It was a society based on the new solidarities of Buddhist monasticism and sectarian Taoism, irrigated rice cultivation, river and maritime trade, and city life. Nanking under the Liang was credited with a population of a million. Liang Wu-ti was an expression of this society. A general by origin, he became completely civilianized, and eventually lost his throne to a military uprising. He became defender of the faith: an extravagant patron of Buddhism especially in its new, idealist Vijñānavāda form, but also protector of the new Mao-shan school of Taoism founded by the alchemist, doctor and scholastic T'ao Hung-ching (456–536). Advised by the famous jurist P'ei Cheng, he was also, rather rare in Chinese history, a legal reformer. A new code was drafted, more in accordance with Buddhist humanitarianism views than the harsh Han code still theoretically in force. These reforms, like the almost contemporary legal activity by Justinian under the advice of Tribonian – the Digest, the Institutes, the Codex, the *novellae* – reflected as well as stimulated the increased legal awareness and business of a more diversified society. Yet the south, with less than a quarter of the population of China, its weak state and unstable leadership, lacked the power to bring about the refoundation of the empire. For that power, China had to look to the strengthening of the state which had taken place in the north, particularly under the Toba, or Northern, Wei dynasty (386–535).

In the north, the period from 311 to 440, the reunification of the northern provinces under the Toba Wei, is known as the 16 states of the five barbarians, the *Wu-hu shih-liu kuo*. As with the new non-imperial kingdoms in the western Roman empire – the Visigoths, Ostrogoths, Vandals, Burgundians, Franks, Lombards and so on, – these states were the outcome less of mass migration than of power vacuums filled by mercenary élites in search of employers. Though the generals and their armies had a variety of often composite linguistic origins – Mongolian, Turkish, Tibetan – and preserved to greater or less extent an ethnic identity, the linguistic frontier changed even less than in Europe. As the Han and Chin empires weakened, barbarians entered the *limes* faster than they could be assimilated and with a greater degree of organization. What had been covert became overt. Moreover, on the imperial margins, in the caravan cities of Kansu and on the coastal plain of Hopei, the barbarian polities could be more than garrisons assigned billets and foraging areas and could draw on, and give support to, local interests. For the most part, however, in the central interior provinces of Shansi, Honan and Shensi, they could find no such basis. It was this which drove them to the first major political innovation of the age: the creation of core support for the state through religious patronage, Taoist or Buddhist. To counterbalance the aristocratic *clientelae*, the state had to create a *clientela* of its own through association with religious solidarities in the same way as, it has been suggested, emperors in Rome used Mithraism to establish an imperial club. Such solidarities might not of themselves provide officials, soldiers and taxes, but they ensured a climate in which other institutions could. They were the extra-mundane fulcrum on which the political earth could be turned: what Ts'ao Ts'ao had dreamed of, but had never had to hand.

It was along this path that the Toba Wei entered. A leading family of the Hsien-pi (a prestigious 'firm' name which Pritsak (1981) connected to Sibir, Serb, Sorb, Bessarab, and others), probably Mongolian speaking and living in the future Chinese province of Suiyuan, they acted as light cavalry auxiliaries of the Chin against the Hsiung-nu armies already established within the *limes*.[1] After the Hsiung-nu ascendancy had been replaced by that of the Tibetans, whose leader Fu Chien, overambitious to conquer the south, then suffered a massive defeat by the Eastern Chin at the battle of Fei-shui in 383, the Toba took advantage of the situation to move their headquarters from Suiyuan to Ta-t'ung in northern Shansi, where they assumed Ts'ao Ts'ao's old dynastic name of Wei. From here they were able to play Chinese politics, taking over the static barbarian states of Yen in the northeast and Liang in the northwest. By the early fifth century they controlled most of north China. They increased their prestige by defeating the outer Mongolian, but probably Turkish-led confederation of the Juan-juan: another prestige 'firm' later transferred to Eastern Europe as the Avars. About this time, now cut off from the steppe and campaigning in Iranian Central Asia, the Toba Wei changed from nomadic light cavalry to Persian-style heavy cavalry. This move altered the social position of the army in north China. The draft, formerly the servitude of the peasantry, now became the privilege of the nobility. With patricians drawn to court and the army, plebeians could be assigned land and tax responsibilities. These military and fiscal reforms were to be consolidated in the *fu-ping* and *chün-t'ien* systems of the T'ang, but they were first adumbrated by the Toba Wei.

Concurrently, involvement in Central Asia brought further contact with Buddhism. For a time, particularly in the reign of T'ai-wu (424–452), the Wei patronized Taoism of the Heavenly Masters sect led by K'ou Ch'ien-chih.[2] Thereafter, patronage shifted to Buddhism, especially the critical sceptical school of the Madhyamika. West of Ta-t'ung, in the rock temples of Yun-kang, carved in emulation of Bamiyan, huge statues of the ruler identified him with the Cosmic Buddha. In the south, the emperor was *chakravartin*, protector of the faith in society. In the north, he was *Buddha raja*, incarnate divinity in the state. In 493, the Toba Wei government, now headed as often by empress dowagers as emperors, moved its capital from Ta-t'ung, now inconveniently eccentric, to a newly constructed, carefully planned city of unprecedented magnificence on the site of the former imperial capital of Lo-yang. Strictly zoned for residence, commerce and religion, the new Lo-yang was the expression of a newly resurgent state, but it was also a Buddhist city with over a thousand monasteries, temples and oratories. In population, Toba Wei Lo-yang rivalled the less-planned Nanking under Liang Wu-ti. Each had one half of the solution to the problem of imperial refoundation: Lo-yang in the state, Nanking in society. It remained to bring the two halves together; this was the accomplishment of the Sui (581–618).

The building of Lo-yang was the last major achievement of the Toba Wei. The pressures it exerted, combined with the unpopularity of Empress-dowager Hu, forced like her contemporaries Theodora and Sophia to balance uneasily between magnates and mandarins, eventually split the state four ways. First, in 528 there was a split between north and south: between the relatively unsinicized, still largely light-cavalry armies of the *limes* and the sinicized mandarins and cataphract magnates of the capital. In this conflict, the *limes* won, the empress being thrown into the Huang-ho, but it could not consolidate its victory. Second, from 534–5, as the magnates resumed control, there was a split between west and east: between the mixed-blood aristocracy of Kuan-chung, the land within the passes in Shensi, and the pure-blood grand clans of western Shantung and the Chinese gentry of southern Hopei. The Toba Wei empire divided into two halves: western Wei with its capital at Ch'ang-an, the old Han metropolis, and eastern Wei with its capital at Yeh, near the site of the old Shang metropolis of An-yang. In the east, leadership was first exercised by what was left of the frontier armies under Kao Huan, but the Kao family soon shifted their basis of support to the Hopei gentry and in 557 established their own dynasty of Northern Ch'i (557–577). In the west, leadership was exercized by metropolitan aristocrats under Yü-wen T'ai who sinified the armed forces by extending the draft as privilege to Chinese families, and established the dynasty of Northern Chou (556–581). In 557, well-ordered, remilitarized Northern Chou conquered chaotic, demilitarized Northern Ch'i. In 581, in the united state, the Yü-wen were replaced by a similar magnate family, the Yang. In 589, Yang Wen-ti (581–604) went on to conquer the kingdom of the south at Nanking, Southern Ch'en, which had succeeded the Liang. He thus reunited China in one imperial state after nearly 300 years of division.

The two Sui emperors, Wen-ti and Yang-ti (604–618) are best considered together since the son was personal assistant to the father and subsequently his viceroy in the south, so that their policies are not easily separable. In personality, however, they were distinguishable, even contrasting. Wen-ti was a canny, reserved northwestern military aristocrat, typical of the Kuan-chung magnates. Yang-ti, converted to the civilization of the south, was an outrageous, extravagant aesthete, his style more like that of flamboyant Northern Ch'i than of disciplined Northern Chou. Together they made a formidable political partnership. The Sui had inherited the military system of the privileged draft and the fiscal system of land assignation. These provided the troops and taxes which placed the court beyond intimidation by aristocratic *clientelae* or military *pronunciamenti* and were maintained. In the policy of enlisting religious solidarities to form a counter, imperial *clientela* of expenditure rather than acquisition, however, there was a change of direction. Though the Northern Ch'i had been Buddhist, Northern Chou had been Taoist, repressing the *sangha* and extending its persecution to the territories it conquered. The Sui reversed this and became systematic patrons of Buddhism. Wen-ti proclaimed himself a *chakravartin* and ordered *stupas*, Buddhist reliquaries, to be created in every administrative district. Yang-ti, more intellectual, took a particular interest in the new southern T'ien-t'ai school, recently founded by the monk-philosopher Chih-i on the basis of the *Saddharmapundarika*, or Lotus *sutra*, which affirmed the availability of salvation by grace to everyone in all circumstances: a hopeful doctrine for a reunited China.

The Sui then took two steps to widen their basis of political support which had profound effects on subsequent Chinese history, though no doubt their full implications were neither intended nor anticipated. First, written examinations were introduced into the recruitment procedure for the civil service. In the long run, particularly after its extension to become the chief criterion of élite social status in the Sung period, the examination system was to subvert the aristocracy altogether and make China the most meritocratic of premodern societies. In the medium term, by the middle of the T'ang, the reign of Hsüan-tsung in particular, it made Chinese government uniquely intelligent and its court aristocracy, some of whom took the exams, unusually innovative. In the short run, it extended membership of the ruling élite from the Kuan-chung aristocracy to the leading circles of former Northern Ch'i and Southern Ch'en. In its immediate effects, the examination system may have been little more than an additional parameter in already complex patronage arrangements, though it is difficult not to think that Yang-ti will have seen further. Second, the Sui constructed the first Grand Canal: from Hang-chou in Chekiang, across Kiang-nan and the Yangtze at Chinkiang and Yang-chou, up through Kiangsu and over the Huai to K'ai-feng, and then west to Lo-yang and up the canalized Wei to Ch'ang-an. The first, and still the longest, arterial canal in the world, it was primarily a transport lane to bring tax rice from the south to the capital, but it also served secondarily as a hydraulic device for irrigation and flood prevention in the Central Plains. Finally, it was an artificial Nile, a rivet linking upper and lower China more permanently and completely. Yang-ti was inordinately pleased with the Grand Canal and spent much time travelling up and down it in a pleasure fleet.

It was indeed a piece of Utopian Saint-Simonian technocracy before its time. Its cost and his preoccupation with it was one of the factors which cost Yang-ti his throne.

The events which brought the T'ang to power in 618 were a readjustment within the ruling aristocratic élite rather than a revolution. Regionalism played a part but imperial reunification was not challenged. The proximate cause of the fall of the Sui was an inconclusive war against the North Korean state of Koguryo. Although undertaken in the interests of the northeastern provinces – Koguryo was an aggressive military state strong in light cavalry and fortified townships – the war, never popular in the northwest, produced maximum friction and eventually revolt in the rear area province of Hopei. Seeing Yang-ti embroiled, the Turks attacked in the northwest. In 615 the emperor visited this front where he did not impress and had to be rescued from a Turkish raiding party by the Duke of T'ang. In 616, there was revolt in Honan by a man associated with senior ministers of Wen-ti's court. Confronted with disaffection or revolt throughout the north, the emperor retired to Yang-chou, where in April 618 he was murdered by his praetorian commander Yu-wen Hua-chi, a member of the former ruling family of Northern Chou. It was a sad end for a creative ruler who, as the Ming historian Yü Shen-hs'ing put it, 'shortened the life of his dynasty by a number of years, but benefited posterity to 10,000 generations'.

Meanwhile, the Duke of T'ang, having signed a truce with the Turks, brought his troops back from the frontier and occupied Ch'ang-an, not clear in whose interests. One of his commanders was his daughter the Ping-yang princess, who raised an army of her own and rode with it: an anticipation of later feminine, even feminist, interventions in T'ang politics. The death of Yang-ti having removed any lingering doubts, in June 618 the Duke of T'ang, subsequently canonized as Kao-tsu, took the imperial title in a new dynasty. There now ensued a three-cornered civil war: Kao-tsu in the northwest, Tou Chien-te, a leader of the Hopei political élite, in the northeast, and Yü-wen Hua-chi in the south and centre. Tou Chien-te eliminated Yü-wen Hua-chi, but was himself defeated in 621 in a battle before Lo-yang whither he had gone to relieve his ally the ex-Sui official Wang Shih-ch'ung who was besieged by the T'ang. Lo-yang then surrendered and Kao-tsu was left supreme. His victory has been represented as one of the northwestern aristocracy over the northeastern gentry, but in reality both regions and classes were divided by over-arching factionalism.

In traditional Chinese historiography, Kao-tsu (618–626) has been eclipsed by his more brilliant younger son and successor T'ai-tsung. He has recently been described as 'One of the most underestimated monarchs in all Chinese history'. His contribution to the architec-tonics of imperial refoundation was considerable. Like Sui Wen-ti, he started as a tough and ambitious aristocratic general. Unlike him, though rather secularist and anti-clerical in outlook, he gave his limited religious preference to Taoism, though not to the extent of persecuting Buddhism.[3] A degree of Taoist messianism had accom-panied the T'ang revolution at the popular level and Kao-tsu went along with it. He accepted the claim of a visionary that Lao-tzu was the ancestor of the dynasty and that under his protection his descen-dants would rule the empire for 1000 years by founding a temple on the site of the epiphany. Though he limited the number of monas-teries, both Taoist and Buddhist, the precedence he allowed to Taoism had long-term consequences in the orientation of dynastic legitima-tion and policy. Confucianism, still more a curriculum than a phi-losophy, was purely Chinese, while Buddhism to many Chinese was still something foreign. Taoism, per contra, pointed to partnership between Chinese and barbarian, in particular between the partly Turkified Kuan-chung aristocracy and the partly Sinified Turkish aristocracy of the further northwest. Thanks to Lao-tzu's supposed journey to the West, Taoism in one of its dimensions was an export religion. A T'ang mission to Koguryo promoted Taoism, Turkish envoys to Ch'ang-an went to a Taoist temple, the *Tao-te ching* was translated into Sanscrit. Necessarily Kao-tsu himself was more pre-occupied with internal than external policy, but the adoption of the Taoist brand name in however limited a fashion had implications for foreign relations which his successors, in particular his grandson Kao-tsung, did not fail to develop. Similarly, Kao-tsu's choice of capital had an external, specifically continental implication. Ch'ang-an was no longer the natural capital it had been in the days of the Western Han. The local irrigation works could not be much extended and the enlarged city no longer had a sufficient agricultural base. Its choice therefore was a privilege, a subsidy even, for the northwest. It was an indication that the regime intended to pay special attention to relations along the intercontinental land routes since Ch'ang-an's principal advantage in 618 was as their terminus. It was the forward capital just as Taoism was an exportable religion.Both Kao-tsu's choices, therefore, had significance and consequences beyond his intention.

The groundplan laid down by Kao-tsu was implemented, extended, modified and embellished by his successor T'ai-tsung (626–649), often regarded as the greatest Chinese emperor. Though later portrayed as a Confucian exemplar, he came to power by the unfilial acts of killing his elder brother and deposing his father. T'ai-tsung was only the second son of his father, but he had played a prominent part in the civil war in operations in the northeast. Through these he had built up a powerful *clientela* of front-line soldiers, ex-Sui officials and eastern gentry. In effect, he headed a Lo-yang party against his elder brother's Ch'ang-an party of court aristocrats, staff officers and senior ministers, though one should not overdo these regional and social differences between what were basically personal factions. Kao-tsu supported his elder son, primogeniture and legitimacy being core values of the T'ang revolution. The crisis came in July 626. On the pretext of a plot against his life, which may have been real enough, T'ai-tsung carried out a coup against his brother and killed him at the Hsüan-wu gate of the capital, being supported here by the armies encamped to the north, which were the main field force of the empire, its *comitatenses*. Two months later, in September 626, Kao-tsu abdicated, living as a semi-captive till 635. The Lo-yang party now took office, but Ch'ang-an remained the capital. The ministers rallied to the new leadership, among them Wei Cheng, who had served both Tou Chien-te and T'ai-tsung's elder brother. His recruitment displayed T'ai-tsung's willingness to accept ability from any quarter. At the new court, Wei Cheng became the outspoken Confucian beloved of Chinese bureaucratic myth, the candid friend of the emperor who could say the unsayable. T'ai-tsung was in many ways the opposite to Yang-ti in personality: a soldier, a man's man, an extrovert, a collegial ruler; but in this openness to civilian talent, he was Yang-ti's successor as well as his father's.

If the preference for Taoism and the choice of Ch'ang-an implied a reorientation to the western frontier, T'ai-tsung implemented it with his campaigns which destroyed the eastern half of the Kok Turk empire. These campaigns, a rerun of those of the Toba Wei against the Avars, involved a military partnership between the half-Turkish border aristocracy and the Kuan-chung aristocracy of China proper. Moreover, following their defeat, the Turks themselves accepted T'ang leadership, so that T'ai-tsung became *Khagan* as well as Son of Heaven. Concurrently, moves were made against the other threat to the northwest, the Tibetans in Chinghai, though more by marriage alliance than by force. In 649 there was T'ang military intervention in northern India. T'ang power was also extended into the Iranian oases of Central Asia and the exiled Sassanids were supported against the Muslims. This area was the heartland of missionary Buddhism, Sarvastivadin in Khotan, Mahayana schools at Kucha. These contacts occasioned a modification of religious policy. Initially, T'ai-tsung was no more friendly to Buddhism, no less anticlerical, than his father. When the monk-philosopher Hsüan-tsang left for India in 629, he did so clandestinely as the emperor was not allowing the free movement of pilgrims. When he returned in 645, the emperor and his court came out from Ch'ang-an to salute him. T'ai-tsung, like Yang-ti, now became a patron of Buddhism. His choice, however, lay not with the popular, universalist T'ien-tai school of the south, but with the elitist, exclusive version of Vijñānavāda, or idealism, which Hsüan-tsang brought back from India, a school at once ecumenical and aristocratic. Buddhism, now became an ingredient in T'ang diplomacy, particularly in relationship to Tibet, the Korean states and Japan. These developments produced one of the most significant innovations of the Sui-T'ang refoundation: the creation round the Middle Kingdom of a system of satellite states based on varying exchanges of status, trade and security; what has been called the Chinese World Order or the Sinophere. China was no longer on the edge of someone else's periphery, but now fully metropolitan, was the core of its own East Asia world.[4]

Lastly, as a final embellishment, T'ai-tsung gave his court a particular style, that special grace which every high civilized moment needs. It was a style derived in part from that of his near contemporary the Sassanid Shah Chosroes Parviz (590–628) but going beyond it in scope and purpose. It was designed to make the T'ang court a place of glamour and to endow it with a magnetism which should not merely attract but hold aristocracy, religion and trade, both Chinese and foreign, in the orbit of Ch'ang-an. That style, hard-riding, polo-playing, but refined and cosmopolitan, is best preserved for posterity in the statues of richly caparisoned horses recovered from T'ang tombs. These horses go back to the six Iranian chargers T'ai-tsung rode during the civil wars. He was devoted to them and commemorated them in paintings, poetry, sculpture and even music. These horses, the Cadillacs of their day, became the logo of T'ai-tsung's outward-looking but court-centred empire, the *Weltreich* of the T'ang.

T'ai-tsung was succeeded, not by his heir apparent for most of his reign, who was eliminated in prolonged in-fighting near the end of it, but by a younger son, the future Kao-tsung (649–683). The substitution was not without effect on the architectonics of the empire. The heir apparent had been a Turkophile and his succession might have consolidated T'ai-tsung's notion of a joint Sino-Inner Asian empire. His removal made the empire more Chinese, encouraged a revival of Turkish independence, and necessitated further military operations throughout Kao-tsung's reign. Generally regarded as a weak ruler, Kao-tsung, like his grandfather, has probably been underestimated because his government was soon subsumed into that of his masterful wife, the Empress Wu. Nonetheless he was capable of initiatives and, despite poor health, remained a factor in politics so long as he lived. His principal initiative was in religious patronage. Against the pro-Buddhist policy of the second half of his father's reign, he reasserted and extended the Taoist affiliation of the dynasty. A Taoist magus Yen Fa-shan was called to court in 650. Kao-tsung and Empress Wu wrote prefaces to fascicles of the Taoist canon. In 666, Lao-tzu was awarded a new cult as *t'ai-shang hsüan-yüan huang-ti*, super emperor of the mysterious origin. In 672, Kao-tsung arranged for his daughter the T'ai-p'ing princess to be given Taoist ordination. In 678 the *Tao-te ching* was made a compulsory subject in the civil-service examinations and the imperial pair made a pilgrimage to the Taoist mountain site at Sung-shan near Lo-yang. From 674 when she took the Taoist title *t'ien-hou*, heavenly empress or empress-regnant, Kao-tsung was increasingly overshadowed by his wife, but it is possible that he should be seen as the partner rather than the puppet of the Iron Lady.[5]

She was born Wu Chao, Wu the Bright, in 627, the daughter, not as was subsequently claimed of humble parents, but of Wu Shih-huo, the fourth son of an aristocrat from Shansi. As a younger son, he had to make his own way and became an entrepreneur in timber in

Szechwan, where his daughter was born. Subsequently, be became an official under the Sui, rallied early to the T'ang, and ended as president of the board of works and a duke. He died in 635, but as a reward to his family, his daughter was taken into the harem of T'ai-tsung in 640 at the age of 13. A concubine in name only, she helped nurse T'ai-tsung through his last illness. Although she had to go into a Taoist nunnery when the emperor died, through contacts earlier acquired, she was brought back to court in 654 as a secondary consort for Kao-tsung. She began to play on the emperor's dislike of the councillors he had inherited from his father and of the official empress chosen for him. In 655 the chief councillor Chang-sun Wu-chi was dismissed, banished, and in 659 ordered to commit suicide. The official empress soon followed, reputedly tortured to death by Empress Wu, though, as the Chinese like horror stories about female rulers, the story may only be prestige advertising. It established Empress Wu's image as a ruthless politician in the mould of Empress Lu of the Han. By the 660s she was a major force in the state and from 674, as empress regnant, co-ruler. In 683 when Kao-tsung died, his posthumous edict ordered her to be joint sovereign with their son and his successor Chung-tsung, whom she quickly deposed for a more compliant son, Jui-tsung. Finally in 690, she changed the dynastic style from T'ang to Chou and proclaimed herself *huang-ti*, emperor under the name Wu Tse-t'ien, Wu the pattern of Heaven. Subsequently, the Chou style which proved unpopular, was dropped and she reverted to T'ang, but her power continued unabated till 705 when, nearly 80 and increasingly eccentric, she was deposed by her own partisans and put into retirement as grand empress-dowager, whence she soon died, less of senility than fury. For over 40 years this extraordinary woman ruled the Chinese empire, leaving a characteristic mark on its refoundation.

Least lasting was her religious realignment. Empress Wu was the most pro-Buddhist ruler in Chinese history except for Liang Wu-ti.[6] In 691 Buddhism was given formal precedence over Taoism, the *Tao-te ching* ceased to be a compulsory subject in the examinations, the empress accepted a prophecy that she was an incarnation of Maitreya the Buddha of the future, and in 704 she allowed Fa-tsang, the Master of the new all-inclusive relativistic Hua-yen school, to preach his famous sermon on the golden lion in her presence. Yet she refused to be dictated to by Buddhist clergy and was not exclusive in her patronage. She continued her husband's support for Taoist mountain cults and promoted Taoist immortality research. Her private office was run by a cool Confucian bluestocking Shang-kuan Wan-erh and the temporary Chou style may be construed as an evocation of that pre-Buddhist golden age of Chinese philosophy.

Most enduring was her further institutionalization of bureaucracy. Although portrayed by later Confucian historiography as a tyrant, Empress Wu was, and had to be, less of an autocrat than her predecessors. Almost involuntarily, she promoted the kind of bureaucratic monarchy Confucians wanted. As a woman, she could not command armies personally nor operate the kind of man-to-man personnel management techniques used by T'ai-tsung. Initially opposed by the established figures of the previous reign, she turned to the impersonal mechanisms of examination, promotion by merit and government by due process. A distinction hardened between the *nei-t'ing* and the *wai-t'ing*: the inner court and the outer court, the palace and the bureaucracy. Though subsequent Chinese government exhibited a see-saw between the two, the bias of the system favoured the bureaucracy. Within the bureaucracy under the T'ang, decision-making at the metropolitan level came to rest with the *San-sheng* or three secretariats. The *San-sheng* was the brain of government. It provided an interlocking mechanism for deliberation and decision, reconsideration and review, and execution. Deliberation and decision took place in the *chung-shu sheng* or imperial secretariat, which was divided into two sections: a lower section of *chung-shu she-jen*, drafting officials, who considered problems arising from provincial memorials or imperial instructions and drafted appropriate decrees; and an upper section, the secretary-general and vice-secretary-general, who made the final recommendation to the throne. Next, if the decision, taken to the ruler by the chief ministers at the next dawn audience, was approved, decrees passed to the *men-hsia sheng*, the imperial chancellery, for ratification. Here again there were two sections: an upper one, the chancellor and vice-chancellor, who reconsidered the principles; and a lower one, the *chi-shih chung*, the policy review councillors, who had a veto in the light of precedents and practicality. Finally, the decree, if it passed the chancellery's scrutiny, was sent to the *shang-shu sheng*, the department of state, for execution. This was divided into six sections, *liu-pu*, later independent ministries: appointments, revenue, rites, war, justice and works.

What was striking about the *San-sheng* was the division of function it embodied and the power it gave to junior lower-section officials who initiated the process and concluded it. It was the perfect vehicle for the intelligence provided by the examination system. It made China a bureaucratic monarchy and not just an oriental despotism ruling through a bureaucracy. Empress Wu accepted the basic Confucian principle that the ruler must consent to take advice from those qualified to give it.

Bureaucratic constitutionalism was carried a stage further under Empress Wu's effective successor Hsüan-tsung (713–758). In his reign the accumulated reforms of previous reigns reached fruition and turned rotten.[7] When Empress Wu was deposed, essentially by the bureaucracy she had reinvigorated, she was succeeded by the successive return to the throne of her two sons, Chung-tsung and Jui-tsung. Both fell under the management of imperial females: Chung-tsung under that of his wife Empress Wei and his daughter the An-lo princess, as advised by Shang-kuan Wan-erh; Jui-tsung under that of his sister the T'ai-p'ing princess. These developments suggest that Empress Wu's gynocracy may have had institutional as well as personal roots. Between 705 and 713 leadership was unstable and there were coups and counter coups, but by the latter year Jui-tsung's son Hsüan-tsung was in control.

Although in his youth a competent politician, in maturity Hsüan-tsung chose to reign rather than rule. In politics he acted as umpire rather than player, exercising his leadership in culture rather than policy or personnel which he left to professional consensus. When he ascended the throne, he invited Yang Ch'ung, a former supporter of Empress Wu, to become chief minister. Before accepting office Yang Ch'ung demonstrated his independence by submitting a list of 10 points, covering both policy and procedure, which the emperor had to accept to obtain his minister.[8] Yang Ch'ung retired in 717. Not himself an examination recruit, he recommended as his successor another protégé of the Empress Wu, who was. Subsequently top ministerial appointments were made more on the basis of factional recommendation than imperial initiative, though the emperor appears to have tried to balance westerners and easterners, military and civilian experience, aristocrats and commoners in composite ministries. From 737, however, there was a change of course when the emperor increasingly gave his confidence to a single minister, the

forceful effective aristocrat Li Lin-fu who dominated the court till his
death in 752. Dominance of the court, however, was not the same
thing as dominance of the bureaucracy, for though chief ministers
held concurrent appointments and supervisory roles within the *San-
sheng*, they, like the emperor, were constrained by its preemption of
decision-making.

The reign of Hsüan-tsung is conventionally represented as falling
in two periods, divided according to emphasis by the rise of Li Lin-
fu from 737, the meeting of the emperor with his new consort Yang
Kuei-fei in 740, or the change in reign title from K'ai-yuan to T'ien-
pao in 742. The first part was a period of peace, retrenchment and
reform, inspired by Confucianism under mainly commoner ministers of generally examination provenance. The second part, more
influenced by Buddhism and Taoism, was a period of greater activism
both at home and abroad under ministers more aristocratic in background, yet often too of examination provenance, since the aristocracy also sought the new prestige of the examinations. Activism
prompted further institutional innovation in special commissions to
extend the range of government and impose the policy of the capital
on the provinces. Thus Yü-wen Jung, an aristocratic member of the
former imperial house of Northern Chou, headed a commission
to get more farmers on the land and tax registers in the south,
while P'ei Yao-ch'ing, with both aristocratic and examination qualification, ran a transport commission to improve the functioning of
the Grand Canal. At the same time, an active foreign policy was being
pursued, directed by Li Lin-fu, but conducted by marshals of non-
Chinese origin: Kao Hsien-chih, a Korean, in Central Asia, Ko-shu
Han, a Turk, on the Tibetan frontier in Chinghai, and An Lu-shan, a
Sogdian on the Mongolian border. Meanwhile Hsüan-tsung and Yang
Kuei-fei concentrated on promoting a magnetic cosmopolitan court
based on patronage both to secular culture, especially Iranian music
and dance, and religion both Buddhist and Taoist, in particular the
new Tantric school of Buddhism propagated by Amoghavajra.[9]
Although these activities produced a moment of rare cultural bril-
liance, their cost and tensions were considerable, and these, following the death of Li Lin-fu in 752, helped generate the rebellion of An
Lu-shan in 755, which brought the era of the Sui-T'ang refoundation
to an end.

## The silver T'ang restoration

The rebellion of An Lu-shan forced the overextended T'ang state into contraction and intensification. The architects of this restoration were ministers, not emperors, a confirmation of the shift from palace to bureaucracy effected by Empress Wu. The two chief figures were Li Mi (sometimes transcribed as Li Pi), national security advisor to emperors Su-tsung (756–763), Tai-tsung (763–780) and Te-tsung (780–805), and Liu Yen, transport and fiscal expert under Tai-tsung. Their policy of doing less but doing it better remained a principle of state so long as the imperial system lasted.

Li Mi, a Taoist and possibly a Manichaean, which religion he may have perceived as the international form of Taoism, devised the overall strategy for the defeat of the rebellion. When Su-tsung, having deposed his father Hsüan-tsung and consigned him to exile in Szechwan, assumed the throne in July 756 at Ninghsia in the far northwest, the fortunes of the T'ang were at a low ebb. Of their four armies, one was in rebellion, another had been defeated by the rebels, a third had been destroyed by the Abbasids, a fourth had suffered reverses at the hands of the Lolo-T'ai state of Nan-chao in the south-west. All the emperor had at his disposal was the Flying Dragon Palace Army (*fei-lung chin-chün*), a professional but small guards unit, commanded by his personal eunuch Li Fu-kuo. Both imperial capitals, Lo-yang and Ch'ang-an, had fallen to the rebels. Those provinces not actively supporting An Lu-shan were either neutral or too isolated to be able to send money, men and material. Yet the dynasty had prestige abroad and reserves of support at home. Except in sections of Hopei, the rebellion was never popular; much of its strength was conscripted rather than volunteered. Li Mi capitalized on these assets. Externally, he mortgaged the T'ang empire in Inner Asia to the Abbasids and the Uighurs, a Turkophone people predominant on the steppe, in return for immediate military assistance, which in the case of the Uighurs could come quickly. Internally, he advocated a side-door strategy to rouse the latent loyalism of the gentry of the Peking area behind An Lu-shan's lines. His plan, however, was rejected by the new heroic but more orthodox commander-in-chief Kuo Tzu-i, who insisted on a front attack on Ch'ang-an, Lo-yang and An-yang. His intention, no doubt, was to put the dynasty back into its heartlands before the rebellion had time to consolidate, but the strategy may have prolonged the war unnecessarily as decisive victory in southern Hopei proved elusive. Nevertheless, Li Mi's diplomacy had provided an army for the empire, even though Kuo Tzu-i found the Uighurs difficult allies.[10]

The next problem was finance.[11] Once back in China troops could be raised, but how could they be paid given the virtual independence and consequent non-payment of taxes of so many of the provinces? It was this concern which was addressed by Liu Yen, aristocrat, examination graduate and technocrat. His solution was the salt administration, an institution both fiscal and economic, which was subsequently maintained not just for the lifetime of the empire but down to the establishment of the People's Republic. Liu Yen grasped that a large fiscal output could be obtained from salt by a small input of administration. Salt was consumed universally, but it was only produced in a few areas: coastal marshes and interior lakes, springs, wells and mines. Control those areas, add a tax to the price of salt as it left them, and the whole country would pay indirectly at the point of consumer purchase. Moreover, because the incidence of the tax was universal, the rate could be low: indeed the lower the rate, the more salt would be consumed, and therefore the higher the returns. Salt was the ideal fiscal object for a weak government with limited territorial control: government in its dawn or dusk. Furthermore, since the major source of salt was the marshes north and south of the Huai river in northern Kiangsu, the so-called Liang-huai, revenue collected there could be used to purchase grain in the south which could then be shipped up the Grand Canal to the capital and its armies. So long as the government controlled Ch'ang-an, the canal zone and the Liang-huai, it possessed a fulcrum by which to move the Chinese world. The salt tax became the core of Silver T'ang finance, the first time that an indirect tax, rather than tribute, levies on land or people, or profit from state enterprises such as mines, had been the primary resource of a major state. It was a significant invention in social technology.

With a core available to pay soldiers and officials, direct taxation too was reestablished though with important modifications. Under the *liang-shui* or double-tax reform introduced by the Treasury Minister Yang Yen in 780, the former levies in grain, cloth and labour on farmers under the land-allocation system were abolished. Instead, taxes in money and grain were collected on the basis of the registers of two supplementary imposts, the *hu-shui*, household levy on people, and the *ti-shui*, land levy on acreages, both graduated according to wealth. The advantage of this was that the tax system was cut loose from the foundering system of land allotment. The state no longer sought to control property and occupation: it could now withdraw its omnipresence from the real-estate market.

With armies and revenue secured and military victories over the Tibetans at the end of the eighth century, Te-tsung's next-but-one successor Hsien-tsung (805–821) could begin to build out from the capital, the canal zone and the saltfields into the provinces. An increasing percentage of provincial governors became imperial appointees. Unmanageable units were subdivided and in 817 the tiresome province of Huai-hsi which overlooked both the Grand Canal and the alternative Han river route was reconquered. The number of troops was reduced, court eunuchs from the palace guard units were dispatched to supervise those that remained, and provincial governors were allowed direct command only over an elite force at their capitals, the *Ya-chün* or governor's guards. Between 820 and 860, under five unremarkable emperors, T'ang China, with imperial power on a plateau, enjoyed an Indian summer or silver age. It is an age revealed to us by the diary of the Japanese tantric monk Ennin who was in China between 839 and 847, mainly in Ch'ang-an itself, where he was warmly welcomed by Ch'iu Shih-liang, chief eunuch, commander of the inspired strategy palace army (*shen-ts'e chin-chün*), and commissioner of merit and virtue in charge of religious patronage. Ennin portrays a well-ordered bureaucratic state: permits and permissions were required, but officials were reasonable and courteous if hidebound by red tape. China was definitely one country, though the northeast enjoyed devolution. There was little endemic social violence from bandits or local bosses and, until the transient persecution of Buddhism and foreign religions in 845, no state-induced totalitarian violence. Though the T'ang empire in Inner Asia had gone, peace had been made with the Tibetans in 822 and the Mongolian frontier was quiet till the middle of the tenth century. Thanks to Li Mi's diplomacy, China was still a superpower. All in all, by the middle of the ninth century the political system had reached a new equilibrium. Contracted in space but expanded in sophistication, it still provided the most advanced government in the world.

## The Sung counter-revolution

It was an equilibrium which did not extend beyond 860. In the last third of the ninth century, a series of tremors, of which the most serious was the revolt of Huang Ch'ao between 874 and 884, a mobile juggernaut of mutinous soldiers and third-layer elements, destabilized its balance. When the structure finally collapsed at the beginning of the tenth century, it was succeeded by a 60-year period of political division known as the *Wu-t'ai Shih-kuo*: the Five Dynasties which succeeded one another in north China, and the Ten, or so, Principalities which coexisted in the rest of the country. Traditional Chinese historiography has always been unsympathetic to periods of disunity, and Western scholarship has followed it in speaking of interdynastic chaos. In fact, as Wang Gung-wu was the first to show, it was a constructive period not only economically and socially but also politically.[12] It may be understood as an attempted revolution of pluralism. As such it was brought to an end by the Sung counter-revolution: a new synthesis of the imperial bureaucratic state which, by a deeper penetration of society, a new professionalism in operations and a more promotive view of its symbiosis with the economy, successfully relaunched the unitary system of the empire.[13]

The Silver T'ang restoration had built out from the capital to the provinces in a sequence of palace guards, allied assistance, imperial field forces, indirect taxes, fiscal officials, direct taxes and local magistrates. The principle was limited not least because the T'ang court, the first link in the chain, cast a raffish and rebarbative image as dominated by palace eunuchs and tantric Buddhists. The Sung counter-revolution was based on the contrary principle of building in to the capital from select provinces to create a nucleus with a more Confucian image which after regional success could be expanded to an empire-wide scale. This was the project of the Five Dynasties which succeeded each other on the north China plain between 907 and 960: Later Liang, Later T'ang, Later Chin, Later Han, Later Chou; who, by fits and starts, two steps forward one step back, relaunched the imperial state which the Sung then extended.

The starting point was military: the *ya-chün* or governor's guards, who came to include civilian intelligence and commissariat officers. When Ch'ang-an fell into provincial hands in 904, officers took over the eunuch military secretariat, the *shu-mi yüan* or bureau of secret documents, which had directed the palace armies. Similarly, their civilian adjuncts were inserted into the metropolitan departments for estimates, indirect and direct taxation to form a financial high command, the *san-ssu* or three offices. Together with a department for general administration, the *shu-mi yüan* and the *san-ssu* became the three highly professionalized super ministries of the Sung period. The basis, laid down by Later Liang, was used by Later T'ang to create an enlarged metropolitan army, the *shih-wei ch'in-chün*, the emperor's personal army, chiefly infantry in composition. Insubordinate in practice, it replaced Later T'ang by Later Chin, who moved the capital to the now more centrally situated K'ai-feng and strengthened the civilian element in the metropolitan administration. Military overconfidence, however, led to war with the Khitan, the first of a new generation of better-organized steppe states, who captured K'ai-feng in January 947. A section of the army continued to resist and its commander on recapturing K'ai-feng in April 947 took the dynastic style of Later Han. When he died in 950, the high-command replaced his incapable son with the commander-in-chief Kuo Wei, who established the Later Chou dynasty. The Chou provided three emperors who showed what the new institutions were capable of. In 956–7 the second emperor fought the southern principality of Nan-T'ang in the Huai and Yangtze delta area, conquering the northern half which contained the Liang-huai salt works. Further conquests were envisaged but were sidetracked by a revolt of a brother of the founder of the short-lived Later Han dynasty in northern Shansi, who established there a minor state known as northern or Pei Han in alliance with the Khitan. It was probably only accident which prevented the Later Chou from constructing an all-China dynasty. In 959 their second emperor died leaving a child as successor. The army was not prepared to accept him, or, more realistically, considered it unsafe to do so. A military mutiny surrounded the tent of the next leading general Ch'ao Kuang-yin and insisted that he take the throne which, after a suitable show of reluctance, he did as first emperor of the Sung dynasty. Sung T'ai-tsu was a typical civilianized desk general of the *shih-wei ch'in-chün* with a programme of troop demobilization and retirement of senior officers. In north China terms his advent represented only a headquarters coup within the military bureaucratic élite.

In all-China terms, however, it represented a counter-revolution against the pluralist tendencies of the previous century. What Later

Chou began, Sung T'ai-tsu (960–976), seconded by his brother and successor T'ai-tsung (976–998) completed. Reunification was pursued steadily, as far as possible by agreement rather than force. One by one, the Ten Principalities were taken over. Shu in Szechwan fell in 965: Southern Han in Canton in 971, and Nan-T'ang at Nanking, still a rich and powerful state despite its earlier losses, not till 975, the year before T'ai-tsu's death. T'ai-tsung, a similar sort of man to his brother, persuaded the king of Wu-Yueh, the richest and most defensible of the southern principalities, to give up in 978. In 979 he was able to conquer Pei Han despite support for it from the Khitan. Throughout this period, unity was the Sung presupposition and the emperor was confident that he was conferring a boon and not imposing a burden in insisting on it. When the king of Nan-T'ang offered to hold his principality as a satellite, T'ai-tsu brushed aside the suggestion: 'What crime has the land south of the river committed that it should be separated from the empire?' Only in Szechwan, where there was a major revolt between 993 and 995 led by disaffected tea merchants turned populists, was there any suggestion of deep-rooted localism. Everywhere else, and eventually in Szechwan too, the educated classes were content to share in the government of the empire through the examination system. As much by the wishes of society as by the policy of the state, that system was extended from civil-service recruitment to being a source of social status defining local elites. The Sung counter-revolution thus consolidated all that had gone before in the Sui-T'ang refoundation and the Silver T'ang restoration by giving the meritocratic imperial state its own uniquely meritocratic ruling class. Traditional Chinese historiography has characterized the Northern Sung (960–1127) as the golden age of the *shih ta-fu*, the scholar-gentry and high ministers. It was this political world, beginning with the reign of Chen-tsung (998–1023) that underlay the miracle of Cathay later revealed to an astonished West by Marco Polo.

## Contrast with the West

China's political achievements between 500 and 1,000 may be highlighted by contrast with those of the four components of western Eurasia: India, Islamdom, the Byzantine empire and Latin Christendom. Their achievements may be characterized as less progress, negative progress, no progress and progress deferred. Here, though the comparison is with China, it is not thereby assumed that the Chinese ideal of a single, bureaucratic imperial state is the criterion of political progress in all circumstances. More pluralistic paths of development may be more in accordance with the propensities of other milieus or with the imperatives of modernity.

## India

The two Indias, Aryavarta and Dravidia, fell into the category of less political progress than China.[14] Indian historians, the heirs of the raj rather than their own remoter past, and intent on making the Mauryas, the Kushans, the Guptas and so on the equivalent of Chinese dynasties, have lamented the failure of the imperial state in the subcontinent between 500 and 1000. Yet the real failure, it may be argued, lay less in the disunity of the whole than in the lack of political development in the parts, particularly in the south where other kinds of development were taking place. India's lesser success lay not in the absence of unity but in the quality of pluralism. India was not so much a failed China as an aborted Europe.

The Indian imperial tradition, derived directly from the Achaemenids, received its longest expression in northern India between 320 and 467 under the five great Gupta emperors. It supplied less a unified bureaucratic state than a periodically renewed paramountcy, recreated by military progresses, exchanges of tributes and gifts at durbars, revised tables of precedence rather than hard administration. The idea of bureaucracy existed, as in the *Arthasastra* of Kautilya, but seldom the fact. Indian imperial states were expensive, more so than their counterparts in China, because they maintained huge armies. But those armies, like those of the Great King which drank rivers dry, were for show rather than for war. They consisted largely of batmen and camp followers and only the core – in India it was an elephant corps where under the Achaemenids it had been the heavy cavalry of the Immortals – were fighting men. Enemies were overawed rather than overthrown and even if defeated might, as in Porus' dialogue with Alexander, expect to be treated royally by the emperor. He, after all, was Shahanshah, King of kings, and what prestige would he have if he had no kings to rule over? Consequently, the Indian imperial state had length, breadth and weight but lacked depth. At times, therefore, it sought a further dimension in religion, whether in the old inherited Aryan ritualism or in the new mendicant codes of the road provided by Buddhism and Jainism. Unlike China, religious patronage in India, recorded in the *sasanas* or endowment charters which became a major source of Indian history after the Gupta period, failed to strengthen the imperial state with new solidarities. Rather endowment weakened the state by reducing its resources and strengthening those of the independent forces of society. India's genius was not political but social. Nevertheless, the imperial tradition was difficult to slough off.

Its last effective exponent was Harsha (606–647), the contemporary of Sui Yang-ti and T'ang T'ai-tsung, whose reign and style of government is known to us through the account of the Chinese pilgrim-philosopher Hsüan-tsang. Unlike those contemporaries, Harsha was not an institutional innovator. Indeed, his preference for Buddhism, though not exclusive and possibly exaggerated by Hsüan-tsang, was an anachronistic return to a policy which had already failed and been rejected by the Guptas. On Harsha's death, unity in the north, already threatened in his lifetime from Gujerat and Bengal, broke down. It was followed by a period of considerable fragmentation until the emergence in the eighth century of a triangle of rival dynasties which lasted till near the end of the millennium. Like the *San-kuo* in China, none of these states was strong enough to overcome the others, all had their periods of advantage, and each had a distinct line of policy. The Pratiharas (780–950) in Gujerat and the west, the first to take the shock of the Islamic attack but also the first to benefit from the Muslim free-trade area, were military innovators. They created a cavalry army based on imported horses and the gentry of the Rajputana. The Palas (750–900) in Bengal, the last Indian Buddhist dynasty, associated themselves with the new Tantric international which had offshoots in Nepal, Tibet and Java, as well as China and Japan. Secure in their swamps, forests and access to the sea, they played magic and spin rather than military force, not unsuccessfully. The Rashtrakutas (760–980) in the centre and south, having first faced north and failed to establish permanent ascendancy on the plain, then looked south and sought to link or transfer their capital, sacred geography and perambulations to the new developments in the south.

For in the south, there was real potential for development beyond the imperial tradition into pluralism. The south had a better economic base thanks to peninsular India's entrepot position between the two halves of the Indian ocean and their routes to the West and Southeast Asia. The triangle Malabar–Coromandel-Ceylon was the turntable of the world's first oceanic economic area, a market for gold, spices, glass and silk. If this potential could be harnessed to politics, new enracinated territorial states with depth, as well as length, breadth and religious height, might be created. For most of the period 500–1000, south India was bifurcated along a line southwest to northeast between the Chalukya in Maharashtra and Karnataka and a succession of dynasties, the Pandyas, the Pallavas and the Cholas in Andhra Pradesh and the Tamil Nadu. As in the north, each half sought to conquer the other, but with little permanent success, the military advantage lying with the northwest, the economic advantage lying with the southeast. Neither, however, took advantage of the potential to create new political structures. The Pallavas came closest to it, but they were succeeded by the militaristic Cholas, who reverted to a thalassocratic version of the imperial tradition with its showy perambulations and magic conquests. The Chalukyas, having to look both north and south, made little effort to break out of the pattern of the *chakravartin, raja-mandala* and *digvija*. The shift to the south, evident in different ways in the Rashstrakutas, the Chalukyas and the three dynasties of the Tamil country did not therefore produce profound changes in Indian political culture or institutions. Nor did it provide a model for relations within a multistate system such as was beginning to exist in Latin Christendom. Instead of political development, there was social development: the extension and sophistication of brahman society in two languages, Sanscrit and Tamil. Society connected with the economy, but the state did not.

### Islamdom

This term, coined by Daniel Pipes to denote institutions established voluntarily, involuntarily or against their will by Muslims, is to be preferred to Islam, the religion itself.[15] Between the Hegira and 1000 the trajectory of political institutions in Islamdom may be described as negative progress in that they lost their original unity and legitimacy without gaining a subsequent one in a system of pluralism. Islamdom ceased to be an empire without becoming a commonwealth.

The sudden explosion of Islam in the seventh century was the most revolutionary event of the second half of the first Christian millennium. According to the reinterpretation by Patricia Crone and Michael Cook, which has so impressed world historians even if Islamists remain unconvinced, the explosion began as a Syrian provincialist protest, with a not fully defined ideology, but universalist aspirations to be a revaluation of all values.[16] It found its initial support in the Third Layer, the people of the routes, in particular the dromedary circuits of the Fertile Crescent, for its connection with west-central Arabia was probably a subsequent transposition of sacred geography.[17] Jerusalem was its original focus and its context was a Syria fragmented between Catholics, Monophysites, Nestorians, Orthodox Jews, Samaritans, Athinganoi, and others, which Justinian's bold initiative of Aphtharto-docetism had failed to unify.[18] Its enemies, once it became clear that neither Christians, Jews or Samaritans would accept its claim to be the final revelation of the Spirit, were all establishments and their upholders: the Basileus, the Visigothic king of Spain, the Shah, the Negus, the Balhara of India, the Son of Heaven. Against these enemies early Islamdom set the *umma*, the community and its leader, the *imam*. He was the *khalif*, the deputy, not of the Prophet, whose role was only gradually defined, but of God.[19] Early Islamdom was a unified, militant theocracy, an explosive big bang which crystallized out of inconsequential antecedent particles and then inflated itself by feeding on an environment stalemated by conflict but not depotentiated. The unity of *umma* and *imam*, society and politics, was central to its achievements. The attenuation of that unity therefore represented both a theoretical regression and a practical loss for the state in terms of legitimacy and power.

As the Islamic explosion reached the limits of camel power and the appeal of its kind of revolution, its lava cooled and crystallized into institutions. Here Muslims invested more in society, the economy and the intellect than in politics. A counter-civilization, after all, had been their objective from the beginning. Towards the end of the seventh century, an Islamic society began to take shape which, led by religious jurists, the bigger merchants and scholars, was to a considerable extent independent of the state. Over time, this development produced a devaluation of the state, a split between society and the state, and a division between the *umma* and the *imam*. These schisms were opposed from the side of the *imams* by the Shiites with their theory of hereditary Alid legitimacy, and from the side of the *umma* by the Kharijites with their theory of community omnicompetence. They were consolidated by the victory in 750 of the Abbasids, who betrayed the Shiite revolution which brought them to power for a conservative acceptance of social power. The Abbasids were content to be deputies not of God, but of the Prophet. A papacy now without infallibility or supremacy, they compensated themselves by a display of monarchical magnificence in contrast with earlier Ummayad republican sobriety. On the ground, much autonomy was allowed to provincial governors: the Ummayads in el-Andalus, the Aghlabids in Tunisia, the Tulunids in Egypt, successive proconsuls in Mawara an-nahr or Transoxania. Administration of the *sharia*, the comprehensive canon law which governed the life of the community, was devolved to local committees of jurists, the *ulema*. A plurality of law schools was accepted. The state as such was not so much secularized as profaned.

This devaluation of politics confronted all state forms with a deficit of legitimacy which translated itself into an inability to enlist talent or raise troops. The regions, particular frontline states engaged with the infidel, were less affected than the centre, because there rulers, could claim the legitimacy of *mujahidin*, exponents of *jihad*, which could be represented as a sixth commandment of Islam, though only proclaimable by a legitimate ruler. Thus the Aghlabids in Tunisia were able to use their prestige as the conquerors of Sicily and Apulia to defy the hostile *ulema* of Kairouan, the capital of the Maghreb's new Muslim society, from their new political capitals of Sousse and Tunis. Appeal to the *jihad* was less easy for the caliphs confronted with the resurgent Byzantine empire of the Amorian Macedonian emperors which threatened defeats as well as victories. The Abbasids are generally considered to have reached their apogee in the reign of Harun al-Rashid (783–809), contemporaneous with the Silver T'ang restoration. His two sons struggled with the problem of political regression. Al-Mamun (813–833) sought to create a new intellectual basis by patronage of the Baghdad Mutazilite or rationalist school of the religious cosmology known as *Kalam* and by accommodation with Shia authoritarianism in the person of Imam Reza.[20] The accommodation was never consummated and while some *mutakallimum* did become propagandists for the Abbasids, Mutazilism with its doctrine of a created Koran never won a firm hold on Muslim intellectuals. Al-Mutasim (833–842), more of a soldier than his brother, focused on the military problem, that free-born Muslims were no longer willing to join the caliphal army, by promoting a slave army of largely Turkish provenance with its own camp city of Samarra.[21] The new, mainly cavalry, army did provide victories against emperor Theophilus, but in the long run the cure was worse than the disease. It widened the split between the military establishment, increasingly Turkophone, and civil society Persian or Arabic-speaking and writing. Privileged slaves became successively auxiliaries, allies, overmighty subjects and finally sultans, recognized power-holders who relegated the caliphs to religion: ecumenical patriarchs not universally accepted since by now there was not only, from 929, an Ummayad caliph in Cordoba, but, from 975, a Fatimid caliph in Cairo. Islamdom, like the Western Roman empire at the mid-millennium had become a congerie of principalities, ruled by barbarian generals, Turkish, Berber, Slav or Kurdish, in a cultural common market. Because Islam did not provide a theory of purely secular authority, they were weak states, unbuttressed by an equivalent of the Christian doctrine of the Divine Right of Kings. Sultans remained mere kings *de facto* in a system which could not confer legitimacy. That did not prevent some local dynasties, such as the Ummayads in Cordoba, the Samanids in Bokhara or the Fatimids in Egypt from producing periods of effective and constructive government, but such periods were limited in duration and not cumulative in effect. In politics, if not in other fields, the change from a single, unified republican theocracy to a multiple, divided set of profane monarchies had resulted in Islamdom in a trajectory of negative progress.

## The Byzantine Empire

Between the reigns of Justinian 1 (527–565) and Basil ll (976–1025), the imperial state based on Constantinople saw advance, crisis, retreat, reconstruction and advance again, but no real political progress.[22] Though at the start of the second millennium it was not yet clear that Christendom would be rebuilt on a Latino-German rather than a Greco-Slavonic basis, the scales were beginning to be weighted against the second alternative. Fertile in means, flexible in topology, the Byzntine empire was rigid in its ends. It was geared into a mechanism of homeostasis set to restore a high initial equilibrium rather than surpass it.

In the sixth century, the East Roman empire (for Latin was still too prevalent as the language of government to justify the term Byzantine) as refounded by Justinian was not unlike the empire refounded by the Sui and the T'ang. Both were military bureaucratic states. Both, for soldiers and taxes, rested on societies of smallholders which they nurtured by limiting patrician power by religious solidarities. Both absorbed about a quarter of their economy's gross national product, spending it mainly on armed forces, whose core was now heavy cavalry. In both, court politics ranged military magnates against civilian mandarins, a polarity mediated by a madamate of imperial women who, as aristocratic but civilian, had a foot in both camps. In both, administration operated to a new degree of rationality: the examination system in China, the extension of Roman law by the Digest, the Institutes and the Codex in the West. Where imperial refoundation differed between China and the West was in the extent of their initial success and their degree of subsequent vulnerability. Where the Sui and the T'ang reunited the whole of the south to the north and extended it, Justinian only reunited half of the west to the east, leaving most of Spain, Gaul, Britain and Rhenania outside. Where the Sui-T'ang reunification brought benefits and reinforcement, Justinian's brought costs and overextension. Where Chinese expansion imported smallpox, the red death of children, which limited population growth but did not alter demographic structures, East Roman expansion imported bubonic plague, the black death of young adults, which, producing huge demographic gaps, invited Slavonic and Semitic third-layer immigrants, boat people and camel drivers. These immigrants, organized by the Avars and the Muslims, confronted the East Roman empire with a crisis with no parallel in the world of East Asia. The crisis was overcome: held at bay by the Heraclian emperors who initiated the themal system of military and naval regions, akin to the *fu-ping* system in China; responded to ideologically and strategically by the Isaurian emperors (717–802); and absorbed and resolved by further reconstruction under the Amorian emperors (820–867) who extended the themal system and began the conversion of the Slavs. From this reconstruction, though placed on a narrower basis than Justinian's, since Egypt and Syria were lost and only a slice of southern Italy remained of the Western conquests, the next dynasty, the Macedonian (867–1050), attempted another *restitutio orbis*.

Under Basil I (867–886) the frontier with the caliphate was stabilized in Anatolia. The Byzantine presence in southern Italy, threatened by Latins, Lombards and Muslims, was refounded by the theme of Longobardia in Apulia, with its essentially new capital of Bari, along with updated salines at Siponto, inherited from the Muslim emirate (847–875).[23] In the reign of Leo VI (886–912), whose controversial four marriages in search of an heir showed the growing importance of the hereditary principle, Justinian's legal system was adjusted by the *Basilika* of 888 and a new set of *novels*, while in the short reign of his brother Alexander (912–913) the parameters of the future Byzantine satellite system were adumbrated in the diplomatic exchanges between the Patriarch Nicholas the Mystic and Symeon of Bulgaria. It was characteristic of the Macedonian period, as of the Silver T'ang, that the head of the government was not always the titular ruler. For most of the reign of Constantine VII Porphyrogenitus (912–959), the author of three very Chinese handbooks, the *De administrando Imperio, De Thematibus* and *De Ceremoniis*, the effective ruler was Romanos Lekapenos. Admiral, father in law of the emperor, father of the patriarch and co-emperor, he consolidated Byzantine naval ascendancy in Italian waters and issued *novels* to protect *protimesis*, the right of first refusal in land sales for the yeoman communities on which the armed forces depended. In the first half of the reign of Basil II (963–1025), power was held by two military co-emperors, Nicephorus II Phocas (963–969) and John I Tzimisces (969–976). The empire was now sufficiently rejuvenated to take the offensive against the Abbasids currently more subverted than supported by their Turkish auxiliaries. In 965 Nicephorus Phokas recaptured Crete, reopening the Levant to Christian seapower, while on land Antioch, Aleppo and even Damascus were briefly reoccupied and John Tzimisces established the military frontier along the ancient sub-montane, supra-desert corridor between Seleucia on the sea and Seleucia on the Tigris, the route of St Simeon Stylites whose basilica of Qalat Seman now became a *limes* fortress. At home, the landed basis of the Cataphract army was consolidated and the budget was adjusted to the advantage of the independent yeomanry. Advance could be resumed.

When Basil II came to conduct government himself he was therefore tempted into a policy of overextension, particularly in regard to the satellite state of Bulgaria which, after the genocide which earned him the name of *Bulgaroktonos*, Bulgar Slayer, he annexed outright. It was a backward-looking move, which jettisoned the achievement of Byzantine diplomacy and reinstated empire for incipient commonwealth, choking off temporarily Greco-Slavonic biculturalism. It put the state into the hands of military magnates who Basil II's civilian bureaucrat successors were unable to control so that the dynasty eventually fell to the Comnenians. Elsewhere Basil II's policy was happier. He made an advantageous peace with the Fatimids, he enjoyed good relations with the Philhellene emperor Otto III in Latin Christendom, he extended imperial authority in Georgia, and, following the conversion of Rus in 988, he married his sister Anna to Volodimir of Kiev, thus opening a new and fruitful field to Byzantine satellitism. Yet no real political progress had been made. The core of the empire remained where it had been when the Heraclians stabilized the situation following the Islamic explosion. What had been made was ecclesiastical progress, by the communion of Orthodoxy, and whatever Byzantine theorists might say Orthodoxy was to prove separable not only from the Basileus but also from any real authority of the Ecumenical Patriarch. Byzantium had not grown, so Orthodoxy was bound to outgrow it, whether in the new Slavonic monarchies or in the Hesychast international whose origins go back to the reign of Basil II. *Restitutio Orbis* had run its course.

## Latin Christendom

Here too imperial restoration was losing relevance, though this was not evident when the first millennium ended with Otto III (983–1002) conducting a showy *Renovatio Imperii Romanorum* with Pope Sylvester II (999–1003) in Rome itself. Not yet evident again, because concealed by the imperial tradition and not yet consolidated under papal leadership, was Latin Christendom's greatest political innovation: the adumbration of a non-imperial a-centric system of territorial principalities, mercantile polities and ecclesiastical palatinates, all new political institutions. The *bilan* of Latin Christendom in the period 500–1000 may therefore be described as progress deferred. It would have taken very sharp sight in AD1000 to have predicted that this congerie of inchoate political forms would one day overtake the mighty structure of China as rebuilt by the Sui-T'ang refoundation, the Silver T'ang restoration and the Sung counterrevolution. Just as China was rejecting political pluralism, Latin

Christendom was investing in it. It did not look like a growth stock, but let us look at the three new institutions from which Western politics were to be born.

First, the territorial principality.[24] The name is unsatisfactory. The states founded by barbarian generals when the Western Roman empire, originally stronger than the Eastern, unexpectedly fell in the fifth century through the loss of its British and African buttresses, were not initially of this character. They were defined not by territory (they were highly transplantable) or even ethnicity (like most armies they were of mixed background, though the leadership might take a prestigious ethnic brand name), but by law and religion. In Byzantine Apulia, a Lombard was someone subject to Lombardic law in respect of marriage and property, while a Latin was subject to traditional Roman law and a Greek was subject to Roman law as modified by Justinian I and Leo VI. Territorialization came slowly through religion. Most of the major barbarian states adopted Arianism brought to them from the east by Ulfilas, the apostle of the Goths. The exception was the Franks who were converted to Catholicism through the baptism of Clovis by St Remi around AD500. The conversion, subsequently attributed to the intercession of St Martin of Tours, facilitated the fusion of the Germanic and Roman aristocracies. It allowed the Franks to survive where the Vandals and the Ostrogoths succumbed to Justinian's reconquest, and eventually both the Visigoths and the Lombards found it expedient to convert to Catholicism, though it did not save the Visigoths from Muslim conquest. By AD600, the time of Gregory of Tours, the difference between barbarian and Roman was disappearing in the Frankish kingdom. A Frank was now anyone subject to the territorial jurisdiction of the Frankish king. It was this new-found unity, associated with the cult of St Martin, the great missionary saint of the West, which allowed the Frankish kingdom first to change dynasty from the Merovingians to the Carolingians, then under Charlemagne to reinvent itself as the Holy Roman empire, and finally under his grandsons to effect the territorial partitions of Verdun and Mersen in 843 and 870 which foreshadowed the future states of France and Germany.[25] Yet national consciousness, even territorial consciousness, remained minimal. John the Scot (Eriugena), the apologist for Charles the Bold, ruler of Francia Occidentalis from 840 and emperor from 875, promoted him as a philosopher king, Solomon and *basileus*, in a synthesis of royal and imperial ideology, who fought for reason and civilization against barbarism in the form of Jews, Saracens and Northmen. Explicitly territorial states in England, Spain and France only emerged in post-Carolingian peripheralization and local inititiave. The dividend of pluralism was deferred.[26]

Second, mercantile polities. They, too, were at first marginal and in the shadow of empires both in the north and the south. In the north Pritsak (1981) has argued that the Vikings or Rus were not a people but a profession: the enforcers of an international trading consortium which was the successor of a Frisian network and the predecessor of the Hanseatic league. Though much of the trade was intraregional, within the narrow seas of the north in commodities such as fish, salt, wood and honey, some of it, in slaves, fur, amber and coin was international, with Ummayad Spain, the Byzantine empire and the Abbasid caliphate. Institutionally these circuits remained primitive: fortified cantonments, intersettlement cousinages, temporary supercargoes rather than permanent chiefs. It was a capitalism of outsiders, its identity affirmed negatively by reluctance to convert to Christianity or even hostility to it. In the south, Amalfi and Venice, the first two Italian emporia, only gradually emancipated themselves from the Byzantine empire to whose trade much of their initial prosperity was due. Amalfi, first mentioned in 596 was part of the Byzantine duchy of Naples till 839 when it gained independence first as prefecture and then as duchy. Subsequently, Amalfitans came to dominate the trade of Bari, the capital of Byzantine Lombardy. They had a Latin church in Constantinople and an Orthodox monastery on Mount Athos. It was they who introduced the cult of St Nicholas, first of Myra then of Bari, to the west, though not possessing the body it could not become a focus of identity for Amalfi as did that of San Marco for Venice. Reputedly founded by refugees from Attila in the fifth century, though more probably from the Lombards in the sixth, Venice long remained under Byzantine rule with the imperial duke the predecessor of the doges. Autonomy, however, was increasingly asserted by a committee of local notables, the future senate. In 828 the clandestine translation of the body of St Mark from Alexandria expressed and enhanced growing civic consciousness. Under Doge Peter Tribuno (888–920), Venice proclaimed itself a self-governing *civitas*, though this did not imply a complete rejection of the empire, still less of Byzantine culture. Venice's unique constitution of interlocking councils and its characteristic organization of business through state-regulated family partnerships, however, were its own. By AD1000, two modes of autonomous mercantile polities, quite distinct from the city states of antiquity, were emerging in Latin Christendom.

Third, ecclesiastical palatinates. The period 500–1000 saw the articulation within the Church of new and exceptional areas of independent action often, as with the territorial principalities and mercantile polities, in association with the semanticizing power of relics.[27] These areas were situated principally in monastic affiliations, Irish, Benedictine and Greek, and pilgrimage centres local and international. In 628 Pope Honorius I granted the first-known monastic exemption from episcopal jurisdiction to Bobbio, the abbey founded by St Columbanus, the Celtic Martin, in 613 and where he died in 615. Though there was no Benedictine order for many centuries, the adoption of the Benedictine rule north of the Alps was already widespread by the middle of the seventh century. Its monks did their best to give aid and comfort to Monte Cassino, notably in the case of St Willihad, from Wessex in 730, who restored discipline to the abbey. Similarly, at the end of the tenth century, St Neilos of Rossano in Calabria brought his Greek ascetic movement to Monte Cassino before moving on to Grottaferrata outside Rome. The Papal state itself was an example of a new emerging ecclesiastical power centre. As site and source of relics, *Roma nobilis*, with its double apostolicity and Marian and angelic epiphanies, was a major pilgrimage centre, particularly attractive to new Christians from England and Germany who gave their name to the precinct of Sassia near the Ponte Sant Angelo. The fortification of the Leonine city to protect St Peter's laid the foundations of the temporal power which was developed by what has been called the Holy Roman republic: the dominance of the Apostolic see by the local senatorial families which produced the unedifying but effective rule of Theophylact, Marozia and Crescentius.[28] Another major pilgrimage centre and power base which was emerging in the tenth century was Santiago de Compostela, though it was not until the eleventh century that, under Cluniac influence, the pilgrimage became of more than local significance.[29] As yet, as so much in Latin Christendom, it was progress deferred, promise rather than performance.

Between 500 and 1000, therefore, there was a massive political shift to the advantage of China. It was not a restoration of balance or a return to a natural centrality, as Frank must suppose, but a new situation. It was brought about less by the decline of the West as by the advance of the East under the extraordinarily capable leadership of the six Sui and T'ang rulers: Wen-ti, Yang-ti, T'ai-tsu, T'ai-tsung, Empress Wu and Hsüan-tsung. China's creativity in this period was exemplary. Its legacy of applied intelligence, executive checks and balances, proper process, distinction between state and government, cosmopolitan receptivity, most evidently displayed in the reign of Hsüan-tsung, have become part of everyone's politics in the current world institution of the common consensus. Politics is not everything but its significance has been undervalued by the tradition, wider than Marxism or Hegelianiasm, which sees economics or sociology as primary. Without proper political achievement, the wealth created by the economy may be dissipated, the order generated by society may be disrupted, and the drive to judgement in the intellect may be sidetracked. When Dr Johnson wrote: 'How small, of all that human hearts endure, that part which laws or kings can cause or cure', he was writing at a time when political violence was at a low ebb, when little was to be feared or hoped from the state. It was not so before or after his time. The better half of politics is the control of violence, whether internal or external. In the reign of Hsüan-tsung, China had achieved it to a greater degree than in the two Indias, Islamdom, the Byzantine Empire or the community of Latin Christendom. No wonder that so many rulers were suitors to his court that China became, for the first time, the centre of the world order. No wonder, too, that the political achievements had implications for the economy and society, as the next two chapters will discuss.

# 3
# Economy: China takes Centre-Stage

In the second half of the first millennium, particularly under the T'ang and most notably in the reign of Hsüan-tsung (713–756), China for the first time took centre-stage in the world economy. In moving from the world of politics to that of economics, one must be aware of a shift in scale: from a few thousand participants to many millions and from some certitude to much conjecture. The Chinese state, thanks to its bureaucratic character and the early invention in China of paper and printing, documents itself well. The Chinese economy, even in the considerable segment where the bureaucracy was involved, does so less well, though further primary material will be found in tombs, yamens and libraries to supplement that retrieved from the caves of Tun-huang and the sands of Sinkiang. Nevertheless, whatever the uncertainty quotient, sufficient material exists and enough research has been done to warrant the assertion that between 500 and 1000, the Chinese economy became the largest in the world for the first time in both gross and per capita terms. Moreover, it began to exercise a gravitational pull on the rest of the world economy, greater than that formerly exerted by the Roman economy or concurrently produced by those of Latin Christendom, the Byzantine empire, the Islamic commonwealth or the two Indias. Probably the world economy as a whole grew between 500 and 1000. Even in Latin Christendom, the fall of the Roman empire and the onset of the Dark Ages was not accompanied by a contraction of total wealth or a decline in overall living standards. The Chinese economy, however, grew fastest. The population increased by 50 per cent from 50 million to 75 million, living standards rose by about the same factor, or a little more, so that the size of the economy more than doubled. Meanwhile, Latin Christendom barely held its own, the Byzantine empire oscillated but on balance expanded modestly, the Islamic commonwealth grew more dramatically, while India redistributed its considerable wealth rather than enlarging it.

Why China ran economically while others walked is the subject of this chapter. First, in three sections, the growth of the Chinese economy will be explained in terms of its milieu, motors and management. Next in a single section, comparison will be made with the economic profiles of the other constituents of the Eurasian supercontinent in the same period. Sub-Saharan Africa and pre-Columbian America will have to be left in their relative marginality, though these were the years of the creation of rain-forest civilizations through the Bantu expansion into the Congo basin and the settlement of Amazonia by manioc.

## The milieu of Chinese economic growth, 500–1000

Two components may be analysed in the milieu in which the Chinese economy operated in the second half of the first millennium: the natural environment and the human ecology. Both provided encouraging circumstances for economic growth.

### The natural environment

Here the most relevant circumstance was climate. Evidence from tree rings, ice cores, glacier measurement, dates of flowering and harvest suggest that, worldwide, climate became cooler and wetter between 500 and 1000, though with remissions and intercalary reversals. Such conditions would have been favourable to China. North China, where the bulk of the population still lived, and the northwest in particular on which the T'ang state was based, suffer from a chronic shortage of rainfall, exacerbated in its effects by long-term deforestation. Drought famine has always been more deleterious to population than flood famine, which is shorter in duration and at least leaves a legacy of fertilizing silt for the future. If northwest China enjoyed a last period of political and economic hegemony under the T'ang, it was due in part to these favourable conditions for agriculture. However, on at least one occasion, the court was forced to flee from Ch'ang-an to Lo-yang in search of food and the primary purpose of the Grand Canal, as built by the Sui and improved by the T'ang, was to transport additional grain from the southeast to the capital. As intermissions and reversals increased and as global warming and drying took hold toward the beginning of the second millennium, Chinese government was forced to retreat even further to the southeast for its sources of food, fuel and building materials: from Ch'ang-an to Lo-yang to K'ai-feng to Hang-chou. Northwest China was left as the exhausted, sunset land so vividly described by Teilhard de Chardin.

The middle T'ang, by contrast, represented an environmental optimum for this original cradle of Chinese civilization. Though massive urbanization and monastic construction made huge demands on the area's already limited timber resources, these demands were somehow met. Both Buddhism and Taoism encouraged conservation by their taste for trees around their own sacred buildings. Wu-t'ai-shan, the great pilgrimage centre of the divinity Manjusri, a bare mountain in recent times, is reliably reported as heavily wooded by the Japanese pilgrim monk Ennin in the ninth century. Cooler and wetter weather will have extended the possibility of Chinese arable farming into the Sino-Mongolian borderlands and along the arid Kansu panhandle towards Central Asia. Chinese Turkestan will have enjoyed a bigger Himalayan snow melt, more extensive irrigation and a less desiccated Lop Nor reached by a Tarim river which went further. In technology, such conditions may have been a factor in the development of successive basin solar evaporation for salt at the An-i brine lake in southern Shansi as the natural product of sunshine there and in the borderland *sebkhas* became no longer enough either in quantity or quality. It was a technique for the better utilization of solar power. Another technique, from the other end of China, which may be seen as a response to fewer hours of sunshine, was the naturalization of early-ripening rice from Champa in modern south Vietnam which commenced in Anhwei in the tenth century. It was the subject of energetic government promotion in the reign of Sung Chen-tsung (998–1022), and became the basis for China's characteristic intensive agriculture of double, or even triple, cropping. Finally, climate benefited distribution. Without adequate rainfall and river flow, the operation of the Grand Canal would not have been conceivable or feasible. Moreover, once set up for transport reasons, its regulation could apply surplus water to irrigation in northern Kiangsu, Anhwei and Honan.

## The human ecology

Here the biological rather than the technological milieu is intended. If climatic change in the second half of the first Christian millennium was broadly favourable to Chinese humanity, ecological change, in common with most other parts of the world, was broadly unfavourable. But it was less unfavourable than in some. Thus China, it seems, did not experience the first pandemic of plague, the *Yersinia pestis* bacillus, which afflicted both halves of Christendom, the Iranian world, though not the two Indias, between 540 and 750.[1] Plague is first mentioned in Chinese medical literature in the *Chou-hou pei-chi fang* of the Chin dynasty Taoist and alchemist Ko Hung, c. 340, but as a marginal disease of the southwest, an exotic challenge to tropical medicine, like Ebola Virus fever today. This report led William H. McNeill to suppose that southeast Asia, specifically the western gorges of Yunnan, was the probable source of plague and the origin of all subsequent plague foci in Mongolia, Kurdistan, Central Africa, Constantinople, California, and so on.[2] Although this is a possible trajectory, the earlier hypothesis of a Mongolian origin between Lake Baikal and Issy Kul remains more plausible, with the Yunnan focus discovered by Ko Hung regarded as its first offshoot and explained by Turco-Tibetan contacts and the introduction of the marmot to the Koko-nor region. At all events, plague in China was not the major aggravation of death it was for two centuries in the West. The expanse of the Gobi and the reluctance of fleas from dead marmots to take refuge on camels were sufficient protection for China. Another medical hazard, less threatening in China than in some parts of the West, were mycotoxins which operating through cereal moulds reduced fertility, increased mortality and injured auto-immunity. Even in wetter and cooler climatic conditions, heartland China of those days was too arid to be much threatened by these, and rye, the principal cereal affected, was never a major crop in China.[3] Leprosy, too, documented earlier in China than elsewhere, perhaps more domesticated and sooner counteracted by tuberculosis, does not seem to have attained the epidemic proportions it appears at times to have reached in the West.

China, however, did suffer from three other aggravations of death. First, this period saw the appearance and establishment in China of smallpox, the viral Red Death of children with its 80 per cent incidence in non-immune populations and lethality of 10 per cent, not to speak of its side effects in pock-marking and damage to sight and hearing. Pierre Darmon supposed that the origin of smallpox was in northwest India or Afghanistan and that it was first widely diffused by the Islamic armies, but the chronology (documented in China by T'ao Hung-ching c. 500 and in Europe by Gregory of Tours c. 600) does not support this contention.[4] Rather, in combination with the differences in incidence, lethality and character of the disease as between North Africa and India, it would suggest an origin in the Horn of Africa or southern Arabia, perhaps through a mutation from a putative camel pox, and a diffusion, not through the Islamic explosion itself, but by the expansion from the third century AD of the camel-using transport network which preceded and grounded it.[5] Whatever the origin and vector, the presence in China from 500 of smallpox will have been a serious restraint on the effective birthrate (children surviving till reproductive age) and hence on population growth. Despite rising living standards (two diseases of affluence, beri-beri and diabetes, are first documented in this period), China's population rose only from 50 million in 500 to 75 million in 750, though the proto-feminism discussed in the next chapter may have had a hand in this too. Next, as Gregory of Tours reports anthrax as well as smallpox, it is likely that China will have received this other human import from the animal kingdom, associated as it was with increased contacts with pastoral people and products. Apart from some notice of rinderpest among yaks in Chinghai, not much research has been done on the history of epizootics in China, due probably to the diminishing significance of the pastoral sector over time. Though low in incidence because non-contagious, an argument against Graham Twigg's theory of its frequent confusion with plague in premodern diagnosis, human anthrax is relatively high in lethality.[6] It may thus have been a factor in population limitation and the decline of pastoral runholding in northwest China as well as in the genesis of the Chinese antipathy to mutton. Finally, the expansion of the Chinese population into regions south of the Yangtze, one of the chief features of Chinese demography between 500 and 1000, exposed migrants and their descendants for several generations to a variety of tropical diseases unknown in the north: widespread malaria, schistosomiasis in the Yangtze overflow lakes, several agents of acute diarrhoea, intestinal parasites, various localized eye diseases, cholera perhaps. Chinese accounts describe northern armies struck down by epidemics, those sent against the Lolo kingdom of Nan-chao in particular, and the south long carried a reputation for miasmas and hidden sources of death.[7] Although their pathologies were more often debilitating than lethal, they impaired quality of life and in the short run at least limited population growth.

In the longer run, however, it has been argued by John McNeill that China's march to the tropics, its latitudinal rather than longitudinal extension, advantaged China's human ecology. It gave China a wider and more varied set of acquired immunities than that enjoyed by any other contemporary centre of civilization.[8] The consequent benefits to life and health only became conspicuous under the Sung, but they were emerging in the Silver T'ang and Five Dynasties periods when the delineaments of medieval China were first adumbrated. China exported disease rather than imported it. Immunologically, its population stood at the opposite pole from pre-Colombian America whose isolation and lack of integration left it so vulnerable to outside pathologies.

As in most traditional societies, medicine was not in a position to do much for ecological improvement. Although some half-effective remedies such as chalmoogra oil for leprosy existed, of the three medical injunctions, 'to cure sometimes, to alleviate often and to comfort always', only the last could be fulfilled by increased medical optimism. In the T'ang period, perhaps prompted by the worsening health context, medicine achieved some major doctrinal enrichments. In particular, it saw the systematization of the complex therapies known as *wai-tan* and *nei-tan* (outer and inner cinnabars), which Needham translated as elixir and enchymoma. Although the new chemical medicine, which later passed to the West to form the basis of the Paracelsian reformation, no doubt gave patients fresh hope, its effect on successful treatment was limited, even negative, some patients dying of mercurial or arsenical poisoning. The same might also be said of the new surgical interventions in eye conditions, notably cataracts, introduced along with the reception of Buddhism from India.[9]

What was positive, however, was improvement in hygiene, in which at this time China led the world. Most notable was the increasing boiling of water associated with the rising consumption of tea, a leading feature of Silver T'ang, Five Dynasties and early Sung consumerism. Dietary handbooks, *shih-ching* (classics of eating), one of which is attributed to Ts'ui Hao a minister of the Toba Wei, were a recognized part of the literature of this period, as were manuals of medical gymnastics. Baths were also more fashionable in China than in the West at this time. Po Chu-i puts Yang Kuei-fei in one at the moment she first attracted emperor Hsüan-tsung, a contrast with the less-revealing bride shows favoured by Byzantine emperors such as Theophilus (829–842), who chose his empress, the second Theodora, instead of the pert Casia in this way. A concomitant of the high level of bathing was the development of vegetable saponin detergents for both persons and clothes, which are mentioned by – among others – the alchemist physician Sun Shih-mo. Meanwhile, T'ang proto-feminism was making gynaecology at least more professional and specialized.[10] Both characteristics, as expressed in medical colleges, qualifying examinations and official pharmacopoeias, were characteristic of T'ang medicine as a whole. By raising medical prestige and its personae, and possibly patient morale too, they may have enhanced therapeutic results. Dentistry, too, in so many medical systems the Cinderella of specializations, was upgraded by contact with India and also contributed to hygiene, an eighth-century painting at Tun-huang showing a monk using a toothbrush.

Alchemical therapies, the precursors of mineral drugs, antibiotics and implant biotechnology, may have been promise rather than performance, but acquired immunities and preventive hygiene were present realities. Joined together, they produced a parellogram of forces where positive factors outweighed negative in the health profile of T'ang China, in so far as we can grasp it. Natural environment and human ecology thus combined to present a favourable context for economic enterprise.

## The motors of Chinese economic growth, 500–1000

In his political autobiography, Nigel Lawson asked the question whence would come new jobs and economic growth, and replied: technology and taste.[11] These motors were present in T'ang China, but in a traditional economy a third motor took priority: territory. For the absorption of new land, by its windfall profits, demand for capital investment, supply of different as well as more products, incentives for enterprise of all kinds provided a powerful economic stimulus even in the absence of changes in technology and taste. Thus the traditional economy of Latin Christendom only really took off with the absorption of American territory in the second half of the sixteenth century, Chaunu's royal cycle of silver in the first age of the Counter-Reformation. Territorial expansion was characteristic of all four primary civilizations in the second half of the first Christian millennium: in the Amazon basin; in southern subequatorial Africa; in the lands east and north of the Rhine and the Danube; and in the jungles and swamps of Dravidian India and its prolongations in Ceylon and Indonesia. But its effects were most profound in East Asia, and specifically in China.

### Territory

Under the T'ang, China began a shift in its economic centre of gravity from the dry, yellow millet and wheat lands of the Huang-ho floodplain to the damp, green rice lands of the Yangtze basin. This shift, consummated under the Sung, was not counteracted until the rise of Manchuria, based on *kao-liang*, soya beans and heavy industry, in the twentieth century. In particular, since Szechwan based on the Upper Yangtze and its tributaries had long been a significant part of Chinese economic space (extending itself further south under the Silver T'ang and Five Dynasties), there was a shift from the loesslands of Kuan-chung in Shensi, Shansi and Kansu to the wetlands of Kiang-nan in the collapsed Yangtze delta of southern Kiangsu and northern Chekiang. In rough terms, whereas at the start of the dynasty 75 per cent of the population was in the north above the Yangtze basin, and only 25 per cent within it in the south, by the end of it the proportions were nearer 50/50. The colonization of Kiang-nan was China's equivalent to the discovery of America; globally it was the most significant piece of territorial extension and exploitation between 500 and 1000.

China's frontier in the south was primarily an agricultural advance, the prime object of colonization was land itself. More space was needed. In the T'ang period, the average size of family farms roughly doubled from what it had been under the Han. This was the result of crop diversification, notably the extension of the female contribution in agriculture in pigs, chickens, ducks, mulberry and silkworms as opposed to the male contribution of cereals. In the north, there was shortage of land and allocations under the state *chün-t'ien* system fell below the statutory acreages. There was thus incentive for the opening of new land and for migration to the south where more intensive farming was climatically possible. Michel Cartier, in a 1991 review of Chinese research on Kiang-nan, considered that until the T'ang the agriculture of the area had been relatively backward. It supported a population of only three million engaged in small farms, often without ploughs or buffaloes, in the production of rice and hemp, the basic foodstuff and dress-stuff.[12] From the seventh century, with a climatic oscillation of warmer weather which increased both the need and opportunity for investment in irrigation and flood control, there was immigration, a move to larger farms (created by polderization) with ploughs and buffaloes, and crop diversification into silk, arboriculture, mulberry especially, and pisciculture in ponds, rivers and on the coast, where salt boiling made technical advances.[13] The Kiang-nan land pattern – rice at the bottom round the T'ai-hu lake created by the subsidence which followed the blocking of exits for deltaic waters; mulberry on the lower, inner rims round the sump; salt relegated to the coast – were set in place under the T'ang. All that was lacking was the later staple cotton, not yet or only tentatively installed, on the higher, outer rims.[14] Further to the south, on the higher hillsides, tea, introduced from Szechwan, began to be cultivated in market-oriented gardens. Everywhere, indeed, in Kiang-nan, basic crops for local consumption began to be supplemented by semi-luxury crops for wider distribution. By the end of the millennium the population of the core area had at least doubled to six million. Kiang-nan was not the only southern area which was developing in this period; the population of Szechwan, boosted by colonization of land taken from the aboriginal peoples in the south and east, rose from five million to eight million.[15] As a result, its own abundant, but still underdeveloped, salt resources were insufficient for its inhabitants and salt had to be imported from the Ho-tung brine lake in Shansi. Tea, grown on the hills west and east of Ch'eng-tu became a major export, while sugar, its technology borrowed from India, became in the T'o valley to the southeast a minor one.[16] It was at this time that Szechwan acquired its reputation as Heaven's inexhaustable storehouse on which subsequent fiscal bureaucrats of the Sung counter-revolution were to lay promotive but heavy hands. Sugar, along with China's first cotton fields, again borrowed from India, was also introduced to the Pearl River delta, where the cosmopolitan city of Canton, still more southeast Asian than Chinese in layout and appearance, was developed to handle the increasing volume of trade, especially in spices and aromatics, with the Nanyang. In southeast Anhwei, the population of the six districts first set up under the Sui, of Hui-chou prefecture, increased from 25,000 to 250,000 between 600 and 750. Through its enterprising gentry clans the area became a major centre for the production or marketing of tea, timber, and the local speciality, ink, for China's rising literacy. Population outgrew local rice supplies despite the local development of early ripening varieties before 1000 and gentry-inspired schemes of tanks, ducts and dykes.[17] To the south, western Fukien was another area of new tea gardens, its product marketed by Hui-chou. In southeast Fukien in the tenth century, Ch'uan-chou came to rival Canton, following its sack by the xenophobic rebel Huang Ch'ao in 871, as an entreprot for the Nan-yang trade, while Foochow in the centre of the province became a regional headquarters under the Five Dynasties and engaged in trade with Shantung to the north.[18]

At the end of the millennium, China and especially its provinces on or south of the Yangtze was still underpopulated and sparsely inhabited, a land of intensively cultivated oases separated by waste, jungle and uncultivated forested upland. It was punctual rather than areal in form, an archipelago more than a mainland, with plenty of room for later infill, but it was beginning to stake out its demographic territory. This process, the conquest of China by the Chinese, was a prime motor of economic growth between 500 and 1000.

## Technology

In the period under review, China both invented new technologies for itself and imported others from more advanced or different economies outside. Broadly speaking, the invented technologies were more significant in the long run and in world history since they were eventually exported and became ingredients in the re-rise of the West, while the imported technologies were more significant in the short run and in Chinese history because of their contribution to the rise of China to become the most advanced economy and the centre of such world economic order as existed at that time. In assessing their impacts in China across the spectrum of state, society, intellect or the economy itself, both sets of technology may be divided into the subsets of physical and social, forming four subsets as follows.

*Invented physical technology*

Here the impact was spread evenly across the spectrum. To the state, in the form of weaponry, new technology contributed co-fusion steel at the beginning of the period and gunpowder toward its end.[19] Co-fusion steel was the osmosis of low carbon wrought iron with high carbon cast iron to produce an intermediate carbon metal with the strength of the first and the acuity of the second minus their malleability and brittleness. The invention, which only reached Europe in the fourteenth century when cast iron became available through the adoption of the Chinese blast furnace, is credited to Ch'i-wu Huai-wen, artificer-general to the Northern Ch'i, towards the end of the sixth century. Its prerequisite was high furnace temperatures. The background here was China's precocity in ceramics and siderurgy and the immediate context was the change, initiated by the Northern Wei, from an army of infantry to an army of knights who needed improved weapons. Gunpowder first appears in a mid-ninth-century text, the *Chen-yüan miao-tao yao-lüeh*, contained in the Taoist patrology, which warns adepts not to play around with mixtures of charcoal, saltpetre and sulphur. By the early tenth century a low nitrate gunpowder was being used as ignition in a naphtha-based flame thrower, its first application to firearms. The antecedents here were, on the one hand, alchemical medicine, saltpetre (potassium nitrate) being described by the Taoist alchemist-physician T'ao Hung-ching in 492, and on the other the importation from the West of Greek fire, the flamethrowing weapon using petroleum, resin and sulphur, which was invented by the Byzantines around 678. Greek fire became known to the Chinese by the end of the ninth century, possibly earlier, and it was used by the Five Dynasties ruler of Wu-Yüeh, or Chekiang, Ch'ien Liu in the tenth century against his neighbour Nan-T'ang which then used it against the early Sung. A silk banner, dated to 950, brought to the Musée Guimet from Tun-huang by Paul Pelliot shows the Buddha, too, under attack by Mara and his demons with such flamethrowers. In reality, the Chinese were slow to apply gunpowder widely to military purposes perhaps because the Sung counter-revolution reacted against the practices of the predecessors. It was not until the twelfth century that, faced with a more serious barbarian threat, gunpowder was used for both propellent and incendiary purposes in rocket-launched fire lances (*huo-ch'iang*) and fire arrows (*huo-chien*), that is projectile devices in defence of walled cities. Europeans did not learn about gunpowder until the thirteenth century, and while it is said to have been used at Crecy in 1346, it did not become a major factor in warfare and the power of the state until Mehmet II's huge gun battered down the cannon gate at the siege of Constantinople in 1453.

Society was affected, too, by invented technology: directly by the rise of alchemical medicine, indirectly through the development of proto-porcelain, the ceramic which became so characteristic of the country as in many foreign languages to give it its name, as silk had done earlier. Alchemy, the anglicized form of an Arabic original which Needham sought to derive from *chin*, the Chinese for gold, was in China as much medical as metallurgical. Indeed, as Jung was one of the first to see, it was psychiatry as well as chemotherapy. It was based, Nathan Sivin has argued, on a notion of time technology whereby the retardation of time in bodies by the ingestion of mineral drugs (*wai-tan*) or by the constellation of anablastic archetypes (*nei-tan*) confered physical immortality, while the acceleration of time in matter would similarly turn base substances into precious. Time, the ultimate substance of all things, could be advanced or reversed into Intemporality, symbolized by jade, the most precious of substances. Alchemy in this sense was not a new notion in the T'ang period, but it underwent greater elaboration and diffusion through its alliance with religious Taoism first made by T'ao Hung-ching, the founder of the dominant Mao-shan school, and its association with the writings, real and atributed of Sun Ssu-mo, court physician to early T'ang emperors. Sun was a prestigious figure in the traditional history of Chinese medicine: for example a leading text giving prescriptions for the treatment of eye diseases, though much later in date, was subsequently ascribed to him because of its use of mineral drugs. The alliance of alchemy, Taoism and court, which was one of the characteristics of the T'ang period, increased the standing and social resonance of all three. It gave Chinese society a new dimension for patronage, expenditure and discourse in both poetry and prose, akin to the permeation of Western society in the second half of the

twentieth century by psychoanalysis and its derivates. In this dimension new medical and ultimately political clientelae could be nucle-
ated. Porcelain, or proto-porcelain, for the Chinese made a less
restrictive definition of this vitrified, translucent ceramic than that
which later became customary in the West, was an invention of this
period, another product of the superior Chinese ability to produce
high furnace temperatures.[20] Its development had implications for
manners, aesthetics and, more generally, civility. Its use inhibited
boorishness, turned tea drinking into an art form, and provided a
new medium for design, colour and decoration. In the T'ang Sino-
barbarian synthesis of values, it reasserted Chinese *yin* against Inner
Asian *yang*. Although scraps of Chinese alchemy had reached the
West in late antiquity before 500 in the form of aurifaction and
aurifiction, medical alchemy only began to surface in the high
middle ages with Roger Bacon, Albertus Magnus and Arnold of Villanova and was not fully absorbed till the Paracelsian reformation,
while porcelain, though noted by Marco Polo and prized by princely
collectors in both Islamdom and Christendom, was not successfully
imitated outside East Asia before the eighteenth century. Exported
under the T'ang notably to Egypt and the Gulf states, porcelain has
been called the first item of global culture.

   To the intellect, T'ang physical invention contributed print and
clockwork: an acceleration of communication and a paradigm of
explanation. When transplanted to the West in the fourteenth and
fifteenth centuries, these new technologies, it has been argued, were
major factors in the genesis of the Renaissance, the Reformations and
the Scientific Revolution.[21] In T'ang China, however, their impacts
were in contrast rather than in complement. The impact of print was
great. Both as civil-service recruitment and as social legitimation, the
examination system needed the more abundant copies of classical
texts which print provided. The eventual triumph of Confucianism
in the examinations and in society owed much to the fact that its
briefer set of texts were more suited to the print industry than the
more voluminous *Tripitaka* and *Tao-tsang*. Chinese print, based on
conserved woodblocks, easy to store, rather than on recomposited
moveable type, favoured short runs, small stocks and customer-
initiated reprints. The author and his public were therefore less
dependent on the publisher than was later the case in the West.
Print culture meant different things in Confuciandom and in

Christendom, while in India and Islamdom, except for Egypt, it was virtually ignored until imposed by European contact. By contrast to print as communication, in China, the impact of clockwork as a paradigm was limited. In Europe, clockwork became the preferred model of physics from Nicholas of Oresme to Max Planck, virtually eliminating the Aristotelian biological model and the alchemical workshop paradigm. In China, the clockwork paradigm never became predominant. Initially, it made little impact in an intellectual world where method predominated over logic, synchronicity over causality and algebra over arithmetic. Subsequently, when it was represented in a modified Euclidean form by the Jesuits, in the sixteenth and seventeenth centuries, it was explicitly rejected by Chinese scholars who instictively preferred paradigms more contextual and processual, less axiomatic and demonstrative. The conclusions of the Jesuits were accepted, and the practice drawn from them, but not their reasoning, epistemology and metaphysics.[22] By the time the Chinese did accept the clockwork paradigm at the end of the nineteenth century, it was becoming obsolete, relativized by field models and quantum mechanics.

Within the economy, the infrastructure was enriched by two pieces of invented physical technology: in production, by the new successive-basin solar evaporation technique for salt developed at the Ho-tung brine lake to supply the new Northern Wei capital of Lo-yang; in distribution, by the wider use of the magnetic compass which became prevalent in the south during the reign of Liang Wu-ti. Though the achievement of practitioners, both had antecedents, if not in Taoism, then in the alchemical outlook with which it was currently associated. The crystallization of salt out of a multichemical manifold of brine could be understood as a contrived emergence of cosmos out of chaos, while the acausal phenomenon of magnetism would not be unexpected in a universe connected by sympathy and synchronicity rather than by mechanism and causality. Salt was already a major item of long-distance commerce in China and the new technique did not become predominant until much later. Nevertheless, even in the short run, its use at Ho-tung improved both the quality and quantity of salt, distributed it over a wider and more unified market, and gave the north a powerful lever at a time when economic power was shifting to the south. Outside China, the technique was taken up by the Muslims, maybe, as with the earlier

Chinese invention of paper, via prisoners taken at the battle of the Talas river in 751 and diffused by them in the Islamic common market from Spain to India. They brought it to Europe via the short-lived emirate of Bari in the mid-ninth century, and from Apulia it was diffused to Christendom, east and west, south and north. That it was diffused and not merely reinvented is indicated by the presence everywhere of a not technologically necessary ratio of catchment, condensing and crystallization areas in a series of 3:2:1, a ratio subsequently modified to suit different climatic, social and economic circumstances. Navigation by magnetic compass, which facilitated sailing outside sight of land and in cloudy conditions, extended maritime shipping both north and south of the Yangtze and out of Canton into the Nan-yang. It turned the Chinese from river and inshore sailors into offshore and far-shore navigators. In Europe, the technique first appeared rather mysteriously at the turn of the twelve and thirteenth centuries in northern waters, where it contributed to the rise of the Hanseatic network. Again, independent rediscovery is unlikely and the agent of transmission must have been the barbarian successor states to the T'ang empire in Inner Asia, most likely the cosmopolitan kingdom of Kara Khitai.[23]

*Invented social technology*

Social mechanisms, and the institutions in which they are embodied, need inventing as much as pieces of physical technology. The period 500 to 1000 saw three major social inventions in China. First dating from the Sui and early T'ang and particularly promoted by Empress Wu, was a system of written examinations in a range of alternative subjects for civil-service recruitment and social accreditation. Initially, the system primarily affected the state, and that only to a limited degree, by introducing an element of meritocracy, but subsequently as extended by the Sung it had profound implications for Chinese society, economy and intellect. A significant recognition and promotion of intelligence in public life, it was only taken up in Europe in the eighteenth and nineteenth centuries, notably after the Trevelyan-Northcote report in England in 1853. Next, the expedient of the Silver T'ang minister Liu Yen, there was the systematic use of indirect taxation, notably on salt, as the main fiscal support of the state instead of direct taxes on land or people. Though socially regressive, indirect taxes are easier to assess and collect, and are less economically harmful than direct taxes. They give a maximum of output for a minimum of input and can be established or maintained in times of political weakness. Indirect taxes, first adopted systematically in Europe in the thirteenth century by Venice and Genoa, resorted to by Palaeologan Byzantium, consolidated as the excise by the Dutch Republic, became fundamental in Germany after 1871 in the division of obligations between the Reich and the Länder, and as value added tax currently form the fiscal basis of the European Union. They still embody the Chinese principle of *wu-wei*: reduced effort to achieve increased effect; in fiscal terms, lower rates and higher yields. Finally, with its system of imperial medical colleges, state examinations for doctors, official pharmacopeias, and forensic manuals for physicians, T'ang invented social technology contributed to professionalism in the state, society and the intellect. Though this was not a theme pursued by later dynasties, the system became the prototype for public health systems as opposed to health regulations such as quarantine, which, because of the lower incidence of epidemics, notably plague, was not, it seems, a Chinese practice. In the West, such state involvement in public health is usually assigned first to 931 in the reign of the Caliph al Muqtadir for examinations for doctors in Baghdad, and to 1224 in the reign of Emperor Frederick II for imperial sponsorship of the medical school at Salerno.[24]

*Imported physical technology*

Mention has already been made of the introduction of Greek fire, and another piece of Greek technology which passed from west to east, most likely from Syria, was glass colouration. Neither had a profound impact on China except perhaps as stimulants to gunpowder and porcelain. More significant were the imported technologies, both from India, of cotton and sugar. Cotton, in T'ang times, was a finished Indian import from Bengal, only marginally grown and processed in China. The chief textile fabrics were still silk for best use, and hemp or ramie (a finer, softer kind of hemp cultivated mainly in the south) for everyday use, with silk, mainly from Szechwan, increasing its market share substantially as overall prosperity grew. But in the long run, from the Yüan period, cotton became China's chief textile fabric, which it is still today, a remarkable Indianization of Chinese culture. Sugar, on the other hand, had a more immediate impact.[25] In T'ang times it established two definite bridge-heads: a major one in Szechwan at Sui-ning on the Fu river to the east of Ch'eng-tu, and a minor one in Kuang-tung in the Canton area, though this was badly hit by the sack during the Huang Ch'ao rebellion. Sugar, its imagery and its reality, came with Buddhism. It came therefore by both land and sea, making its first China-falls at Tun-huang in the northwest and at Yang-chou in the southeast before moving to more favourable locations further south. Cane sugar production involves five processes: growing, crushing, boiling, purifying and refining. The first four are documented for T'ang times. They produced both a softer and darker granulated product (*sha-t'ang*, sand sugar; *shih-mi*, stone honey) and a harder, lighter granulated form (*t'ang-shang*, sugar ice). Refining, generally in the form of washing in clay rather than reboiling, which resulted in hard white caster sugar (*yang-t'ang*, foreign sugar) or icing sugar (*ping-t'ang*, sugar ice) had to await an export market and imitation of foreign tastes in the seventeenth century. Until then, it seems, the Chinese preferred sugar large-grained and coloured, perhaps in conscious contrast with salt which they preferred small-grained and white. Salt and sugar were associates, not least in their common use of the *lou* or filter, the first to enrich brine before boiling, putting something in, the second to remove molasses and caramel after boiling, taking something out. The *lou* itself, unknown in Han times, was another piece of recent imported physical technology, probably from the southeast Asian cultural zone of still aboriginal south China.

*Imported social technology*

In the period 500 to 1000, China entered more deeply into two distribution networks which, while they involved physical techniques, were primarily pieces of social technology. The first was the camel network: the fusion of the Arabian and Bactrian transport subsystems which both preceded the rise of Islam and was extended by it. Before the T'ang period, the camel was low on the Chinese horizon; it was known as an occasional draft animal in the marginal agricultural lands of the northwest. It was known, too, as a pack animal in the same area, but, thanks to efficient equine harness, secondary to the horse-pulled cart. Because it was not a major food-producing animal in East Asian nomadic pastoralism, the number of Bactrian camels on or beyond the frontier was not large. With the unification of the

Arabian and Bactrian networks and China's return to Central Asia, the number of camels and their visibility on Chinese horizons, as expressed by tomb figurines, the Tun-huang cave paintings and literary references, rose and reached a peak in the first half of the T'ang period. Behind conspicuous numbers, however, lay social invention: a veritable Baltic exchange of breeders, trainers, brokers, charterers, operators, the world of the caravanserai, which in the West had already collapsed many classical gridiron plan cities into the *souk* cities of early Islam. Because the cart held its own against the camel, this did not happen to the same extent in China, but it did occur in the caravan cities of the Kansu panhandle where the Chinese orthogenetic model ceased to apply, as it did eventually in the *hu-t'ung*s of Peking where camels became the principal conveyors of coal from the local mines. The second distribution network into which China entered more deeply was the circuit of cross-Indian ocean and double-monsoon navigation which linked the West and China. It, too, involved social as well as physical invention, though here the contribution of China through the kingdom of Wu, ship design, fore and aft rig and the maritime compass, was greater than on land. Much of the organization, however, was non-Chinese. Cosmas Indicopleustes regarded Ceylon as the pivot of the circuit, while early Muslim authors emphasized the role of the Sumatran city of Srivijaya. Till the sack, Canton remained dominated by foreign mercantile communities. Both by land and sea China enriched herself by what had been initiated by others.

The new distribution networks brought changes to production and consumption through the greatest intellectual importation.[27] Buddhism came to China from two areas more highly developed: northwest India and southeast India, Gandhara and the Tamil Nadu. Moreover it came via areas of greater economic mobilization: the oasis city states of Central Asia and the estuarial city states of Southeast Asia. It therefore brought with it, in its saddle bags and cabin luggage, economic and social notions, practices and institutions unknown in China. Among these, L.S. Yang (1965) identified auctions, compound interest, equitable mortgages and the money club, to which Gernet (1956) added the monastery itself as the first, permanent non-kinship association, and via the notions of karma, the accumulation of merit and the Bodhisattva's self-giving, the distinction between risk capital and repayable loans, equities and bonds.

Buddhist monasteries in China, unlike Benedictine monasteries in the West, drew the greater part of their income not from the land, but from commercial activities such as money or grain lending, royalties from hydraulic flour mills and oil presses, and gifts from the faithful solicited by means akin to modern advertising and fundraising. In addition Buddhism revolutionized business by providing new objects for consumption and consumerism in buildings, statuary, incense use, celebration of festivals, giving of banquets to monks and making of pilgrimages to holy places. Mahayana Buddhism, like Counter-Reformation Catholicism, was a lavish extravagant religion, which surcharged expenditure and redirected demand. To society, it gave new forms of prestige and status, to the state new opportunities for patronage and clientage, and to the intellect a register of critical thinking, a new technical vocabulary and a fresh iconography. If any one factor, apart from political genius, took China from the periphery of the Eurasian world to its centre, it was the reception of Buddhism.

## Taste

By the reign of Hsüan-tsung, if not earlier, China's economic growth had been sufficient to bring into play, at least for a segment of the population, a third economic motor: taste or fashion which surcharges by turning high consumption into discriminating consumerism. Taste implies choice and, as Braudel (1974) argued, in a premodern economy, choice in any branch of consumption – food, dress, habitation or utilities – was a privilege confined to a few. Nevertheless, given the antecedent and concurrent dynamics of territorial expansion and technological innovation both invented and imported, that privilege could impart a further dynamic of its own as the creative periphery of the economy. Here it could act as what Gilles Lipovetsky, the historian of fashion called 'le rien qui fait tout'.[28] Fashion, as opposed to luxury, did not really exist in antiquity either eastern or western except episodically. Lipovetsky regarded it as 'une réalité sociale-historique caractéristique de l'Occident et de la modernité elle-même'.[29] He pursued its origins back into the later middle ages, especially as manifested in the Netherlands, but it may be suggested that there was a prehistory in T'ang China, that the Valois court of Burgundy was receiving light from the long-dead megastar of Hsüan-tsung's court at Ch'ang-an.

In the second, T'ien-pao era, half of his reign, when Ch'ang-an reached its greatest size and impact on the economy, the court of Hsüan-tsung displayed many similarities with the world of fashion, as described by Lipovetsky. First, there was the same restless search for novelty: in dress, hairstyles, furniture, calligraphy, sport, poetry and theatre: but most of all in music, where the welcome of new orchestral groups and instruments, song styles and dances, often imported from Central Asia, punctuated the life of the court. Not all the music was highbrow. One of the dances, the Western Twirling girls, in which Hsüan-tsung and Yang kuei-fei became accomplished performers, sounds like a sort of twist or rock'n roll. Patronage was extensive; by the end of the reign, several thousand musicians were given employment by the Palace. Second, there was the same mixture of the secular and the sacred: 'un lien intime, bien que paradoxale, unit *l'homo frivolus* et *l'homo religiosu*s du cas spécifique chrétien'.[30] In the case of China, the religious inspiration was not only Nestorian Christianity, whose influence has until recently been underestimated, but also Tantric Buddhism, Mao-shan and Ling-pao Taoism, and late Sassanid Zoroastrianism. It was characteristic of these religions that they gave spiritual value to matter whether in the Incarnation, the unity of *samsara* and *nirvana*, the possibility of physical immortality and transcendence, or the use of matter by Ahura Mazda to fight spiritual evil. Even Manichaeism, which divorced spirit and matter absolutely, could inspire a sort of punk anti-fashion in Ch'ang-an as in Uighur Turfan. Secular culture provided the details. The steppe world supplied falconry and furs, Iran perfume and horsemanship, India polo and chess, southeast Asia aromatics, pearls and exotic foods, China itself silk and tea. Third, while T'ang fashion never ceased to be bi-gendered, there was the same tendency for it to become feminine and for males to lapse into age-differentiated uniformity. The second tendency was strengthened by the Sung counter-revolution which universalized the scholar's gown among the elite, while any proto-feminism was curtailed by the male-designed but female-enforced practice of foot-binding. Finally, while T'ang fashion was elitist, it already displayed some of the phenomena which Lipovetsky associated with modern mass fashion: destabilization of social distance, enlargement of public space, ideological meltdown, substitution of advertisement for propaganda, cult of glitterati and media personalities at least in the case of poets, and a focus on the present rather than the past or the future in a conscious empire of the ephemeral.

T'ang consumerism was not confined to the court and Ch'ang-an. Moreover, the overthrow of Hsüan-tsung by the rebellion of An Lu-shan, far from destroying consumerism, diffused it to regional centres where court exiles took refuge. It spread to Yang-chou, where the Grand Canal crossed the Yangtze, the future headquarters of the salt administration, and in later times a famous centre for gastronomy, gardens and the theatre. It spread to I-chou in Szechwan, the future Ch'eng-tu, the centre of the booming silk and tea-producing area watered by the Min river barrage, which served as capital for Hsüan-tsung in 756, for Hsi-tsung in 881 and for the subsequent states of Anterior and Posterior Shu in the Five Dynasties period. I-chou was a major focus for the printing industry which supplied the book-sellers quarter later famously copied in Peking. It possessed a power-ful gold and silversmiths' banking guild which provided credit, and it was the place of the first private paper money to supplement liq-uidity. In the Silver T'ang period, these cities, renowned for rows of shops, night markets and festive atmosphere became the number-two and number-three metropole is of the empire and in the Five Dynasties period the capitals of independent states. Subsequently, K'ai-feng, the Northern Sung capital, became a major centre of con-sumerism, though the Sung counter-revolution redirected taste back to the classical mimesis of Confucian affluence. Throughout the period 700 to 1000, taste was a serious motor of economic growth; its golden if gaseous corona where as Lipovetsky put it 'Protée et Promethée sont de même souche'.[31]

## The management of Chinese economic growth, 500–1000

Motors, however powerful, require management, and as every investor knows it is on the quality of the managers that the success of enterprise capital depends. So it was with China Incorporated between 500 and 1000, though the form of management changed markedly with the transition from Golden to Silver T'ang around 750. In the first half of the T'ang period, that form may be described as capitalism without capitalists, a set of arrangements analogous with the Eparchic capitalism characteristic of the Byzantine economy under the Macedonian dynasty. Following the caesura of 750 a new form developed which for the first time in Chinese history comprized native big business as well as small business. Both forms may be delineated with reference to a grid consisting of a vertical axis public/private and a horizontal axis micro to macro. Before 750, management effectively occupied only three of the four quadrants; small-public, large-public, small-private. What was lacking till after that date was large-private, except in so far as this was provided by non-Chinese, intruded by the global economy via the camel and maritime distribution networks. This schema may now be unpacked more concretely.

First, the state macro-sector. The *tsu-yung-tiao* – grain, labour and silk – assessment imposed on the *chün-t'ien* assignment of land to farmers, of which the silk was the most valuable component, gave the state a controlling interest in food supply and luxury dress, especially in the major urban centres. In Ch'ang-an, the eastern market where such goods arrived from the Yangtze valley was conducted under official supervision as to prices and outlets. The arrival was dependent on the state-constructed and maintained Grand Canal whose barge people were state employees and which served hydraulic as well as transport purposes, especially in Anhwei and Honan. The grain tribute service was China's equivalent of the *annona*, though considerably surpassing it in capacity. In the western market, too, where large-scale foreign merchants and embassy agents took the initiative, the role of officials was nevertheless considerable: in diplomatic counter-tribute of silk, the military requirements of the army for large horses, and the civilian demand of the court for prestigious objects, such as jade, from Central Asia. Though the Chinese economy at this time was only partly monetarized and Hsüan-tsung's Confucian minister Chang Chiu-ling defended private coinage to increase money supply and reduce deflation, under his aristocratic but also technocratic successor Li Lin-fu government monopoly of coinage was increasingly asserted. It was reaffirmed after the rebellion of An Lu-shan, especially when taxation surcharges begin to be collected in money and fixed quotas made deflation advantageous to the government. In Chinese monetary theory coinage was regarded as a boon conferred on society by the state, one whose value needed to be maintained, but whose primary purpose was prestatory to facilitate the payment of tax. Another area where the Silver T'ang extended large-scale state control was in Liu Yen's salt monopoly which asserted a regalian right of first purchase and resale, rights subsequently extended to wholesale and sometimes even to retail. In the Five Dynasties and early Sung, similar rights were asserted over tea and urban leasing, though with less success. Finally, under the T'ang the state operated at considerable cost an imperial postal service for official correspondence which covered, by horse and boat, 20,000 miles of routes.[32] The state macro-sector was therefore large and pervasive.

Second, the state micro-sector. The largest part of this was rural: the millions of farmers who, especially in north China, received land allocations under the *chün-t'ien* system and became in effect sub-managers of agriculture for the state. When modern historians first read the T'ang land statutes with their complex assignments of large working-life grants (*k'ou-fen t'ien*), small grants in perpetuity (*yung-ye*), and intermediate transitional grants for the retired, widows, dependents, and so on, they found it difficult to believe that their implementation lay within the resources of a premodern bureaucracy. The discovery at Tun-huang and other sites in the northwest of actual working papers of the system, however, has made it clear that the statutes were put into effect for a considerable period of time. Admittedly the practice was less comprehensive than the theory. Some land was always held outside the system, especially by monasteries and the still landed aristocracy. There was not always sufficient acreage available to make allocations in full, since even in theory the system gave out more land than it took back. Nevertheless, down to 750 the system did establish a class of highly competent micro-managers, smallholders, female as well as male, with a mixture of usufruct and ownership, a possible optimum for the Chinese peasantry. For viability, however, the system demanded the constant acquisition of new cultivatable land through internal colonization. That new land, by the same token, was not the creation of the state, but, especially in the south, of colonial entrepreneurs, monastic and lay, and the *chün-t'ien* system was difficult to apply to it. With the rebellion of An Lu-shan in 755 and the long period of civil war which followed, the land allocation system broke down altogether and for the next 1000 years the Chinese state was increasingly pushed off the land except as tax collector. In the medium term, the Five Dynasties and the Sung, the beneficiaries were the colonial entrepreneurs. The attempt by the Southern Sung statesman Chia Ssu-tao to reverse the process by a scheme of land nationalization or *kung-t'ien* was a major reason for a flight from the dynasty by estate-holders which resulted in the replacement of the Sung by the Mongol Yüan. In Hsüan-tsung's reign, however, the state's involvement in micro-agriculture, though showing signs of strain and having to be reinvigorated in the 730s by another well-born technocratic minister Yü-wen Jung, was still in place in the countryside. Similarly in the cities, especially in the luxury and armaments industries, many artisans were in effect government employees or sub-contractors. The frontier between the public and private sectors was ill-defended and permeable.

Third, the private micro-sector. Small-scale private enterprise, though circumscribed by official supervision and guild regulation, certainly existed in T'ang China. Indeed, Hill Gates (1996) has argued that at least from Sung times, and it would not be unreasonable to extrapolate back in the Silver T'ang, such petty capitalism has been the chief motor of Chinese economic growth.[33] China, it may be argued, was the earliest nation of shopkeepers, the first country where enterprise culture and propensity to business were more than minoritarian and part of a collective ethos. In Gates' Marxian terminology, a petty capitalist mode of production coexisted with a state or tributary mode of production in a relationship, not without contradiction and conflicts (such as the characteristic Chinese protest by cessation of business), yet predominantly mutually reinforcing and symbiotic. Because such production, especially in silk, was domestic, in a patriarchal kinship-gender system imposed from above, the losers by this system were women and children, who became an exploited class, an alternative proletariat. Much of this analysis could be restated in non-Marxian terms, but it should be noted that not all such micro-business was domestic in character. One which was not was the building industry which, whether conducted by neighbourly mutual assistance or professional small-scale contractors, took place necessarily outside the home, often on an itinerant basis. Another, of growing importance in the southeast, was inshore and offshore fishing where, as in Europe, women were left minding the home base, a position of responsibility rather than subjection. Most service industries, it is true, such as restaurants, hairdressing and retail generally, were domestic in character, but it is not clear that women were always passive and exploited. Even in the silk industry, perhaps especially in the silk industry, the superior delicacy of female fingers

sometimes provided opportunities for self-employment and independence, especially, it seems, in the south where Han and non-Han
cultures overlapped.³⁴ Domesticity, moreover, did not imply isolation. Micro-business had to be flexible and responsive to demand. It
required intersubjective mutual trust which went beyond kinship
relations. Such trust was provided by specific religious affiliations,
Taoist or Tantric more than élitist Buddhist, and less specifically
by the temple management committees arising from indigenous
Chinese religion. These mini chambers of commerce were probably
at the height of their influence during the Silver T'ang and Five
Dynasties periods before being downgraded by the kinship-gender
institutional revival of the Sung counter-revolution, though this took
time to operate.

Fourth, the private macro sector. In the aristocratic, state-
dominated world of the T'ang, big business, which had existed in the
early days of the Han as described in a famous chapter of the *Shih-
chi*, was slow to assert itself. Despite those earlier examples of private
wealth and acumen, big business before the impact of Buddhism, was
held back by the absence of key economic concepts, notably the
notion of capital itself. Most large-scale enterprise, in the caravan
cities of the Kansu panhandle and at Yang-chou and Canton for the
seaborne trade, was foreign, predominantly Iranian in language, but
also by land Syriac and Turkish and by sea Singhalese, Arabic, Tamil
and Malay. This situation was not regarded unfavourably as a sign of
underdevelopment or threat of imperialism. On the contrary, since
Ssu-ma Ch'ien's chapter was read negatively and big business seen as
socially disruptive, it was better that it be foreign rather than domestic, a view still held by Vietnamese Confucianism as late as the nineteenth century. In China itself, however, it could not be maintained.
Following the rebellion of An Lu-shan, with the reduction of China's
links with the outside world and the requirements of physical reconstruction and cultural refinement at home, a genuine Chinese grand
capitalism began to emerge. It developed particularly in salt where
the need for capital was enhanced by the state monopoly with its
insistence on prepayment of tax by wholesalers; in timber, the prime
requirement in house construction, shipbuilding, much artisan work
and most fuel, which often had to come from a distance; and in tea,
the new cultural exigence driven by the currently fashionable innovation of Ch'an Buddhism, which was also a specialized import from

the south as processed in Szechwan and southern Anhwei. Medicines, vegetable and mineral, prompted by a new valetudinarianism, and spices, especially aromatics, propelled by a new sensitivity in smell, were other areas in which big business could show to advantage since large outlay, distance and time were involved. In the Silver T'ang and Five Dynasties periods, there was a shift in demand from the court to regional capitals, such as Ch'eng-tu, which widened the opportunities for the large-scale private sector because there the official presence was less overpowering. By the end of the millennium, the Chinese economy rested on a firm tripod of state, grand and petty enterprise which constituted not so much multiple parallel modes of production as a dynamic hierarchy of modes of consumption, distribution and production, integrated from the top down. It was this hierarchy, established under the T'ang, which lay behind the equal, if not greater, economic achievements of the Sung, until its management system was eroded by the promotive statism introduced by Wang An-shih and his successors.[35]

## Cross – economic comparison, 500–1000

China's economic growth, in gross and per capita terms, was not only absolute but also relative. This may be seen by comparison if the economic fortunes of the other major Eurasian areas of civilization are considered. Here again there are uncertainties about more than details, but the main outlines can be established and are compelling as to the fact of China's new precedence.

First the two Indias, Aryan and Dravidian. At the outset of the period, India possessed both the largest economy in the world and the highest per capita distribution from it, even if its political arrangements were less impressive than those of the Roman world or of Toba Wei China. India had the best basic cereal, rice; it had the best luxury foodstuff, sugar; it had the best everyday fabric, cotton; it had the strongest domesticated animal, the elephant; and it had the most sophisticated mathematical notation, 'Arabic' numerals. When Fa-hsien visited India during the reign of Chandragupta II (370–415), a period of good governance, he regarded it as a Utopia, as Marco Polo would regard China under Khubilai Khan. Magadha, in the middle Ganges valley, the heart of the Gupta realm, was the most urbanized, richest and most prosperous, most virtuous place on earth, a witness to the truths of Buddhism, even though these were now in partial eclipse under a Hindu dynasty. Hsüan-tsang, in India in the reign of Harsha (606–647), a pro-Buddhist ruler, was still admiring but no longer astonished: China and India were parallel Buddhist civilizations. By the end of the period, however, the Indian economy had definitely been overtaken by the Chinese in both absolute and per capita terms, the first despite the fact that the two Indias may still have had a population in excess of China's. Only particular parts of India, especially in the south and in Bengal, continued to impress. India's wealth, it appears, redistributed itself rather than grew.

How had this happened? It happened, it may be argued, as much by political as economic factors. The cooler and wetter weather of the natural environment should have benefited the drought-threatened northwest and challenged the wetter east and south, but if so it was a challenge responded to by the economies of the Palas in Bengal and the Pallavas of Madras, while the economies of the Pratiharas, the Chalukyas and the Rashtrakutas saw their benefits dissipated by the bellicose politics of their rulers. Infrastructure could not flourish under a destructive superstructure. Similarly, in human ecology, though neither India nor China suffered from the first plague pandemic 500–750, Indian sociology allowed a strong demography to multiply production rather than productivity. India not China was the true land of sanctimonious poverty. In the absence of plague, India was not in a position to obtain its occasional positive side-effects in a higher propensity to consume and greater capital intensification, such as occured in the European Later Middle Ages according to David Herlihy (1997) and Norman Cantor (2001), and may have occured too in early Byzantium.[36] The Indian economy did not draw significant new power from changes in its motors. Internally its territory did expand, but not, except in Bengal and the Cauvery delta, to any depth. Externally, its prolongation into Southeast Asia in one direction and into the Himalayas in another, was cultural rather than economic, though there were commercial advantages, especially to the Tamil Nadu, in the export of Buddhist and Hindu institutions to Java, Sumatra and Cambodia. In technology, India, from its advanced position, exported more than it imported: an advantage to the rest of the world, China in particular, but less so for India herself since she lost her monopoly of sugar and cotton.

India's only two significant technological imports in the period under review were the spinning wheel from Iran and successive-basin solar evaporation for salt from China, both late and through Islamic vectors. In taste, however, the coming of Islam did not bring the across-the-board change Buddhism brought to China. Rather, it brought only a new stratum or sediment to lie parallel to those Indian society was already creating for itself in embryonic castes and through the new cults of Siva and Vishnu which were turning Brahmanism into Hinduism. Management, too, saw little development, an effective tripod of princely patrons, great merchant partners and artisan clients already existed, and seemed to require little improvement as an influx of gold continued to lubricate the economy as well as satisfying the demand for thesaurization. India was beginning to suffer from what has been called the law of the retarding lead.

Second, Islamdom: first the single state empire of the Ummayads and early Abbasids, then the multistate commonwealth of the later Abbasids and their successors, Arabic, Iranian, Turkish and Berber. Next to China Islamdom was the greatest economic growth area of the Dark/Light ages. It was, however, a forced hot-house growth with shallow roots, achieved by the resynthesis of assets which already existed rather than by their creation. Moreover it was inhibited in its heartlands by a low ceiling in the key energy resource of timber.

Here early Islamdom was favoured by the cooler and wetter natural environment, whose moisture provided more trees for construction, fuel, workshops and shipyards, as well as refreshing the parched lands to the south and east of the Mediterranean. In human ecology, if the argument given above is correct, Islamdom was relatively immune from the demographic ravages of smallpox. While it suffered from those of the first plague pandemic, it was in a position to use its economic opportunities, coming as it did from the Fertile Crescent where labour was always scarce and developing high consumer expectations as it conquered. With regard to the motors of growth, the Islamic *umma* saw territorial expansion unmatched since the post-Alexander the Great conquests of Hellenism and unsurpassed till the post-Chinggis conquests of the Mongol *ordo*, but, except in Africa, it was a unification of civilized lands rather than their extension. In technology, Islamdom inherited from the Roman world (glass), acquired in Iran (perfume distillation, brass, *qanat* hydraulics, windmills), imported from India (sugar, cotton, numerals) and China (paper, successive basin solar evaporation, further installments of alchemy, steel technology, medical institutions) and diffused, but itself invented little. In taste, Islamdom was from the beginning dangerously self-sufficient and inward-looking, apart from the predilection from the Fatimid period onwards of its élites for Chinese porcelain, a taste which was eventually to transform production and tastes in China itself. The Islamic explosion, at once a cultural revolution by provincials and a spending spree by parvenus suddenly become patricians, tolerated exotic diversity, but did not welcome it to the same degree as T'ang cosmopolitanism. As regards management, the early Islamic economy suffered from the growing gap above it between state and society: between sultans with power but no legitimacy and the *sadr* of canon lawyers, landowners and great merchants with legitimacy but no power; a schism which underlay the transformation of the empire into a commonwealth. Islamic sociology favoured capitalists, both grand and petty, and encouraged both individual and corporate enterprise. It is not so clear that it promoted capitalism in the sense of independent, self-regulating market mechanisms. If the state and society were too distinct, the economy was too embedded in society. It remained a moral economy rather than a free one. Similarly in the macro-economy, Islamdom provided a free-trade area, but it did not evolve into a genuine common market such as was provided by the Chinese *Weltreich*. Only in particular states, generally of medium size, such as Ummayad Cordoba, Aghlabid Tunisia, Fatimid Egypt and Samanid Sarmarkand was management sufficiently supported in independence to produce sustained growth once the windfalls released by dethesaurization were past.

Third, the Byzantine empire which, with the conversion of Rus in 988 and the tacit recognition of the independence of Georgia shortly thereafter, was turning into a Byzantine commonwealth where the frontiers of the imperial state were no longer coterminous with those of Orthodoxy. In overall terms it may be said that the Byzantine economy grew between 500 and 1000 but only modestly. This statement, however, conceals a U-shaped trajectory: prosperity in the sixth century, collapse in the seventh and eighth centuries, and recovery in the ninth and tenth centuries, a recovery which then accelerated after 1000 in the Late Macedonian and Early Comnenian periods. Constantinople illustrates this pattern. Its population passed from 400,000 in 500 to 100,000 in 750 to 400,000 again, or more in 1000.[37]

Milieu was the key factor in this trajectory. In the natural environment, wetter and cooler weather was to the advantage of Sicily, Tunisia, Egypt and Syria where the agricultural base of Justinian's empire lay. When these provinces were lost to the Muslims, the weather continued to benefit the new basis that the empire found for itself in Apulia, the Morea and Western Anatolia. The coming to human ecology of plague, smallpox and anthrax, however, was highly deleterious both in the demographic losses, which were especially serious in the large urban sector, and in the compensatory inflow they provoked which included the politically disruptive Slav migrations and Muslim invasions. The truncated empire of the Heraclian and Isaurian dynasties suffered from reduced revenues from a contracted economy. The downturn, though deep, however, proved temporary. The plague episode with its 11-year pulsations came to an end around 750. There are signs that the Byzantine economy, like that of Latin Christendom in the Later Middle Ages, gathered some positive side-effects from plague in increased capitalization and heightened consumptivity. These are particularly evident in the spread in the production and consumption of silk from Constantinople to Thessalonika, Thebes, Athens, Corinth and the Peloponnese which acquired, probably from its mulberry trees, its new name of the Morea. The different phases of the silk business became highly specialized. If there is little indication of machinery or new sources of energy, there is plenty of the systematic division of labour: the first occurrence in a major industry in Europe of Adam Smith's prime-mover.

The motors of this post-800 economic growth were various. Territorial expansion was exemplified by the recovery of Southern Italy, Cyprus and Crete, the re-Hellenization of Slav immigrants in Greece, their conversion to orthodoxy, political conquests in the northern Balkans, and the extension of Byzantine influence north and east of the Black Sea through the conversion of Rus. At times the Byzantine world extended as far as Prague and Novgorod. Though technological invention was thin on the ground, except for Greek fire, technological importation was considerable: silk, collar harness, stirrups, lateen sail, successive-basin solar evaporation, paper, windmills. Taste too changed. With the decline of the decurion class in the cities with its euergetist mode of consumption expressed in the classical public amenities, there was a shift to a style more interior, domestic and familial, as exemplified by the small, internally jewel-like, later Byzantine churches as contrasted with the earlier, externally magnificent basilicas. Management was similar to that in the first half of the T'ang. In the countryside there were smallholders protected by the state; in the towns, if one follows the *Book of the Eparch*, there was a mixture of state enterprises and private workshops subordinated to craft guilds under official supervision. There was a relative absence of merchant guilds and great merchants. But whereas in China after 750 great merchants began to substitute themselves for foreigners, in Byzantium the role of foreigners – Amalfians, Venetians, Pisans, Genoese, Rus – grew ever larger. The Byzantine economy chose to invest in industry rather than commerce, no doubt because higher risks were seen in distribution rather than production. Its tumultuous course between 500 and 1000 left the Byzantine economy with a reluctance to assume or manage risk, and that function therefore fell to the Latins.

Finally, Latin Christendom. To reiterate, the Dark Ages were dark only in that they have left few written or archaeological vestiges so that many problems remain obscure. It must not be imagined therefore that it was a period of general economic regression or fall in living standards. The disappearance of the imperial superstructure and part of the urban proliferation it had fostered, both costly, brought gain as well as loss. Overall, although the judgement is qualitative as well as quantitative, the economic balance between 500 and 1000 was positive, though many of the favourable items were in basic consumption. In its lack of conspicuous progress Latin Christendom was at the antipodes from T'ang China. Rome, once the centre of the world order, was now at its periphery, but as Silvester II, Pope in the millennium year may have dimly perceived, it had not lost all hope of restoration.[38]

The milieu was not favourable. The natural environment, with its cooler and wetter weather, made the chosen line of investment, the colonization of forest and marsh by assarting and defrichement, more difficult. The same weather, in human ecology already burdened by plague, smallpox and anthrax, promoted the additional handicap of the mycotoxicoses, fungal poisoning derived from mushrooms, mildews and moulds.[39] Ergotism was injurious in itself, lowered resistance to other infections and damaged the immune system. By reducing fertility and increasing mortality, it was a serious factor in demography, particularly where rye was the principal cereal crop, as it was in much of the new land being brought into cultivation east of the Rhine. To overcome these impediments, the Latin economy required powerful motors. Territorial expansion was the most significant: outward to Ireland, upwards into the Alps and the Cantabrian highlands, downwards into the wetlands of the Rhine and Po deltas, but above all eastward into Germany and the confines of Poland, Bohemia and Hungary where it disputed Byzantine hegemony. In technology, contrary to popular impression, the fall of the Roman empire brought no serious losses, but the innovations, invented or imported – the heavy plough, the collar harness for horses, successive-basin solar evaporation for salt, improved script and musical notation – produced results only slowly. Taste was limited by absence of consumer choice and until the rise of Romanesque architecture, remained within the confines of late-antique and Byzantine paradigms. Management did its best with the motors, but it too was limited. Below the territorial polities, the ecclesiastical palatinates and the mercantile communities, all still embryonic, was the landed estate. Variously named and multiform, *Massa* in Central Italy, *Shire* in Northumbria, it was less a piece of realty than a complex of activities, rights and obligations involving many stakeholders: a punchbowl of ingredients into which spoons of various sizes might be dipped in accordance with more or less self-enforcing legal rules.

The best-known of such structures is the Benedictine monastery, for example Pomposa in the Po delta, which Newman saw as the characteristic institution of the Latin Dark Ages, the Benedictine centuries. In theory, it was a self-contained cell: 'the monastery ought if possible to be so constituted that all things necessary, such as water, a mill, and the various crafts may be contained within it', as the sixty-sixth chapter of the Rule put it.[40] In practice, the cell did not exclude pseudopods beyond its ring-fence – rights to salt were often held at some distance – and it was capable of wider connections and federation, as the model of Cluny was beginning to show. It was in this basic infrastructural unit that Latin Christendom invested most heavily. Here, at the grassroots, was an institution, the monastery, which was common to the Far West at the periphery of the world economic order and to China at its centre in a pattern of universal, but uneven, economic growth. For wherever the monastery was situated, in town or country, whereas in the West the sources of monastic wealth were predominently agricultural and rural, in China they were commercial and urban. The Benedictine monastery was at the periphery of an economic world, the Buddhist monastery at what had become its centre.

# 4
# Society: A Multiple China

Between 500 and 1000, Chinese society underwent a process of diversification from relative simplicity to manifest complexity, which made it by the reign of emperor Hsüan-tsung the most sophisticated in the world. Some of the differentiation effected successively by the Sui-T'ang reconstruction, the Silver T'ang restoration and Five Dynasties regionalism was subsequently curtailed or rehomogenized by the Sung counter-revolution, but enough survived, or in some cases was extended, in the following millennium to substantiate images in the West of China as Social Utopia: Marco Polo's consumerist megapolis, Matteo Ricci's ethical meritocracy, François Quesnay's peasant physiocracy. The reality, however, was more far-reaching than the images. Social diversification under the T'ang penetrated the interface between the economy and society, the matrix of social activity, the anthropology of marriage and gender relations as well as non-kinship institutions, associations and ethnicity. These constituents of Chinese sociology will be outlined before making a comparison with the other civilized centres of Eurasia during the same period.

## The interface between the economy and society

In reaction against a Marxism which reduced society to an epiphenomenon of economy, recent historical investigations of economic and social institutions have emphasized their distinction and interdependence. Thus the economy provides wealth and acquisition, where society provides status and recognition. Both are fields of meaning and sources of messages, but where the economy regulates things by compulsion, society rules people by values. Yet each is constrained by the other in a binary system. The economy is constrained by demand, since production and distribution are only rational in terms of consumption, which is ruled by society. Society is constrained by supply, since consumption is only feasible in terms of production and distribution, which are regulated by the economy. The interdependencies between basically independent variables necessitated periodic or local readjustments of both means and ends. Characteristic of premodernity was the pursuit of common and unchanging social priorities by different and changing strategies in a variety of economic circumstances and conjunctures. Such adaptations might, with the onset of modernity, terminate in partial or total shifts in priorities once new circumstances made them feasible. A study of binary adaptations and reversals of this kind of particular suggestiveness for the emergence of a multiple China is that of Gérard Delille (1985) with regard to Naples and the Neapolitan kingdom in the second half of the second Christian millennium, at a time when that city was the most dynamic urban complex in the Spanish empire.[1] Here Delille presents the contrasting yet complimentary economics of Campania and Apulia, the silk, wine and olives of the first, the cereals, pastoralism and salt of the second, their different rates of natality and mortality, opposite marriage localizations, alternative approaches to clientage and God-parenthood, as nevertheless coordinated by a single set of basically endogamous, lineage-oriented, social priorities. This set of values persisted from the fifteenth to the twentieth century and found expression not only in the layout of rural communities – villages and townships – but also in the topography of Naples itself, 'macrocosme gigantesque' of the twinned economies and sociologies of Campania and Apulia.[2]

To the historian of T'ang China what is most suggestive in Delille's study is its juxtaposition of often intensive agriculture and super urbanization on the one hand, with a strong sense of lineage and a preference for endogamy on the other. Thanks to the territorial expansion, which was one of the motors of its economic growth, T'ang China, though cross-latitudinal rather than cross-longitudinal, like the Neapolitan kingdom, had a binary structure. Its northern and southern moieties corresponded with Campania in the west and Apulia in the east. Like the Neapolitan kingdom again, the relationship between the two components was originally colonial in character. But whereas Apulia remained colonial, a land of immigration, primary products, repatriation of profits, attempted compensations and ongoing dependency, Southern Szechwan and Kiang-nan, because of higher levels of investment and the growth of secondary and tertiary sectors, escaped colonial dependency and became first equal then dominant partners with the north, going on to establish colonies of their own in Kweichow and Fukien. The underlying duality, however, remained, and in the face of a binary economy T'ang China, like the Neapolitan kingdom, adopted a dual sociology. This was most evident in its double system of marriage, a duality which nevertheless expressed a single underlying set of social priorities and values. Indeed, in China, diversification went further than in the Neapolitan kingdom in that eventually four systems of marriage emerged (discussed later, this chapter), as China south of the Yangtze added a new frontier with its own colonies to that which it already had with its northern parent. A further difference from the Neapolitan kingdom was that whereas in Delille's story the underlying traditional set of values was eventually eroded by the onset of both economic and sociological modernization, in China the traditional set of values was reinforced by the Sung counter-revolution, so that its multiple strategies were preserved into modern times to constitute what might be called an alternative model of modernization. That reinforcement of tradition was the product not of either economic or social institutions, by themselves, or even of their interaction, but rather of sociology's other interface, that with the intellect, which will be taken up in the next chapter. What is emphasized here is that with the economic developments outlined in the previous chapter, the interface between the economy and society became increasingly multifaceted and fractalized. Society had to update its game in the face of greater complexity and followed suit with a corresponding multiplicity.

## The matrix of social activity: family and friends

It is commonly held that the family, in some sense, has always been of special, perhaps defining and unique, importance among Chinese social institutions. *Hsiao*, filial piety, it has been argued, is the characteristic Confucian virtue, as charity is the characteristic Christian virtue. As between East and West, an ethic of deference confronts an ethic of equality.[3] At the same time, particularly with regard to the present, it is recognized that *kuan-hsi*, relationship or connections, not necessarily of kinship but also of place, age, education, employment and *curriculum vitae*, play a crucial part in determining an individual's fortune or status, in China as elsewhere.[4] In the past, *chung*, loyalty, variously to dynasty, teachers, friends and firm, ran *hsiao* a close second as a Confucian virtue. In both cases it was a question of the We surrounding the I: the matrix of social activity; humanity as membership rather than individuality. In China, as in other sociologies, in T'ang China as in the People's Republic today, individuals can be seen as acting always in two planes presented along two axes. First, there is a vertical axis of family relationships: parents, siblings, cousins, marriage partners, in-laws, children, descendants and forebears, kin of one kind or another; this is a biological axis, even if the kinship is selective or fictive, pseudo-kinship by protocol rather than by genetics. Second, there is a horizontal axis of friendship and association: real friends, acquaintances, partners at work, neighbours at home, customers, clients, class contemporaries, fellow countrymen: this is a sociological axis, even if sometimes expressed in kinship terms, social proximity being familiarized into God-parents, *alma maters*, Dutch Uncles, brother officers, unrelated aunts, and so on. Along both axes one may arrange institutions according to size, concreteness, complexity and abstraction. Thus along the vertical family axis are set the married couple, the nuclear family (children or grandparents), the multiple family (more than one nuclear family, living or acting together), the extended family (all parts of at least three generations of common descent), the lineage with a longer and wider definition, the clan as established by joining lineages into genealogies, the tribe with only presumed genetic linkages arising from the blood group and genomic differential. A similar list may be made on the axis of association: school friends, close contemporaries in place or purpose, business or professional contacts, age cohorts, class profiles, tax brackets, psychological types, ethnicity, language, ecology, gender. Again the list runs from concrete to abstract, from small to large.

In relationship to the axes of the social matrix, an individual's position will vary in two ways: first, by what the axes have to offer, that is what kind of society it is; second, by his or her own particularities of age, gender, personality, wealth and social status. Thus everyone starts in the nuclear family and the lower levels of the biological axis. With education and career, there is a move to higher levels along the sociological axis. Marriage brings reconnection with the family, while retirement implies at least partial withdrawal from association. Finally, death in premodern societies is familial, in modern ones it is more likely to be extra-familial, in hospice or hospital. Our focus of interest at present, however, is less the trajectory of the individual than the structure of the social matrix itself. Here three questions are worth asking about any society. First, where along each axis do the principle institutions of the society lie? Second, which axis, kinship or association predominates in the institutional milieu? Third, what is the specific character of the leading institution among those of the dominant axis? These questions will now be put to T'ang society as it developed and diversified between 500 and 1000.

On the family axis, institutions in China may be identified through the four terms in current use: *chia*, *tsu*, *tsung* and *hsing*. *Chia* was the ordinary word for household in the sense of related persons co-resident under one roof, sometimes together with unrelated servants, guests and lodgers. Two kinds of household were distinguished: the *hsiao-chia*, or small household, of two generations, that is the nuclear family; and the *ta-chia*, or large household, of more than two generations, that is the extended family, or in the case of coresident married brothers with children, the multiple family. *Tsu* was the lineage, a larger, sizeable group defined by common ancestry, more abstract because not generally co-resident even in a family compound, but linked by the possession of a lineage hall, a burial ground, and common funds for welfare and education.[5] Some lineages were designated by a choronym, the Wangs of so and so, though the link was often honorary and vestigial and did not necessarily imply substantial landed property in the locality. The lineage, halfway along the family axis, was the preferred institution of the Sung counter-revolution. *Tsung* was the clan, a larger, older, more notional assemblage, which ran to several thousand members and mixed kinship with pseudo-kinship and the clientage of *k'o*, 'guests' or retainers. In later times, the *tsung* was confined effectively to the imperial house which managed its affairs through a bureaucratic imperial clan court, but in the T'ang period the imperial house was only *primus inter pares* in a network of allied but competing aristocratic clans. Such clans, ascendant since the Eastern Han, had dominated China during the period, and some, sometimes descended from former dynasties, enjoyed social status and matrimonial prestige higher than that of the T'ang themselves. Such prestige was important in a society where male hypergamy was the rule and where honour went through the female line, so that nubility, in the sense of desirability of marriage alliance, was nobility. Consequently, the T'ang found it necessary to issue official genealogies to counteract the superior marriage claims, in particular, of a number of ancient, great clans linked choronymically to the Confucian homeland province of Shantung. Finally, *hsing*, the present-day word for surname, also had the connotation of tribe or race. Then, as now, there were comparatively few surnames in China: Wang, Li, Chang and Ch'en might cover 80 per cent of the population; but there was, and is a feeling that people of the same surname should not marry. The presumption was that they must be ultimately related and form part of an immense superclan. Endogamy, *per se*, as in most traditional societies was not much objected to, indeed within limits was enjoined to preserve property and maintain connections, but its prohibition was upheld at the abstract level of the *hsing*, all other things being equal.

Which of these forms of family organization was most significant for most people in the T'ang period? The *hsing* was vestigial. The *tsung* was hardly less so, except in the care of the imperial house, which was endeavouring to put itself above all others. The other great aristocratic clans, which had dominated society under the Hou Han, the *San-kuo* and the Chin, were changing their portfolio strategies and losing interest in vast numbers of kin and pseudo-kin. Quality rather than quantity was now the hallmark of a good clientela: court office, exam success, army command. Kuo Tzu-i, victor in the rebellion of An Lu-shan and defender of the empire against the Uighurs and the Tibetans, was the last founder of an aristocratic clan in the old sense: as a military man he needed numbers and his descendants' marriages with the imperial house for five successive reigns made his clan in effect a consort family or *wai-ch'i*.[6] The real issue, therefore, was between the *chia* and the *tsu*: the household in its two forms, small and large, nuclear or extended, and the lineage. Here ecology was determinant. On the North China plain, where the *chün-t'ien* system of land allotment was strictly applied, the household was the operative unit, and given prevailing death rates and life expectancies, the nuclear rather than the extended household. On the other hand, in the newer colonial territories of the south, where agricultural rice paddies were effectively being created out of wetland and forest by large-scale entrepreneurship, the lineage was predominant over its component households. However, not all internal colonization was done by lineages. In Szechwan it was the work of *t'u-hao*, local strongmen, a mixed group of landowners, charismatic adventurers, frontier merchants and converted native chiefs whose fortified hamlets and hillforts (*chai*) eventually gave way, as security improved, to isolated household farms rather than lineage villages as the predominant pattern of settlement.[7] Except in Kiang-nan and its subsequent colonies in Fukien and Kwangtung, one must conclude that it was the household, and generally the nuclear rather than the extended or multiple household, which was the most significant institution on the family axis. The same possessive individualism which, it is argued, later characterized medieval European society was thus precociously evident in 'Dark Age' China.

On the friends' axis, too, there was a similar predominance of institutions on the smaller, more concrete levels: the stall, the workshop, the partnership, the shrine, the cell rather than the firm, the corporation, the temple or the monastery. Nevertheless, while the average size of family units was probably declining, the average size of associative units was probably increasing. The rise of Buddhist and Taoist religious houses in the first half of the T'ang period contributed to this molecularization of atoms, as did the development of large-scale commerce in tea, salt and timber in the second. The increase in the level of urbanization from maybe only 5 per cent of the population to around 20 per cent turned the street and the road, and perhaps even more the river and the canal reach, into effective sociological entities. Inside the burgeoning cities, immigrants from a particular area often took up a common line of business and congregated together to form the *t'ung-hang* and *t'ung-hsiang* groups of later Chinese history with their striking *hui-kuan* or community halls. The presence of coherent foreign communities in Ch'ang-an, Yang-chou and Canton-Uighurs, Koreans, Japanese, Malays, Persians and Arabs – was beginning to provoke a xenophobic backlash and the embryonic sense of Chinese ethnicity, even Chinese racism, which one finds in Confucian writers such as Han Yü. Associative reference was widening. This contrast between the movement upwards on the friends' axis and the movement downwards on the family axis no doubt reflects a mechanism of compensation. The more the family atomized, the more alternative social institutions needed to aggregate and the further they did so the further independent households could operate outside larger kinship networks. Individualism and corporatization went hand in hand as they did in later northwest European society in the early modern period.

It may now be enquired which axis, kinship or association, predominated in the social milieu of T'ang China. The answer is clear. Despite urbanization and the growth of new institutions at the higher end of the sociological axis, the family axis continued to prevail if society is taken as a whole. Indeed urbanization, in its Chinese pattern of male immigration with wives initially left behind with their parents in law, may have helped sustain this prevalence. In this sense, the conventional picture of China as a country whose society was unusually permeated by kinship and its values is correct. The course of events is its illustration. The eventual relativization of Golden T'ang, the court-provinces duality of Silver T'ang, the failure of the Five Dynasties and Ten States to revolutionize China, and the victory of the Sung counter-revolution, all owed something to the ongoing predominance of kinship institutions in society. Once again, one is reminded of Delille's kingdom of Naples where massive urbanization, cultural originality and institutional pluralism were sustained by kinship rather than association in the Mezzogiorno's alternative model of modernization. Since kinship, however, is as broad a term as association, this assertion of the prevalence of family over friends is insufficiently specific about the character of T'ang society without a further enquiry into what must always be the key factor in any system of kinship: marriage and its anthropology.

## An anthropology of Chinese marriage

The study of marriage as an institution in China is in its infancy even for modern times,[8] and to attempt to reconstruct its profile in the remoter past therefore involves speculation. Nevertheless, the subject is of such importance for understanding the dynamics of a family-oriented society that the attempt must be made. It is best to begin with what is known of current, or recent past practice, and from there to extrapolate to earlier conditions and developments.

The most striking feature about marriage in China in the recent past was that it was, as an institution, multiple rather than unitary. This would not have surprised a Roman of classical antiquity or an early Muslim, but it did surprise Europeans of current modernity for whom, since Justinian I defined marriage as cohabitation and Ivo of Chartres redefined it as cohabitation by consent, matrimony has been a unitary institution. It was not so in premodern China either in theory or practice. Marriage was multiple in order to match a variety of social and economic circumstances and imperatives. So far research has isolated four varieties of marriage in premodern China. No doubt others await discovery, quite apart from the marriage systems of the minority peoples, such as Tibetan polyandry or Tungan polygamy.

First, most esteemed, there was major marriage, which was presumed everywhere as the norm, though in many areas this was not justified by the facts. Major marriage was virilocal or rather parentolocal, the groom's parents' residence. Neolocality, a separate home for a newly married couple, was not a Chinese ideal nor, except in the case of some urban immigrants, a Chinese practice. Following the payment of *p'ing-chin* or brideprice and accompanied by the transfer of *chia-chuang* or dowry, a girl aged 18 left her home with much ceremony – her procession took precedence in the streets over that of even the highest mandarin – and went to live in the home of her husband aged 23. The dowry should be more valuable than the brideprice since it was presumed that the bride's family was higher in social status than the bridegroom's and thus required its status to be displayed. The bridegroom might be less than 23. In Shantung and Chihli, rich older girls marrying poor younger boys might be older than their grooms. On marriage, the girl ceased to be a member of her parental family for ritual purposes and joined that of her husband; but her brother, if any, retained some responsibility for her. If she died, he must inspect the coffin and might lecture her children, especially the males, as to their filial duties. There was some sign, therefore, of what anthropologists call an avunculate: the special relationship of a mother's brother to his sister's sons. In general, major marriage was very much a family affair. It was a formal alliance. It established a patron/client, host/guest relationship between the bride's family and the bridegroom's or lack of it. For a common pattern was for high-status gentry-lineage girls coming from a *tsu* to marry the son of a nouveau riche low-status merchant with only a *chia*. Marriage alliances of this sort fed into *kuan-hsi*, networking, and served some of the purposes of God-parenting in the West, at least in the Apulian rather than the Campanian version of that institution. Major marriage came with strings attached.

Second, there was minor marriage. This too was virilocal, but in very different circumstances. It was not prestigious, no mandarins yielded precedence to its processions, but it was widely practised and was much more common than most Chinese believed. Under it, a girl variously known as *t'ung-yang-hsi* (daughter-in-law reared from childhood), *hsi-fu-tzu* or *sim-pu-a* in Hokkien, was brought into the household of her prospective bridegroom at a very early age, sometimes even before weaning, and only married formally 15 or so years later generally without much ceremony. Frequently no brideprice was paid, often only a minimum dowry followed, and no strong ties were created between the in-laws, a situation reminiscent of God-parenthood in Campania where only the midwife might be nominated to satisfy canon law. Minor marriage was tantamount to adoption, a practice which Chinese Confucianism, like traditional Christendom but unlike Japanese Confucianism, did not favour. Once transferred, *sim-pu-a* were treated as daughters in their new homes. Sometimes they were not married later to the son of the household, but were married out into a different family in major marriage. Alternatively they were taken in before any sons had been born, as there was widespread belief, for which there is basis in anecdote if not in science, that such adoption promoted fertility in the adopting mother. As Maurice Freedman put it in 1975, the *sim-pu-a* was really 'an all purpose female': servant, concubine, daughter, daughter-in-law; the only difference from an adopted child being that she had *some* prospect of marriage with a son of the family. In recent times, the giving and taking of girls as *sim-pu-a* was a widespread practice: in some areas amounting to 70 per cent of girls from all income brackets. For minor marriage was not confined to the poor and it was not the same as selling daughters into prostitution in time of famine, a practice which like female infanticide was not uncommon in China. Traffic was not all in one direction. Some families which gave away real daughters in minor marriage also took in adopted females as *sim-pu-a*. Minor marriage was a valued if unavowed tactic in family matrimonial strategy which effectively implemented the values sought in the kinship system as a whole. To these values we will return shortly.

Third, there was uxorilocal marriage. It again was not esteemed: in one form the groom was known as a *ming-ling tzu*, boll weavil son. But in recent times it occurred more frequently than the investigators were led to expect and it was probably practised even more widely in T'ang times. Under uxorilocal marriage, a boy, a teenager characteristically, though he might be older or younger, left home and went to live in the household of his bride's parents. Marriage rites followed shortly without much ceremony. The groom generally retained his own name and birth-family membership, children being distributed equally between the two houses, but in some more adoptive forms he lost both. Sometimes a small groomprice was paid, but there was no inverse dowry, and both the financial and the *kuan-hsi* components were as a rule kept minimal, though there were exceptions to this. Unlike major and minor marriage where the initiative in the approach to the matchmaker came from the mother of the groom, in uxorilocal marriage it came typically from the father of the bride. Uxorilocal marriage was really a contract between a father-in-law and a son-in-law, generally for labour but sometimes for status. The most common case was a widower with daughters but no sons. Here the imported son-in-law was little more than a servant to the older males of his bride's family. In other cases, and these may have been more common in T'ang times, boys of good pedigree and connections but poor, though possibly with brains and examination prospects, were taken into the households of wealthy merchants in an exchange of status, *kuan-hsi* and intelligence for the finance needed to valorize these assets. Moreover both families stood to benefit through the eventual distribution of grandchildren. In both its forms, uxorilocal marriage was characteristic of colonial situations: that is, shortage of agricultural labour, especially where, as in Apulia, so in south China because of new diseases, male death rates were high; new wealth without status; insufficiency of social infrastructure; dissonance of power and legitimacy. Here, despite its disesteem, uxorilocal marriage provided answers.

Fourth, there was delayed transfer marriage, a practice first discovered in 1989 by Janice E. Stockard (1989) in her researches in the Canton delta. Generally virilocal, though uxorilocal forms did exist, it seems to have been derived from the practice of the non-Chinese, but not uncivilized or purely passive, aboriginal people of the south. Thus it is found today among the P'u-i of Kweichow, the Chuang of Kwangsi and the Li of Hainan, all Thai-speaking ethnicities.[9] If this is so, it too was a phenomenon of the colonial frontier. Under delayed transfer marriage, a girl was married out with the same pomp, brideprice dowry and rituals as in major marriage, but her transfer to her husband's home was delayed three to four years. Sometimes it was never effected, she or her parents preferring to buy themselves out of the contract. In the cases studied by Stockard, this kind of marriage was associated with silk-producing families, whose daughters' sensitive fingers in cocoon reeling had considerable economic value, though it has always been assumed that sericulture was a Chinese rather than aboriginal invention. It may also have been associated with high female death rates, or high female infanticide, so that girls were in short supply, but this is contradicted by the relative absence of female infanticide in the areas concerned. For the groom and his family, delayed transfer marriage indeed represented a kind of girl future which might or might not be honoured by the seller. For the bride and her family, it represented a matrimonial insurance policy, cashable at any time but with no premiums and present retention of income. During the period of delay, the putative bride visited her future in-laws' home occasionally and maybe got used to them, but if she did not like what she saw, or her parents decided the groom's family were not worth investing in, she was operating in a sellers' market and could cancel and, if need be, start over again. The result was almost a proto feminism where, because of their earning power, many girls, very unusually in most Chinese contexts, chose not to marry at all and were supported in this by their families. Some joined sworn sisterhoods, reminiscent of the Beguines of medieval Europe, and were unsurprisingly suspected of forming a lesbian subculture parallel to the larger and more real bachelor subculture produced by the surplus of marriageable males resulting from female infanticide. Others, to obtain the advantage of married status, including the right of relatively free remarriage, contracted so-called spirit marriages with unmarried males already dead, so that delay became permanent. Delayed transfer marriage among Chinese may have been primarily the product of the silk industry, which enjoyed considerable expansion in T'ang China especially in Szechwan, but it was also the expression of social values: the endogamous desire to keep property and profit within the household and the lineage, itself the expression of deeper values about community and gender.

Before isolating what those deeper values were and how they were schematized into multiple matrimonial strategies, it is necessary to describe the geographical distribution of the different forms of marriage in recent times. This will provide living archaeological clues to past developments. Major marriage predominated in the older lands of North China in the Yellow river valley and also in the newest lands of the southwest, especially Szechwan. Minor marriage was nowhere in the majority, but it was a substantial minority, and sometimes ran major marriage a close second in the lower and middle Yangtze valley, in the southeast and in Taiwan. Uxorilocal marriage was in a small minority, except in the Yangtze delta, but there is reason to believe that at one time it was much more widely prevalent throughout the Yangtze valley, including Szechwan. Richard von Glahn (1987) speaks of uxorilocal marriage enjoying unprecedented popularity there in early Sung times when the practice began to be objected to by Confucian theorists.[10] In their eyes, it was destructive of lineage solidarity and coresidence by *pieh-ch'i i-ts'ai* 'establishing separate households and partitioning the family estate', that is the rise of neolocality in marriage and the encouragement of conjugality rather than filiality as its principle. Finally, delayed transfer marriage was largely confined to the Canton delta, though its possible aboriginal provenance, association with silk and proto-feminist possibilities may have given it wider diffusion before the Sung counter-revolution. Like uxorilocal marriage it was rooted in the more spacious days of the T'ang.

Behind its multiplicity of forms, it may be thought, Chinese marriage concealed a single content or dynamic. Wolf and Huang (1980) believed that the essence of marriage in early modern China was better expressed in minor than in major marriage.[11] Minor marriage was not essentially different, it merely expressed the same aims more clearly because the circumstances were simpler. Minor marriage was major marriage without trimmings and writ large; consequently it revealed better the underlying principles. The chief reason why Chinese mothers-in-law chose minor marriage for their sons rather than major was that they thereby acquired a more amenable daughter-in-law who was bound to them by almost maternal ties of upbringing. Conversely they avoided too close ties between husband and wife, which were always feared in Chinese extended households as 'pillow ghosts'. In minor marriage conjugality was weaker than in major marriage. As confirmed by modern statistics, fertility was lower, infidelity more frequent, and divorce rates, when this became an option, higher. Young people disliked minor marriage as quasi incestuous. You suddenly had to marry someone you had regarded as your brother or sister: 'like going to a movie you've seen 2 or 3 times', a modern victim told Wolf and Huang.[12] Romance, as also between *kibbutzim* children in Israel, was impossible. For parents, however, and in particular for the mother-in-law of the girl, minor marriage had many advantages. It softened domestic frictions, gave greater purchase on sometimes unruly sons and avoided affinal commitments: the patron/client relationship with another family which might be desired, but could be felt as constraining and no longer necessary as alternative connections along the friends' axis developed. Minor marriage was mother-in-law's optimum. She arranged it, she kept her options open, for if the *sim-pu-a* proved unbiddable she could be treated as a daughter and married out; the adoption, it was believed, increased her own chances of conceiving, and if in the end the girl did marry the son, she would prove submissive, not too closely united with her husband, in a word, filial.

Filiality, it may be suggested, was the key value pursued in all Chinese marriage forms, just as conjugality was increasingly the key value sought in the single marriage form of traditional Christendom. In delayed transfer marriage, it was the income of the parents which was the prime concern. Uxorilocal marriage was more concerned to provide a handyman for a father of daughters or an examination hopeful for an ambitious but unlettered or unconnected household than a groom for a bride. Minor marriage was open in its disregard of conjugality. Major marriage, too, emphasized filiality. The groom's first duty remained to his parents rather than to his wife. The imported wife was servant to her mother-in-law rather than partner to her husband; her prime duty was to provide a son, not so much for him, as for the family line, that is a grandson for her mother-in-law. Indeed, in Tientsin, the economic capital of north China, getting married was, for a girl, known as 'finding a mother-in-law'. In all the marriage forms, filiality, in the sense of domestic harmony and the deference on which this had to be based, was valued over conjugality. That, of course, did not mean that strong conjugal ties could not exist in China, but ideologically and in social practice they took second place to filiality.

Although filiality was couched in patrilinear, patriarchal terms, its real focus was the matriarch, the grandmother. In premodern medical conditions, she lived longer than her male counterparts, her prestige increased with age while those of elderly males diminished whatever lipservice was paid to greybeards, and she often ended as effective head of the household whether as lifetenant, trustee or manager of its property. At the most intimate level of Chinese society, within the household, the status and power of older women was considerable. This was particularly so in the T'ang period when China was open to barbarian influence, from the steppe to the north, from the forest to the south, both of which had distinct if different traditions of female activism. This preeminence of dowagers was reinforced from within by the rise of silk production and other aspects of farming such as ducks, poultry and vegetables which were under feminine supervision. It formed the social counterpart and supplied the infrastructure to the madamate at the political level: the power of arbitration exercized by imperial women in their triangular relationship with magnates and mandarins. In this perspective, the Empress Wu, far from being the outrageous anomaly portrayed by later Confucian historians, was simply a successful Szechwanese widow writ large: a figure who, by suitable remarriage, managerial skills, intelligent propaganda, a team of female assistants, plus a few toyboys and hatchet men, kept herself at the top of a nominally patrilinear system and thereby ensured her grandson a long and prosperous headship of the family firm. The matriarch was the strongest link in the family chain, the best hope of its survival as household, lineage or clan, and so deserved and received the support and self-sacrifice of its members. China became a civilization of dowagers where kinship predominated over association, filiality was preferred to conjugality, and gender convention and economic circumstance made the mother-in-law the residuary legatee.

It is now possible to conjecture the evolution of multiple forms of marriage in the T'ang period, a multiplication which gave Chinese society more power to pursue its ends in a variety of new economic contexts. Major marriage, it must be supposed, came first. It was probably the only form of marriage before 500. Not only did it receive a primacy of esteem which only antiquity could confer, it also accorded so completely with the circumstances of the Yellow river valley, the old heartland of China where it began and retained its preeminence. The rural communities of north China, less well-endowed with water communications than those further south, suffered from both isolation and fragmentation, since under the *chün-t'ien* system the land was farmed by smallholders in nuclear households. The main difference between major and minor marriage was that the first, but not the second, provided ongoing affinal relationships, something desired in a situation threatened by lack of structure. It put families into a hierarchy of marriage-givers and receivers while preserving patrilinity through virilocality. As population expanded to the south, as living standards rose, as female work became as valuable as male, the model of major marriage ceased to be optimal. Instead, probably from around 700 and the first signs of problems in the *chün-t'ien* system, there developed, in the new colonial lands of the Yangtze valley, the new uxorilocal model which von Glahn found so prevalent in Szechwan in the early Sung period. It was one answer to the problems of the colonial household, one evolved from within. Another was delayed transfer marriage, borrowed from the colonists' aboriginal partners on the silk frontier of Chinese civilization. Neither model, however, succeeded in sustaining themselves as more than minoritarian in the longer run. Uxorilocal marriage retreated towards the Yangtze delta, delayed transfer marriage became a peculiarity of the Canton delta. Both were rejected by the mainstream. Uxorilocal marriage offended too deeply against the prejudice in favour of patrilinity. Moreover, an imported adult son-in-law was unlikely to enhance the position of a matriarch, except sometimes relieving her of pressure to remarry. Indeed, it threatened a conspiracy of conjugality against her. Similarly, delayed transfer marriage might put a son under greater obligation to his wife than to his mother. Both forms, therefore, were increasingly subsumed into the new form of minor marriage. The new form rejected conjugality more radically, it avoided the affinal connections no longer required in the more mobilized and socialized south, and it reasserted dowagerism in its most naked formulation. Major and minor marriage agreed in their basic values. Uxorilocal marriage and delayed transfer marriage had the potential to generate alternative values. The T'ang period therefore was the time of greatest multi-

plicity of marriage values in Chinese history. It was a period of exper-
iment between two conservatisms, pre-T'ang and post-T'ang.

It remains to consider the wider implications of the multiple
Chinese marriage system and in particular the high value it placed
on mothers-in-law and dowagers. Francis Fukuyama (1995) looked
at the Chinese family from the point of view of information-
processing and trust-creation: two key elements in the genesis of
modern society, separate but not unrelated. He argued that the
Chinese emphasis on kinship and on *hsiao*, filial piety, in particular,
inhibited the development of non-kinship associative relationships
and the formation of social capital in the community necessary to
modern society. It is difficult to sustain this argument for the T'ang
period, whatever its merits for later, post-Sung, times. On the contrary, as will be detailed in the next section, non-kinship flowers
often had kinship roots, particularly through the activities of women.
Thanks to their relatively privileged position in the family system,
older women played a considerable part in the flowering of religious
institutions and the rise of consumerism which were characteristic
of the age. Here again the Empress Wu was not alone as patron nor,
on a more secular level, Yang Kuei-fei alone as customer. Judged by
the extent to which female intelligence and initiative is drawn on
in society, T'ang China was an advanced civilization. Dowagerism,
of course, was not feminism; it rested upon patriarchal assumptions,
it presumed a sharp distinction of gender roles between the community and the household and it involved the systematic intragen-
der oppression of young girls by older women as evidenced in the
practice of foot binding, where origins go back to the Five Dynasties
period though it only became widespread under the Sung.[13] Nevertheless, it is arguable that Chinese endogamous dowagerism, given
the patriarchal context, made better use *de facto* of feminine intelligence and enterprise than Christendom's option for exogamous conjugality which, while it might have greater potential in this direction,
for most of the time fell far shorter in performance. Christendom
might be laying good foundations, but T'ang China was doing more
actual building.

To conclude, the Chinese marriage system, based on kinship solidarity and focused on the mother-in-law, may be seen as forming
part of an alternative model of modernization with later parallels
in southern Europe. Even Fukuyama, who is critical of all forms of

familism, found economic merit in the more uxorilocal model
of it practised in Japan and in the Korean modification of major marriage which surrounded smaller households with larger lineages;
both subsystems with antecedents in T'ang China. Moreover, he
praises what he calls the Italian 'Confucianism' of the small high-
technology or fashion firms of contemporary Emilia, while the
reviving south Chinese lineages of post-Maoist China have
discovered a role as vehicles for the repatriation of capital from the
*hua-ch'iao* communities of Southeast Asia.[14] The family and the association need not be enemies as the record of T'ang China in
building non-kinship institutions indicates.

### Non-kinship institutions: a multiple associationism

The T'ang period saw the development of a gamut of non-kinship
institutions which ran, like those on the kinship axis, from small and
concrete to large and abstract. Some were rooted in the family, but
reached out to a wider contituency and gave the lie to the notion
that kinship solidarities *per se* were inimical to associative ties. Others
consciously and deliberately transcended kinship. Seven innovations
at different levels of organization may be adduced in support of this
picture:

- First, at the more concrete end of the spectrum, in the villages
  shaped by the *chün-t'ien* system especially, there was a proliferation of non-kinship bodies such as crop-watching cooperatives,
  lion-dance groups, martial-arts clubs, temple-management committees and so on, which further south were joined by mediu-
  mistic therapy groups and dragon-boat teams. Some of these
  appealed directly to those outside established family networks,
  such as long-term bachelors.
- Second, along routes and in the towns they connected and served,
  there developed so-called secret societies, really mafias or unions
  for people involved in transport businesses such as coolies, carters
  and boatmen. Their activities were often located in the inns
  and restaurants which reached a new degree of articulation in the
  T'ang period.[15] Soochow was already famous for its restaurants
  in the tenth century, round tables were preferred to rectangular
  to avoid any suggestion of patriarchal precedence, and Ch'ang-an

establishments provided a floor show with geishas from Sogdia and Tokharistan.

- Third, in both town and country, the new medical fashions of *wai-tan* and *nei-tan* together with the exorcism therapy of the Heavenly Masters school of Taoism (particularly developed in Szechwan) created new communities of physicians and patients which endured beyond the medical emergencies which gave rise to them. Hence the notion in the West that in China the patient paid the doctor when he was well, but the doctor paid the patient when he was ill.

- Fourth, T'ang religiosity created new solidarities around shrines, temples and monasteries, not only Buddhist and Taoist, but also Zoroastrianism, Nestorian, Manichaean and Muslim as well as the new sacralities being evolved out of the indigenous Chinese religion, such as the cult of the Fukienese shamaness Ma-tsu or Shennu, the divine woman, whose origins go back to the Five Dynasties period. Many of these solidarities, Buddhist monasticism in particular, were criticized by contemporaries for being deleterious to family values.

- Fifth, at the more abstract end of the spectrum, there were the new 'same year', *t'ung-nien* linkages of education and the examination system. In Chinese eyes the award of a degree created an obligation between the successful candidates and the examiner in rather the same way as cure created an obligation to the doctor. As regards social mobility, in the past too much has been made of the effects of the examination system at least immediately. It did not so much replace aristocracy by meritocracy as make aristocracy more meritocratic in that education and exam success now became part of the preferred portfolio of a noble family along with court office and high military command. Even this limited promotion of intelligence, however, was significant in moulding the ethos of society. It had effects on the marriage system, literate and intelligent wives being preferred by mothers-in-law to supervise the early education of their grandsons. It was from such educated girls that Empress Wu was able to recruit her bluestocking secretary Shang-kuan Wan-erh and her female private office.

- Sixth, as T'ang China expanded in space, there came to be a greater sense of regional solidarity, *t'ung-hsiang*. One of the objectives of the examination system had been to obtain a better regional balance in the composition of the bureaucracy and provincial families of good standing were one of the chief beneficiaries from it. From 643 an annual imperial assembly, *Ch'ao-chi shih*, was held of delegates from the 300 odd districts of which the empire was composed. Residences for each district were constructed at the capital which became the seats of permanent delegations. From the reign of emperor Te-tsung (779–805), these bodies became part of a national banking network, *fei-ch'ien*, whereby the delegates borrowed money from metropolitan merchants to meet their tax obligations in return for cheques on their localities whence the merchants drew their supplies for consumption at the capital.[16] In this way no actual coin or bullion would have to travel in either direction. It was these new regional solidarities, which formed the basis both for the Silver T'ang dualism of court and provinces and for the devolution of the Five Dynasties and Ten States. The pluralist, even parliamentary, possibilities of the *Ch'ao-chi shih* were not, however, pursued by the Sung counter-revolution which preferred centralization, pure bureaucratism and a law of avoidance which forbade officials serving in their native provinces. Nevertheless, this could not prevent the formation of regional cliques in Sung politics or, in later dynasties, the *ching-kuan*, or capital officials from a particular province, from acting as that province's pressure group in the corridors of power.

- Finally, concrete as well as abstract, the solidarity of solidarities, there was the planned imperial city, Ch'ang-an itself. In the Han period and before, Chinese cities had generally been irregular in their street plans even if confined within rectangular walls, with private buildings growing up haphazardly round palace complexes. Under the T'ang, a much greater degree of state planning was instituted, even if the development of the blocks (*fang*) laid out by the gridiron plan was left to private initiative. The first example of the new approach to urbanization was the Northern Wei city of Lo-yang to which that dynasty transferred its capital from Ta-t'ung in northern Shansi in 493, but the principle attained its fullest embodiment in Ch'ang-an under Hsüan-tsung when the emperor sought to make the city the shop-window of empire. Cities, it has been argued, are always semantic and semiotic fields as well as a collection of structures, but Ch'ang-an was consciously designed as an image and instrument of imperial power.[17] Government offices were concentrated into an imperial city (*huang-ch'eng*) to the north just below the palace complexes, and the rest of the urban area, divided east/west by a north/south arterial avenue, was carefully zoned for aristocratic palaces, imperial monasteries, public markets, recreational lakes, with workshops, retail outlets, restaurants and commoner residences allowed to grow in the interstices. The whole heterogeneous life of urban humanity, which subsequently was to create the serpentine China towns of the south, was here in the north directed into imperial channels and subsumed into an overall unity. Yet Ch'ang-an was a unity of multiplicity not a monolith. Unlike many Indian capitals, it could survive the transfer of the seat of government and become Sian, shrunk within its walls no doubt, but still, like Sh'eng-tu, another planned city, a regional capital. In terms of urban typology, Ch'ang-an was less a Brasilia, Canberra or Ankara, created by state fiat, than a Manhattan or Washington, self-creating within its framework of avenues and streets. It was a social as well as a political space, heterogenetic as well as ortho-genetic, which drew on the conjoined and complementary forces of kinship and association across a spectrum of small and large, concrete and abstract, all under the aegis of a cosmopolitan court.

## Cross-social comparisons, 500–1000

In comparison with China, the four other major civilized centres displayed either less diversification in their societies between 500 and 1000, as in the case of India, or actual simplification as in those of Islamdom and the two Christendoms, Byzantine and Latin. The last in particular experienced a profound *reculer pour mieux sauter* which at the turn of the millenium, gave few indications of future take-off.

### India

The origins of the distinctive modern system of caste found in both Hindu and Dravidian India remain obscure and a matter of controversy. On the one hand, by those who stress *varna*, the ancient abstract formal distinctions between *brahmans*, priests; *kshatryas*, knights; *vaisyas*, merchants; and *sudras*, commoners, it is put back to the Aryan conquest, whether in Renfrew's long chronology contemporaneous with the introduction of agriculture c. 8000BC or in his short chronology contemporaneous with a military conquest by charioteers c. 1000BC. On the other hand, by those who stress *jati*, the modern term for the more numerous, smaller, concrete groups in trade and manufacture, it is brought forward to the post-Muslim period, perhaps as late as the Delhi sultanate in the fourteenth and fifteenth centuries. Taking a middle path or third way, however, it would not be unreasonable to place the crucial phase of the development of caste in the period 500 to 1000 when the political superstructure was in decline, the economic infrastructure provided new resources for social development, and the post-Buddhist intellectual environment lent legitimacy to a revival or pseudo-revival of ancient Hindu categories. Caste, it might be argued, took up the slack from empire, as India, unlike China, experienced no imperial reconstruction, but did experience a similar return to classical sources and canonical books. In this interpretation, caste would be less a direct response by Hindu society to the advent and superimposition of Islamdom, though the invasion of Muhammed ibn Qasim in 708 and Mahmud of Ghazna c. 1000 were factors in the total situation, as compensation by society for the fragmentation, militarization and growing irrelevance of the state in a time of economic redistribution. As such, it should be regarded as a remarkable and constructive social development.

The Indian caste system, in the sense of *jati*, has seldom had a good press from Western sociologists who have accused it of being both inherently undemocratic and inhibitory of social mobility. Neither accusation is well-founded. On the one hand, the caste system served to limit the power of the state, whether alien and predatory as under the Delhi sultanate and the Mughals, or alien and promotive as under the *raj*. Caste supplied the solidarities on which the countervailing power of society was based and whose micro-units could later be harnessed to mass machine politics both locally and on an all-India scale. On the other hand, though the movement of individuals between castes may have been inhibited, the castes themselves were often in a state of Brownian motion with respect to each other as economic circumstances changed. In premodern conditions, collective mobility was probably of more significance for the generality than individual mobility. It provided sustained, cross-generation change in status rather than episodic, atypical cases with no overall significance. Outside periods of change, moreover, caste functioned as a set of cards of social identity whose use conveyed expectations and elicited appropriate responses effectively. It was a useful system of information so that historians of India have spoken of the modernity of tradition. Where India's traditional sociology was more vulnerable to comparison with China's was in the lesser diversity of its marriage systems and in its more patriarchal interpretation of filiality in kinship. Though female intelligence and initiative were not ignored in traditional India, a different schematization of gender plus the absence of the printing press and the examination system afforded them less expression than in T'ang China.

## Islamdom

In its sociological dimension, the Islamic cultural revolution produced, over its vast area, uniformity rather than diversity. Islamic cities, for the focus of the new religion was urban, Islamic societies everywhere, had a family likeness, from al-Andalus to Mawara-an-nahr. It was a simplified likeness of the late antique world against which Islam had reacted when it began as a Syrian provincial counter-world of the marginalized. Thus the new Islamic cities, though they might begin orthogenetically on the model of Roman fortified camps, continued heterogenetically as complexes of lanes and markets, *souk* cities, in a pattern beginning to be imposed by the replacement of the cart by the camel in late antiquity. Within these cities, the Islamic *sadr*, the local oligarchies of urban landowners, canon lawyers and greater merchants replicated and repristinated the late antique decurionate without its particular euergetisms and with a different *paideia*, the word of the Koran rather than the words of Cicero. Outside the city, in the *chora*, the desert palaces of the early caliphs and the encampment of the pseudo-Arabian tribes, which resulted from the Muslim conquests, echoed the villas and aristocratic estates of the former Greco-Roman world. Beyond the city, on the frontier and in the *ribat*, the slave armies of early Islamdom, set apart from its culture and irrelevant to its lifestyle, mimicked the barbarian armies of the later Roman empire in their position of power without legitimacy. Similarly, opposition to the establishment found expression in schism (*shia*) and secession (*kharij*) just as it had done in the days of the Monophysites and the Donatists. Islamdom was the truest heir of antiquity: religion without barbarism, as Gibbon might have argued. It was sophisticated, but not innovative except in giving slavery a new lease of life as the legal form of various kinds of adoption, concubinage and military indenture. For the slave was the substitute for the child, to be used, abused and sometimes privileged in a society with, by premodern standards, a low birth rate because of polygamy and contraception and a high death rate through war and urbanization. Islamdom was constantly at risk of demographic poverty. Slavery supplied it with the brains, beauty and brawn it could not always provide for itself. Its simplification of some human relations to those of property was acceptable to a society in which, in principle, all were the slaves of Allah. Paradoxically, slavery was part of the social egalitarianism of early Islamdom.

In the sociology of the family, the notion of equal but separate gender roles in a single form of marriage, as practised in early Islamdom, contrasted with Chinese multiple marriage in its results. Dowagers were not privileged nor, on the whole, was female intelligence and initiative so widely utilized even within its separate sphere. Though Valide Sultans, often of non-Muslim or slave origin, did later achieve preeminence within the Ottoman political machine, that was due more to the particular institutional circumstances at the beginning of the seventeenth century than to the general thrust of Islamdom which was against matriarchy. What Islamdom did promote in its early sociology was a work ethic and a socially responsible individualism which put the community ahead of the family.[18] One indication of this orientation was the preference for burial with individual headstones in communal cemeteries rather than in the family gravesites favoured by Chinese tradition. In China, Muslim social cohesiveness found expression both in the Tungan community of the northwest and in pioneer commercial and missionary activity in the Nan-Yang. Like its antique antecedents, Islamdom was a culture of the *agora*: not the classical *agora* of temples, baths, gymnasia, theatres and circus, but the late antique *agora* of basilicas, martyria, narrow streets, recycled palaces and in-fill. It was against this background and in this likeness that the Islamic revolution undertook its revaluation of all values and built its community, the *umma*, in a style both ancient and yet new.

## Byzantium

Although Eastern Christendom was the most direct heir of late antiquity, its sociology between 500 and 1000 showed less continuity with its antecedent than did early Islamdom. This may be seen in both kinship and non-kinship institutions.

In kinship, the discontinuity was conscious, deliberate and profound, though not all the effects were envisaged or intended. Two changes affected marriage, one minor, one major. The minor change was Justinian I's unification and democratization of marriage by his redefinition of it as simply cohabitation. It was minor because it did not really affect parental control of marriage or promote conjugality between the partners. As Eve Levin (1989) noted in her study of gender among the Orthodox Slavs: 'the conjugal relationship was secondary to family interests'.[19] Nevertheless, the change was significant because it separated, theoretically, the marriage contract, its validity, licity and sacramentality, from any property arrangements of dowry, counter-dowry or bride price which might accompany it. This simplification of marriage was a change in the opposite direction to what was happening in China: one form instead of four. The major change, however, was the attack on family and lineage endogamy by the extension of marriage impediments by reason of consanguinity, affinity or spiritual relationship (God-parenthood), to the sixth or seventh degree. These impediments were codified in the reign of Justinian II by the canons of the Council in Trullo in 692, the so-called Quinisext because it completed the work of the fifth and sixth ecumenical councils. The reasons for the late Palaeo-Christian passion for exogamy have been much debated. Jack Goody (1984) supposed that it came from considerations of property: the Church's desire to facilitate bequests to itself by will in default of lineage heirs.[20] Certainly the Church benefited from bequests, such as that of a whole *massa* and several *fundi* by Flavia Xanthippe to Santa Maria Maggiore in Rome in the early seventh century.[21] However, its new dislike of endogamy was more than economic. Though in the East not yet committed to conjugality in marriage as an ideal, the Church was aware both of the aristocratic stranglehold fostered by endogamy and the obstacles it imposed on the free flow of information as well as property. The cult of virginity, another Christian innovation, reinforced the attack on endogamy. As Peter Brown has pointed out, virginity was directed more at the family or lineage than against the body or carnality, while Eve Levin noted that, 'For medieval women, the anti sexual aspect of Christianity was more liberating than constrictive.'[22] Virginity, celibacy and exogamy were serious limitations to the power of kinship: a partial deconstruction of what had been the most powerful social institution.

In the non-kinship dimension, too, the discontinuity was profound, but it was passive, unintended and largely unwelcome. This was particularly evident with regard to urbanization, the highest form of association. The demographic parabola of high point, sharp decline and slow recovery suffered by Constantinople and other eastern Mediterranean cities between 500 and 1000 as a result of war, plague and commercial reorientation had sociological consequences. In the capital, households, it is believed, became smaller and more nuclear. Courtyard compounds and multistoried *insulae* lost their raison d'être. In provincial cities, the late-antique decurionate was replaced as the local élite by bureaucrats and ecclesiastics. In consequence, in both capital and provinces, the topography of civic euergetism was replaced by that of churches, monasteries and public offices. In the capital the centre of gravity shifted from the hippodrome where races became rarer and factional *stasis* tranquillized by ritualism to, on the one hand, parish churches and monasteries like the Studion further out towards the wall, and, on the other, to the docks on the Golden Horn, the nucleus of the future Eminonu and Galata bridge area: that Bund which made Comnenian and Palaeologan Constantinople a medieval Shanghai. Similar changes may be identified at Thessalonika and Smyrna as the ancient city collapsed itself either outwards or inwards or both together. Civic consciousness changed. Poverty and wealth began to be conceived in more economic and less sociological terms and class took the place of status in stratification.[23] The solidarity of the bishop with his flock which had given rise at Rome and other places to the system of stational liturgies – the whole city coming together on certain days to a single point – in the East gave way to more diffused and localized sacral solidarities focused on parish or monastery, even individual ikons. Only in times of emergency, notably external military threat, would Constantinople come together and the Iconoclast emperors failed in their attempt to institutionalize the sense of crisis in more permanent form. Within the immense walls provided by Theodosius II, on which the Comnenians preferred to live at the Marian shrine of Blachernae, the populace of Constantinople continued to manifest a certain Cockney independence, as evidenced by the *patrias* or mythical histories of the city, but it was increasingly directed more against the Latins than for the emperor or the patriarch.[24] As the Old Rome became depopulated, so the New Rome was deconstructed into the simpler components reflected in the *Book of the Eparch*. Similarly, after 650 the *Annona* was privatized to independent sea captains or *naukleroi* less vulnerable to crises, while in the countryside, small-holders, upheld by the emperors as the source of themal soldiers by the right of *protimesis* in the purchase of local land, made progress at the expense of the *dynatoi*, the powerholders of late antiquity. Eastern Orthodoxy was building its base in village communities, both urban and rural.

### Latin Christendom

Here there was greater and more prolonged contraction of both political superstructure and urban infrastructure. These were greater discontinuities with late antiquity and in society a more profound shift from association to kinship.

Bernard Lonergan (1970) saw the fall of the Roman empire in the West as a shift from social order to intersubjectivity: 'The collapse of Imperial Rome was the resurgence of family and clan, feudal dynasty and nation.'[25] No institution was more affected by the return of kinship than the Church. Forced to swim in a different sea, it redirected its energies to the conversion of the barbarian aristocracies both within and beyond the *limes*. The second half of the first millenium was the age of *Adelskirche*: the captivity of the Church by kinship, but also her conquest of it. Richard Fletcher writes: 'The European *Adelskirche* had many shortcomings . . . However its positive contribution may be seen in the harnessing of aristocratic loyalties in the service of the Christian faith as such persons understood it. The directing elite in the barbarian kingdoms were prepared to divert colossal, staggering resources into the service of new spiritual ideals': episcopal households, monasteries and parish communities.[26] Moreover, though magnate monks like St Wilfrid might rule, kinship was undergoing modification. First, Justinian I's definition of marriage as cohabitation was further redefined, most notably in the codification of St Ivro of Chartres, as cohabitation by consent: the consent not of the parents, but of the bride and groom. This opened the way to other changes: the greater involvement of clergy as witnesses and guarantors of free choice; emphasis on the wedding rather than the betrothal as the moment of choice; and the assimilation of matrimonial choice to monastic vows, hence irrevocability and more than entry to the religious life, sacramentality. Second, Justinian I's imposition of marriage impediments to the sixth and seventh degree was interpreted more strictly in the West by the adoption first articulated by St Peter Damian but adumbrated earlier, of the so-called German as opposed to Roman method of counting. Third, particularly in derivation from Lombard law taught at Pavia and Benevento, there was a new emphasis on a wife's property rights in dowry, brideprice or counter-dowry and *morgingab* or second counter-dowry which might be more than both.[27] The existence of these rights and the fear of their exercise was another factor in the promotion of marriage indissolubility against the kinship preference for the flexibility of divorce. Kinship predominated over association at the end of the first millenium, but it was being fragmented into small or more nuclear, more conjugal units with corresponding need for non-kin accessory institutions. Reurbanization, though by 1000 less pronounced than in the East, and partly based on kinship initiative, pointed in the same direction.

Latin Christendom suffered from deurbanization more severely than the Byzantine world because its cities depended more on state subsidization. Rome itself, with a population in its palmiest days of a million, was by the tenth century down to 10,000. Its people had withdrawn from the hills, as the Aurelian walls became indefensible, to the Campus Martius and the bend of the Tiber. From here they only emerged with monastic promotion of new houses, notably by Abbess Ermingarde in the eleventh century, in a kind of spiritual uxorilocal recolonization.[28] For much of the period, Rome was a denucleated post-city without a centre: an archipelago of hamlets with gardens and farmlets, vinyards and flaxfields, clustered round wells and the acqueducts repaired by Pope Hadrian I (772–795). The great basilicas such as Santa Maria Maggiore continued to offer their stational liturgies and to receive gifts from the Popes, but their processions must often have been through grass-grown streets and such information as we possess concerning their staff indicates dominance by the Roman barons from their high towers scattered around the former urban space.

Nevertheless, an embryonic Curia, based on the Lateran palace or the new Leonine city on the right bank of the Tiber, was beginning to offer careers as meritocrats to the petty gentry of Latium, though it was miniscule compared to a Chinese yamen. Beyond the Alps it was worse. Calleva Atrebatum, possibly deliberately deurbanized, virtually disappeared, its Christian community retreating from the centre of town to the shelter of its still defensible walls, while the amphitheatre became a quarry for outlying farms. Roman Bath became a shadow of itself, while the continuity of Roman and Saxon London, though increasingly established, has been a matter of dispute. When reurbanization began – at York through Viking trade, at London through Saxon government, at Durham through the cult of St Cuthbert – although it had deeper roots than in late antiquity, its new associations were at an as yet too low a level to make much headway against the surrounding power of kinship. It was the same on the continent. At Tours, Martinopolis, the would-be Rome of the north, all three institutions concerned with the cult of the saint, the abbey, the basilica, the cathedral, remained embedded in the aristocratic lineages of the Loire valley.[29] The scale of urbanization was just too low. Around AD 1000 Byrhtferth of Ramsey credited York, as the second city in England after London with a population of 30,000.[30] Many Chinese provinces already had dozens of places of this size. Moreover, York was only a revival, albeit on a new basis. Many Chinese urban nucleations, such as Lu-chou where the T'o joined the Yangtze and the old territories of Shu met the new territories of Pa, a centre of the cross-border trade in salt and timber which sent lichees to Yang Kuei-fei at Ch'ang-an, were new developments. The preeminence of T'ang China in its multiple sociology was not a restoration to a perennial Sinocentric norm, but an innovation in the unrolling of world history. In society, as in economics and politics, China achieved greatness. It was not born great nor did it have greatness thrust upon it.

# 5
# Intellect: China's Complex Pluralism

If political genius was the source of China's rise to centrality in the world order between 500 and 1000, complex pluralism in thought was its summit. Source and summit were mutually supportive. Political foundations provided the secure environment for the economy to grow and society to consolidate. Intellectual fruition supplied the semantic field for conceptualization, the semiotic medium for communication and action, and the syncretic forum for legitimation. In the rise of the East, China's complex pluralism in thought was no mere epiphenomenon. To be itself, China must be for itself. Charles Morazé's dictum, 'destin de la pensée, destin du monde', was as much in point in the world of the T'ang as in the Victorian world for which he enunciated it.[1] Complexity and pluralism were not identical. Complexity refers to the number of logical registers engaged, while pluralism refers to the range of alternatives presented across and within them. China enjoyed a high degree of both. Other civilizations in the period lacked either the complexity or the pluralism or both, or, in the case of India, where both were present, a lesser degree than China. Thus the Islamic world was more plural than complex, the Byzantine world more complex than plural, while the world of Latin Christendom, though rich in promise, in performance displayed little complexity or pluralism. China's intellectual preeminence, both cause and effect of its overall centrality, was most conspicuous in the reign of emperor Hsüan-tsung (713–756), where our primary focus will once again rest, though with a secondary focus on the millennial year at the end of the period.

China's intellectual spectrum will now be evaluated from the double perspective of complexity and pluralism. It was China's greater depth in the first and greater breadth in the second which secured her the intellectual preeminence of that time. These characteristics were not an inheritance from the past. On the contrary, though initiated in late antiquity under the Hou Han, the *San-kuo* and the Chin, western and eastern, they were the achievement of the Nan-pei ch'ao, the Sui and the T'ang. It was a surprising achievement because, before these developments, the intellectual world of China had been provincial, static and monochrome, whereas after them it became cosmopolitan, dynamic and polychromatic.

## China's intellectual complexity

This may be assessed by reference to a grid composed of two axes, one horizontal from paradigmatic to syntagmatic, the other vertical from categorical to critical. The grid provides four registers of intellectual activity: paradigmatic–categorical, categorical–syntagmatic, syntagmatic–critical, critical–paradigmatic. The contrast paradigmatic/syntagmatic is between, on the one hand, intransitive, self-referent, declaratory thinking such as mathematics, myth, music or other art forms and linguistic syntax; and, on the other hand, transitive, other-referent descriptive thinking in theories and hypotheses, as may be found in science, scholarship, theology and metaphysics. The contrast categorical/critical is between prior, first-order thinking, whether about paradigms or syntagmata, and posterior, second-order thinking, thinking about thinking, whether in the intransitive arts or in the transitive sciences. The degree of complexity, or intellectual depth, may be measured by the number of registers in which intellectual activity is taking place, while the degree of pluralism or intellectual breadth may be measured by the number of alternatives within each register.[2]

In the T'ang period Chinese intellectual activity may be found in all four registers, but it had not always been so. In the preimperial period of intellectual efflorescence known as the Hundred Flowers, Chinese thought was heavily slanted towards the paradigmatic-categorical register and moves in other directions were short-lived. Of the five classics traditionally recognized by Confucian scholars, three, the *Shih-ching* (classic of poetry), the *I-ching* (classic of change) and the *Li-chi* (collection of rites) were patently paradigmatic, while the *Shu-ching* (classic of history) and the *Ch'un-ch'iu* (Spring and Autumn annals) were generally given an exemplarist interpretation. A sixth, lost classic, the *Yüeh-ching* (classic of music) was most likely similarly structuralistic in character. In post-classical literature, the *Lun-yü* (Analects), the laconic, rather contextless collection of sayings ascribed to Confucius about a century after his death, is an educational and linguistic primer rather than an ethical or political tract. Its pedagogy is in the form rather than the content, the medium more than the message, what Confucius is doing rather than what he is saying. What he is doing is *cheng-ming* (rectification of names): the enunciation of a logic of definitions to prestructure future discourse. In the next generation, Mencius, the self-proclaimed successor of Confucius, attempted to go beyond such paradigms and formulate a syntagmatic ethical and political system. The book of his sayings, the *Meng-tzu*, has a quite different character from the *Lun-yü*, in being both provided with contexts and pursued discursively. In reaction, however, his successor Hsün-tzu returned to an emphasis on ritual and protocol which subsequent Confucian philosophy never really escaped.[3] Indeed, the last two considerable philosophical works of the preimperial period, the *Chung-yung* (Doctrine of the Mean) from the school of Mencius and the *Ta-hsüeh* (Great Learning) from the school of Hsün-tzu, survived significantly as incorporated in the *Li-chi*. As to the classics of Taoism, the *Tao-te ching* and the *Chuang-tzu*, they are best understood not as fountainhead of a rival philosophy to Confucianism, still less as the origin of the later Taoist religion, but as inverted Confucianism, an anti-linguistic, sceptical and negative but equally paradigmatic tendency within the *Ju-chia*, the community of scholars.

In the two Han periods, western and eastern, the paradigmatic–categorical register continued to be dominant, though with two exceptions, one major, one minor, neither sustained. To take the minor exception first, in the reign of Han Wu-ti (140–87BC), the *Hsin-wen chia*, the New Text school founded by Tung Chung-shu on authentic texts and broad interpretation, read a speculative metaphysic of correlation out of the Confucian classics. It incorporated Tsou Yen's *wu-hsing* (five processes) theory to advance a universal system of mutual production and destruction by phase transition and pan-cosmic resonance. Over time, however, the system became less a theory of everything and more a set of *a priori* classifications like the *I-ching*. Moreover, the *Hsin-wen chia* was soon displaced, from the usurpation of Wang Mang and especially under the Eastern Han, by the *Ku-wen chia*, the Old Text school. It was founded by Liu Hsin, spin-doctor to the new emperor. Rationalistic in tone, based on spurious texts but strict interpretation, it retreated from speculative cosmology to positivistic philology. Confucius again became a teacher of mindstyle and manners rather than a philosopher of humanity and nature. The major exception to the prevailing paradigmatic mode of thought under the Han was the consolidation of the Chinese historical tradition. History-writing found its legitimacy in the *Shu-ching* and the *Tso-chuan* commentary to the *Ch'un-ch'iu*, but it went far beyond their exemplarism in the *Shih-chi* of Ssu-ma Ch'ien written in the days of Han Wu-ti. With the *Han-shu* of Pan Ku in the first century of the Eastern Han and the *Hou Han-shu* of Fan Ye in the early part of the Eastern Chin, the first two dynastic histories, it became an orthodox genre, the production of which for its predecessor was incumbent on each successive dynasty as a sign of the orderly transfer of the mandate of heaven. Nevertheless, it may be thought, something was lost between Ssu-ma Ch'ien and Pan Ku as a result of the paradigmatic priorities of the *Ku-wen chia* with its exemplarism, positivism and emphasis on style. Ssu-ma Ch'ien wrote history for a public, taking responsibility for what he said. His successors assembled material and compiled precedents for officials in the belief that documents spoke for themselves. True, Ssu-ma Ch'ien was not without his secret agendas and exemplarist modelling, as in his account of Ch'in Shih Huang-ti as a negative image of Han Wu-ti, but he endowed his prototypes with a spontaneity lacking even in Pan Ku's famous portrayal of the last days of the magician emperor Wang Mang. Even Pan Ku, master of style, was constrained by the intellectual parameters of his time.

For Chinese thought to move beyond its sophisticated but monocentric concentration on one intellectual register, three steps were necessary. Advances must be made in the underdeveloped critical–paradigmatic, categorical–syntagmatic, and sytagmatic–critical registers. They were made successively by Confucians, Taoists and Buddhists to give China a more complex panoply of intellectual activity than that of any other major civilization of the time.

Long shrouded in half-conscious provinciality, China, suddenly, under the T'ang displayed itself as the world's intellectual cynosure.

## Confucianism

The first step, into the critical paradigmatic register, was taken by Confucians, if that term is understood in its contemporary sense. Until the time of the Sung counter-revolution, indeed some way into it, Confucianism was not the name of a distinctive philosophy, but of an educational curriculum: the Chinese *paideia*, the study of the classics and their adjunct literature through which literacy was acquired and membership of the élite established. As such, it was no more incompatible with the new upsurge of religiosity, Taoism from within and Buddhism from without, than was the *paideia* of the West with Christianity, though in both cases there might be occasions for friction and discomfort. The curriculum provided the basic skills of reading and writing *wen-yen*, the literary language as opposed to the *pai-hua*, the spoken vernacular, the demand for which was being swelled by bureaucracy, paper and print, the latter two Chinese inventions. Beyond these skills, the curriculum sought to impress paradigms of language, thought and behaviour, all expressing themselves in protocol, *li*, the manners of the civil society described in the last chapter.

It was from this pedagogic milieu, among people who reflected on what they had been taught or were teaching, that emerged the first two critical–paradigmatic works in Chinese literature. These were the *Wen-hsin tiao-lung* (The Literary Mind and the Carving of Dragons) of Liu Hsieh, early in the sixth century, a work of literary criticism, and the *Wen-hsüan* (Literary Selections), an influential anthology by a prince of the Southern Liang dynasty. It was subsequently extensively commented on, notably by Li Shen who collected previous commentaries and added one of his own in the *Wu chen-chu Wen-hsüan* (the Wen-hsüan with five commentaries) published in 719 as part of the Confucian revival in the early days of Hsüan-tsung. Critical appraisals of painting, already a major art form though its golden age was not to come until the Northern Sung, were also produced, of which the most notable was the *Li-tai ming-hua chi* (Notes on the Famous Painters of Past Ages) of Cheng Yen-yuan, which was published in the ninth century.

Last but not least, in this context of entry into a new intellectual register, mention should be made of the Silver T'ang Confucian hero Han Yü (768–824), scholar-official from Honan, author of the *shih-lu* or veritable records of the T'ang emperor Shun-tsung who had a brief but controversial reign in 805, and famous for his opposition to imperial veneration of the bone of the Buddha and for a rationalist sermon he preached to the crocodiles in his place of exile in South China. Han Yü was an intellectual magnifico. He was a critic but more than a critic. He became the Leavis of China for whom the literary style of antiquity, laconic and grave, inspired both a morality and a political attitude. Antiquity, he insisted, is now, and he reinterpreted the *paideia* to draw a sharper line between Chinese and barbarians, Confucians and non-Confucians, than had been current in the Golden T'ang period. He was the prophet of the days of the Sung counter-revolution when Confucianism first became a philosophy in the categorical–syntagmatic register. Han Yü elevated Mencius above Hsün-tzu as the true successor of Confucius and reinterpreted the *Ta-hsüeh* in Mencian terms. Confucianism, transmitted through an orthodox succession of teachers, was now presented as a message as well as a medium.[4]

## Taoism

In the exploration of the categorical–syntagmatic register, although Confucians like Han Yü were drawn into it, as were exponents of the historiographical tradition like Tu Yu (732–812) whose *T'ung-tien* (General Statutes) was the first Chinese institutional history, the main thrust came from bodies of thought which may be called Taoist. In few branches of Sinology has there recently been as much progress, as in the study of Taoism, the Taoist religion in particular. Until the work of Holmes Welch, Michel Strickmann and Nathan Sivin, Taoism was misconceived.[5] It was seen as either, or both, an anti-intellectualist private mysticism advanced in opposition to rational Confucian public moralism, as with traditional sinology, or as with Joseph Needham a protosocialist empirical naturalism underpinning a subculture of skill and practice in counterpoint to high Confucian theoretical humanism. Both views sought to derive Taoism from the philosophy supposedly contained in the *Tao-te ching*, which was understood as the foundation document of the whole movement. Neither view was wholly false, but they did not express the whole truth about Taoism and its place in Chinese intellectual life. In particular they did not deal adequately with the Taoist religion as based on the *Tao-tsang*, the Taoist canon and patrology. This massive collection of texts was assembled in 745 in the reign of Hsüan-tsung. It was first printed in the early Sung in the reign of Chen-tsung, reprinted with additions in 1119 under Hui-tsung, and then definitively, following further printings around 1190 under both the Chin and the southern Sung, in an enlarged if also expurgated edition of 1445 in the reign of the Ming emperor Cheng-t'ung. It is from study of the *Tao-tsang* texts that a better understanding of Taoism is being obtained.

The *Tao-tsang* is divided into two parts: the *San-tung*, the three caves or revelations of the three principal Taoist schools; and the *Ssu-fu*, four supplements, one attached to each of the schools and one to the corpus as a whole. The *Ssu-fu* texts were in fact older, and known to be older, than those of the *San-tung*, so that they constituted a *praeparatio evangelica* rather than an apocrypha.

The *San-tung* were the three gospels or arcana of religious Taoism, but they were not accorded equal weight. The first, of greatest weight, was the *Tung-chen*, the cave of truth. It contained the *shang-ch'ing*, highest purity, scriptures of the Mao-shan school. They were first revealed by a celestial bureaucrat Dame Wei to a visionary Yang Hsi around AD 370, then transmitted to the aristocratic Hsü family, high officials at Nanking under the Eastern Chin, and finally edited at their mountain retreat of Mao-shan by T'ao Hung-ching (456–536), scholar, scholastic and alchemist in the days of the Southern Liang. He was regarded as the first patriarch of the school. It was the most doctrinal of the three schools and to it was appended, as a prefiguration, the *Tao-te ching* itself. Next, in listing and weight, was the *Tung-hsüan*, the cave of the mystery. It contained the Ling-pao, spiritual treasure, scriptures. They were ascribed to a revelation made to another Eastern Chin visionary, the aristocrat Ko Ch'ao-fu around AD 395, but probably not written till later and only consolidated into a school in the North in the sixth century, that is after Mao-shan. Ling-pao was the most liturgical of the three schools, and for this reason the most appealing to royal courts. To its scriptures was appended the *T'ai-p'ing ching*, the classic of the Great Peace, a text prophetic of a Utopian therapeutocracy to be established by a prince of high virtue, *shang-te chin-chün*, associated with the revolutionary movements at the end of the Han. Third, in order and value, was the *Tung-shen*, the cave of divinity. It contained the scriptures of the *San-huang*, or three divine emperors, school, supposedly conveyed to another visionary, Pao Ching, around AD 300, who was portrayed as the teacher of the aristocratic Hsü family involved in the transmission of the Mao-shan texts. Represented as the earliest it was probably the latest of the *San-tung*. It was the most occultist of the three schools, concerned with divination, theurgy, exorcisms, incantations, talismans, as well as techniques, sexual and respiratory, for callisthenics and therapy. To it was appended writings on alchemy, including those of Ko Hung, the author of the *Pao-p 'u tzu*. Finally, appended to all three schools, were *cheng-i*, orthodox unity, texts associated with the *T'ien-shih*, Heavenly Masters, sect, the successor to the Five Pecks of Rice revolutionary movement in Szechwan at the end of the Han, from whose line of hereditary patriarchs of the Chang family, the so-called Taoist papacy, relocated in the late T'ang time to Lung-hu Shan in Kiangsi, was to emerge in Sung and Ming times.

The body of thought discovered by recent research into the *Tao-tsang* was neither traditional sinology's anti-intellectualist mysticism nor Joseph Needham's empirical naturalism. Nor was it lower class or anti-establishment in constituency. Rather it was devised by aristocrats for aristocrats in an aristocratic age. It was, as Michel Strickmann put it, 'China's indigenous higher religion based on the Taoist Canon'.[6] It was a religion of the Word like the contemporary revelations of Christianity, Mithras, Krishna, Manichaeism and Islam. Derived from the revolutionary movements at the end of the Han, it unleashed a wave of religiosity in China which lasted well-beyond the Sung counter-revolution in politics and society.[7] As a revealed religion, its rich content of theory and practice involved a further colonization of the categorical–syntagmatic register of thought which represented a new departure in Chinese intellectual history. Religious Taoism was self-consciously Protean and unafraid of incoherence. Despite a luxuriant iconography, its *Tao* was indeterminate and unnameable, the *wu-chi*, the extreme of nothing, the ultimate of negation. Nevertheless, a number of attempts have been made to state the central notion of its strange, asystemic universe. Thus Nathan Sivin (1977) has portrayed alchemy, independent in origin from religious Taoism but in the T'ang period annexed to it as cosmological foundation, rather in the way Aristotelianism was to

Christianity by scholasticism, as time technology.[8] Alchemical procedures could accelerate time to turn base metals into gold or jade, or they could decelerate time to prolong human life indefinitely and produce bodily immortality by a revealed chemotherapy. N.J. Girardot (1983) thought that the central notion of Taoism was that the true order of the universe lay in chaos, which was both primordial and ongoing. It sought techniques to return the pseudo-cosmos to chaos in order to recover its original immortal nature: a redemption of nature through man and of man through nature.[9] Isabelle Robinet saw the revelation itself, the scripture revealed by the divinity or saint to the adept, as metaphysically ultimate.[10] The universe was constituted by books and diagrams. Here one is reminded of Derrida's *Urtext*, which stands before all writing and is uncovered by the deconstruction of pseudo-texts: the *Tao* is logograph, the primordial Chinese character. While there is something to be said for all three interpretations – time-cosmos, chaosmos and cosmic equation – they all suffer from an essentialism alien to the philosophy of Taoism. A better approach may be through the writings of a representative individual, the court Taoist Tu Kuang-t'ing at the turn from the Silver T'ang to the Five Dynasties who has been the object of major studies by Franciscus Verellen, and Suzanne Cahill.[11]

Tu Kuang-t'ing may be considered as representative of T'ang Taoism. He was considered a patriarch in both the Mao-shan and Ling-pao schools, and was, if not a wonderworker himself, a chronicler of thaumaturgy. He received late in life a high rank in the Heavenly Master's hierarchy, and was if not an alchemist himself, a devotee of the Queen Mother of the West, a patron saint of alchemy. An ecumenical Taoist, who sought to reconcile the schools in the face of the emerging Confucian counter-revolution, he was an avid collector of texts, both manuscripts and incunabula, an activity which facilitated the first printing of the *Tao-tsang* early in the Sung. In addition, he was an active propagandist for the final courts of the T'ang and their successor in Szechwan.

Tu Kuang-t'ing's own writings, many of which found their way into the Taoist canon, fell into five categories. First, doctrinally most significant though second by number, were sacred topographies such as the *Tung-t'ien fu-ti yüeh-tu ming-shan chi* (Record of Grotto-Heavens, Blessed Places, Holy Peaks and Conduits, Famous Mountains) published in September 901. This described, along with their associated divinities, the five holy peaks and rivers, the 36 pure hermitages and grotto-heavens where saints had lived, the 72 blessed places from which transcendence was obtained, and the 24 dioceses of the Heavenly Master's organization, which together constituted the meta-geography of the Taoist world. Second, closely allied with topography, was hagiography. Such a work of Tu's was the *Yun-ch'eng chi-hsien lu* (Record of Immortals Assembled at Yun-ch'eng), the home in the K'un-lun mountains of the Queen Mother of the West, the *Hsi Wang Mu* whose sacred history was included among the biographies of Taoist adepts. She was the principal Mao-shan female divinity, *Chin-mu yüan-chün*, Metal Mother and primordial ruler, ultimate of yin, the giver of immortality and revelation. Suzanne Cahill comments here that the 'people of the T'ang united two of the greatest human longings in their worship of the goddess: the wish to conquer death and the desire for perfect love'.[12] Third, most numerous, were liturgies, re-edited or newly devised, for the splendid ceremonies with which the court approached this sacred universe and greeted new portents and hierophanies. Such was the large *T'ai-shang huang-lu chai-i* (Grand Ritual of Fasts in the Yellow Register) produced by Tu Kuang-t'ing in 880 just before the fall of Ch'ang-an to Huang Ch'ao. These ceremonies, and the interpretation of events which preceded them, were the daily bread of the Taoist spindoctors who were responsible for the appropriate ritual response. Fourth, there were thaumatologies or *mirabilia*, such as the *Lu-i chi* (Record of Marvels) of 921–925, a record of anomalies, prodigies, spiritual close encounters, supernatural visitations in Szechwan. It was designed to read the signs of the times, to prove the province a focus of divine action and so legitimate the Ten Kingdoms' state of Shu as a true successor to the T'ang, whose mandate, Tu Kuang-t'ing had now reluctantly to admit, was superseded. Finally, there were works of exegesis and hermeneutics. Such was the *Tao-te-ching kuang-sheng-i* of 901, Tu Kuang-t'ings massive explication of the commentary and annotations to the *Tao-te ching* written or sponsored by emperor Hsüan-tsung in 723. It surveyed previous commentaries, extended the emperor's and developed the theory of Lao-tzu as the Cosmic Person first fully recognized by his descendants, the T'ang.

Topography, hagiography, liturgy, thaumatology and hermeneutics added up to a sacred cosmography linked together less by natural causality than by supernatural coincidence, in a fluctuating hierarchy where nothing was absolute. It was a remarkable body of descriptive speculative thought, a powerful piece of transitive semanticization of space and time. It was a mannner of thinking less familiar in Europe where the nearest equivalents might be Wilhelm Gumppenberg's *Atlas marianus* or Athanasius Kircher's *Mundus Subterraneus*, both composed at a time of maximum Paracelsian, alchemical and Taoist influence in Christendom.

## Buddhism

In the T'ang period, in perhaps the most dramatic intellectual development, Chinese thought also established itself in the syntagmatical–critical register. Here, though the historiographical tradition launched by Ssu-ma Ch'ien produced the first Chinese critique of history in the *Shih-t'ung* (Generalization on History) by Liu Chih-chi (661–721), the broadest advance was made by the new Buddhist critical scholasticism of the Mahayana tradition, which reached a peak of influence on China in the reign of empress Wu, in a sermon preached before her by the Hua-yen monk Fa-tsang.

Buddhism first came to China from Iran in the Eastern Han in its early Hinayana or Theravada form. Early Buddhism, possibly influenced by Greek philosophy, especially if the recent later dates for the Buddha prove correct, has been described as a metaphysic secreting a religion.[13] In China, the metaphysic, as taught by the Parthian missionary prince An Shih-kao, was that of the realist Sarvastivadin (Everything Exists) school. Its phenomenalist ontology reduced both *samsara*, the everyday world of illusion, and *nirvana*, the transcendent world of true reality, to their basic constituents, the *dharmas*. The religion, as propagated by the Indian monk Buddhabhadra, had at its core, meditation, *dhyana* or in Chinese *Ch'an*. This term is more familiar in its Japanese form of *zen*, but in China, originally in a Hinayana rather than a Mahayana context, it referred to discursive meditation on the Four Aryan Truths (Suffering, its Origin, Cessation and Path to that Cessation) and the ontology in which they were grounded, rather than the later sense of acquired contemplation. Early Buddhism in China was in effect a psychotherapy by which to move from the insubstantial yet painful world of *samsara* to the supersubstantial and blissful world of *nirvana*. Endemic first in foreign communities, it was then taken up by court circles, especially the *wai-ch'i*, the raffish *nouveaux riches* consort families, and finally became epidemic among non-court or anti-court intelligentsia and gentry as the turn to religion initiated by Taoism intensified and extended itself. So far Buddhism did not imply a move into the critical register. That only came with the introduction to China of Mahayana schools in the *San-kuo* and Chin periods. In particular, it came with the implanting of the Madhyamika school of Nagarjuna by the Central Asian monk Kumarajiva, the St Augustine of late antique China who was brought to Ch'ang-an in 408 by the Tibetan warlord emperor Fu Chien of the later Ch'in dynasty, one of the ephemeral regimes of the *Nan-pei ch'ao*.[14]

Mahayana, in its new *prajnaparamita* (Perfection of Wisdom) scriptures, taught the doctrine of double vacuity. Its slogan was 'all the *dharmas* are empty [*sunya*]': all the elements are vacuous. Whereas for Hinayana schools only the *dharmas* of *samsara* were vacuous, while the *dharmas* of *nirvana* were more substantial, for the Mahayana schools the *dharmas* of both were *sunya*. There was no metaphysical difference between *samsara* and *nirvana*. Early Mahayana schools may have treated *sunya* (empty) and *sunyata* (emptiness) as categorical terms, but in the *Madhyamika* which became predominant in India from the third century AD they took a critical turn which moved their reference from categorical ontology to critical epistemology. *Sunyata*, now referred not to reality but to thought. In *Madhyamika*, in particular in the *mahaprajnaparamitasastra* (Commentary on the Greater Perfection of Wisdom) ascribed to Nagarjuna but in fact belonging to a later generation and going beyond his position, which was introduced to China by Kumarajiva and translated into Chinese, the slogan 'all the *dharmas* are empty' became an assertion of the radical incapacity of thought to reach reality.[15] None of the four fundamental categories of thought: being, not-being, both being and non-being, neither being nor non-being; were applicable to reality, which was thus *sunya*, empty in the sense of incomputable. As Çandrakirti, Nagarjuna's seventh-century disciple, put it, 'the son of the barren woman is neither black nor white'.[16] Initially the Chinese found this critical turn hard to grasp. They interpreted *sunya* categorically in terms of the ontological dichotomy *yu* and *wu*, determinate and indeterminate, familiar to them from the *hsüan-hsüeh* (School of the Mystery) scholars of the previous generation, for whom *hsü*, space, was cosmically ultimate. Eventually, however, Chinese Buddhists, notably Seng-chao (384–414), saw that *sunya* was not appropriately translated by *hsü* and gave it a better transation as *kung*, vacuity, which conveyed its reference as cognitional and not ontological. With the reception of *Madhyamika*, Chinese thought crossed into the sytagmatic–critical register. Indian critical philosophy, however, did not stop with *Madhyamika*. It was propelled forward by that school's own logic which has been described as all dialectic and no doctrine. As with Wittgenstein's aphorism at the end of the *Tractatus*, it was objected that to assert an unbridgeable gap between thought and reality involved a counter-position, an implicit self-contradiction, because it bridged the gap by saying something about both. This objection was already raised in the *Mahaprajnaparamitasastra*. To avoid it, the author had to go beyond Nagarjuna's purely negative parameter which he had used to deconstruct Sarvastivadin metaphysics. He deconstructed his own deconstruction through the notions of *sunyata-sunyata* (emptiness of emptiness) and *atyanta-sunyata* (open-ended emptiness) to advance the concept of *anupalambha-sunyata* (unseizable or non-reified emptiness) which could validly be posited of the *sarvadharmanan-bhutalaksana*, the true essence of all things. *Sunyata*, thus glossed, became both the last term of cognitional analysis and the first term of ontological analysis. If the unknown was conceived not as an insoluble antinomy but as a yet uncomputed mystery, then the mind could run on empty, and thought and reality be reconjoined in critical metaphysics. This reversal of the counter-position was not pursued in India. There, instead, the brothers Asanga and Vasubandhu founded the Vijnanavada (in Chinese *Wei-shih*, consciousness only) school, which opposed *Madhyamikan* dualism with a consistent Idealist monism. The mind, knowing its own incapacity, at least knew itself, so that thought was reality and reality thought. This school, which developed considerable psychological elaboration, was brought to China in the reign of Liang Wu-ti by the Southern Indian monk Paramartha and then again in later form by Hsüan-tsang when he returned from India in the second half of the reign of T'ang T'ai-tsung.

In China, consonant with its preference for realism over idealism, *Madhyamikan* dualism was resolved in a different way by the Tient'ai school of critical metaphysics which stood more in the line of the *Mahaprajnaparamitasastra*. This was founded by Chih-i in the south at the time of the Sui unification and was developed in a later text, the *Ta Ch'eng chih-kuan fa-men* (Methodological Principles of Mahayana Contemplation and Meditation), probably to be ascribed to the reign of Hsüan-tsung. Chih-i argued that reality was neither in the subject nor in the object, but only in their conjuncture, just as sound was neither in the drum nor in the drumstick, but only in their collision. Reality was relational. Moreover, while it might be true, as the *Madhyamikans* argued, that the subject could not reach the object, that did not mean that the Object, the Cosmic Buddha, endowed with infinite skill in means (*upayakasaulya*) could not reach the subject. Man might be imprisoned within his own mind, condemned like Plato's cinemagoers in the cave, to know only his own projections, as the Vijnanavadins argued, but the Buddha mind could enter the cave, or was already present in it, to turn any scenario to its own salvific purposes. Reality revealed itself. That was known because negation ended in affirmation: in the metaphor of the handkerchief made into a rabbit by a conjuror, 'do not take the non-existence of the rabbit to be the handkerchief'.[17] This was the critical metaphysics which the T'ien-t'ai school read out of, or into, the *Saddharmapundarika-sutra*, the Lotus or *Lien-hua ching*, one of the most impressive of the Mahayana scriptures. Through its association with the Lotus, T'ien-t'ai, named after a monastery not far from Nanking, became the mainstream of Chinese, indeed East Asian, Mahayana Buddhism. It was to this school and its *sutra* that the great Japanese monk Nichiren gave his adherence. In China, T'ien-t'ai was known as the orchid of the spring, the perfection of pristinity.

It was run a close second by the chrysanthemum of the autumn, the masterwork of maturity, the Hua-yen (Flower Garland) school, so called from its reliance on another impressive Mahayana scripture, the *Avatamsaka* (Flower Garland or Ornament) *sutra*.[18] This text, composed in India, never there became the basis of a distinctive school. In China it did so become and the school, reinforced by an improved text and an expert translator Siksananda, both fetched from Central Asia, reached its greatest réclame in the reign of empress Wu with the Sermon on the Golden Lion (*Chin Shih-tzu chang*) preached before her by Fa-tsang (643–712), himself of Central Asian extraction though Chinese birth.

In the sermon, Fa-tsang took a gilded lion, doubtless of Chinese type, as a metaphor for the relations between the Absolute and the relative: the total lion the single noumenon, its component metallic hairs the multiple phenomena. Hua-yen continued but transposed T'ien-t'ai. It accepted Chih-i's discovery that reality was relational, thereby transcending the categories of being, not being, both being and not being, neither being nor not being, the tetralemma with which *Madhyamika* had started. It extended that insight to cover not only the coexistence of noumenon, *li*, and phenomena, *shih*, as T'ien-t'ai had done, but also what it regarded as more basic, the mutual codetermination of the phenomena themselves – what was designated *shih-shih wu-ai*, the absence of obstruction between one phenomenon and another. It accepted, too, the Tien-t'ai belief that reality could communicate itself to minds imprisoned within themselves, but argued that such communication would be more than skill in means, more than information conveyed according to the capacity of the recipient. It would be both total, an unrestricted act of understanding, and constitutive, the knowers becoming what was made known to them, so that the term of critical analysis could only be the Omega Point of a multiple Godhead constituted by the circumincession of an infinity of divinized persons. It was this cosmotheism or theocosmos which Fa-tsang tried to convey with his metaphor of the lion and its hairs. In the *Avatamsaka* itself it was conveyed by the two interrelated metaphors of Indra's net and the Tower of Maitreya. In Indra's net, the image of *shih-shih wu-ai*, each jewel reflected the others and its and their reflections to infinity: 'Inside a single hair pore, innumerable lands. With various bases, many as atoms. In each of them a universal illuminator. Expounds the truth in the midst of the crowd'.[19] The Tower of Maitreya, the Buddha of the future, represented the final destination of the pilgrim:

> He saw the tower, immensely vast and wide, hundreds of thousands of leagues wide . . . Also, inside the great tower he saw hundreds of thousands of other towers similarly arrayed . . . yet these towers were not mixed up with one another being each mutually distinct, while appearing reflected in each and every object of all the other towers.[20]

Hua-yen, as expounded by Fa-tsang, was the high point of Chinese Buddhist critical thought, but also a dead-end. Without a further injection of categorical thinking from religion, science or scholarship on which to exercise its critical digestive juices, it had nowhere further to go. Its synthesis was so complete and perfect as to be felt inadequate and constraining. Everywhere the Buddhist mind turned away from critical thinking as expressed in the four schools of *Madhyamika*, *Vijnanavada*, Tien-t'ai and Hua-yen; it sought new enlightenment and fresh expression in the four new schools of Hinayana fundamentalism, Pure Land evangelicalism, Tantric esotericism and Ch'an or Zen illuminism, none of which operated in the critical register. Except for Hinayana fundamentalism which found its homeland in Ceylon, Burma and Thailand, all three schools were represented in China from the reign of Hsüan-tsung, and Pure Land and Ch'an or a combination of the two went on to become the dominant strains in Chinese Buddhism in modern times. Critical scholasticism, however, went into eclipse.

The emergence of cognitive complexity through the deployment of a fuller panoply of categorical and critical registers had a multiplicatory effect on Chinese intellectual history. An intertextuality or synergism was created whereby what was fact in one register was metaphor in another, terms being transposed between fields to express new shades of meaning. An example of this cross-fertilization may be found in poetry, one of the glories of the T'ang period and the most significant enrichment then of China's original paradigmatic–categorical register. Tu Fu, Li Po and Po Chu-i are sometimes described respectively as Confucian, Taoist and Buddhist poets in that they used imagery and themes from these bodies of thought. They did so, however, for poetic rather than propagandist reasons, taking advantage of the further possibilities for allusion, resonance and mood-creation that the new intellectual registers and their vocabulary afforded. T'ang poetry, it may be argued, has retained its primacy in the Chinese canon because it was able to draw on the widest and deepest pool of ideas at the moment of their freshest and most immediate impact. It was golden poetry in the sense that C.S. Lewis applied this term to English verse in the Jacobethan period. These indirect dividends from one register to another were probably more significant in the growth of intellectual capital than direct borrowings between Confucianism, Taoism and Buddhism. Intertextuality was an important if invisible source of a multiplication of semantic currency under the T'ang, difficult to account for in any age, but neverless palpable.

## China's intellectual pluralism

The formation of intellectual capital and semantic currency under the T'ang was furthered by the presence of a degree of intellectual pluralism unique in Chinese history. Gerard Manley Hopkins distinguished between freedoms of pitch and freedoms of play in literary composition. Complexity with its annexation of new registers extended freedom of pitch. Pluralism provided more variegated play within it. Two leagues of players may be distinguished: the major league of Confucianism, Taoism, Buddhism and what, on the model of Hinduism, may be called Sinism, the endogenous religion of China; and a minor league of imported ideologies which, while they did not succeed in becoming naturalized as did Buddhism, nevertheless in the atmosphere of T'ang cosmopolitanism were not without impact. Such were Zoroastrianism, Nestorianism, Manichaeism, Judaism and Islam, all potential major players if more favoured by circumstance. The relationship of these diverse bodies of thought to each other and to the imperial authorities ran a gamut of indifference, rivalry, toleration, mutual enrichment and occasional confrontation, but their co-presence on a complex and far from level field enhanced the vitality of Chinese intellectual life. Pluralism diversified complexity to remultiply meaning, messages and media.

### Major league

Here Confucianism deserves again to be taken first, not so much for its achievements at either the categorical or critical registers in the T'ang period, as for its guardianship of ancient Chinese literature and its provision thereby of the curriculum which, whether in schools or more frequently in the hands of private tutors, used print to sustain rising literacy. Confucius in his T'ang interpretation was essentially the Teacher of 10,000 Generations, rather than his previous or subsequent incarnations as uncrowned king, prophet, sage or philosopher. In a sense, all educated Chinese in the T'ang period were Confucians. One famous educator, under the Sui, was Wang T'ung (584–617), later credited with thousands of pupils but having no official status. Most Confucians were anonymous.

Yet already some were Confucians in a special, more conscious sense. Such had been the agnatic aristocracy of the Eastern Han who wished thereby to distance themselves from both the raffish, uterine aristocracy of the consort families, the patrons of Buddhism, and the barbarian aristocracy of *foederati* and conquest dynasties who often, because of Lao-tzu's supposed sojourn among non-Chinese, favoured Taoism. Such too were the super aristocracy of Western Shantung, Confucius' home territory, whose matrimonial prestige exceeded that of the T'ang imperial house itself. Such too were some ministers and bureaucrats, not necessarily of examination provenance, like T'ai-tsung's candid counsel Wei Cheng or Hsüan-tsung's imperious premier Yao Ch'ung or Tai-tsung's high-flying technocrat Liu Yen or Li Te-yu, minister to Wu-tsung (840–846), anti-Buddhist, connoisseur of camellias. For these the value of the Master lay less in filial piety and family solidarity than in moral independence and professional responsibility. Women were not excluded from these standpoints under the T'ang. Shang-kuan Wan-erh, empress Wu's secretary and head of her private office, was a noted Confucian bluestocking, widely admired for her poetry and only reluctantly murdered by her regular civil service opponents.[21] Finally, in the Silver T'ang period there were intellectuals and officials like Han Yü and Li Ao (d. 844) who began to extract philosophy from the *paideia* and to redefine Chinese identity in a shrunken empire in culturalistic rather than dynastic terms. Han Yü was a Renaissance man. He combined fundamentalism, the meaning of antiquity in the style of antiquity, with modernism, antiquity is now, and expressed both in a Housman-like clarity and pugnacity. Subsequently these T'ang Confucianisms, general and particular, formed the basis for the radical, missionary Confucianism of the Sung counter-revolution, the golden age of the *shih ta-fu*, the scholar gentry and high ministers for whom education in the literary language was both a communications system for government and a set of social shibboleths for an élite. Then, from within these paradigms, there emerged in the eleventh century the adumbration of syntagmatic metaphysics with Idealist and Rationalist wings. Yet, even then, it is now maintained, such formal Confucianism remained minoritarian, and was aggressive for that reason. Confucian China was long in the building, and was perhaps never complete.[22]

By the same token, Taoist China was long in the dismantling and even under the Sung counter-revolution developed new forms to attract both imperial and popular patronage. Nevertheless, if Confucian China had its grey dawn in the Silver T'ang period, Taoist China, it may be argued, had had its high noon in the preceding Golden T'ang period. The meridian came in the second half of the reign of emperor Hsüan-tsung, whose temple name, Mysterious Ancestor, and final reign title *T'ien-pao*, had distinct Taoist resonances. Whereas the development of Confucianism was shaped by the requirements of successive patrons who sought different things in a fixed canon of classical literature, the development of Taoism was set by additions to the canon itself as it broadened to include new texts. In the one case the readers were active, in the other the writers. As a result, the Taoist canon became unwieldy to its own ultimate disadvantage in a print world where brevity was prized.

The Taoist religion, in the sense of the body of doctrine and practice contained in the *Tao-tsang*, began in the revelations to Chang Chüeh in Shantung and Chang Tao-ling in Szechwan which inspired the revolutionary movements of the Yellow Turbans and Five Pecks of Rice at the end of the Han. These movements, often miscalled peasant rebellions, were penitential and therapeutic in character and secessionary in effect. They were instigated and led by dissident intellectuals, members of the *shih* or gentry, who had been radicalized by eunuch repression out of conventional politics and into religious messianism and social utopianism. Some details of the utopia were derived from confused reports of Roman constitutionalism. The Yellow Turbans were suppressed by the forces of Ts'ao Ts'ao, the enlightened, antinomian military dictator, adopted son of a eunuch, whose own philosophy, a mixture of Machiavellianism and mysticism, nevertheless had affinities with Taoism. The Five Pecks of Rice, on the other hand, directed by Chang Tao-ling's grandson, Chang Lu, survived by accommodation. It became a regional theocracy in northern Szechwan and southern Shensi, but was accepted as part of the political establishment by the Shu Han and the Chin. When the Chin moved south to Nanking early in the fourth century, it took this orthodox, *cheng-i*, Taoism with it. Here at the turn of the fourth and fifth centuries it reverted temporarily to its revolutionary origins in the rebellion of the magician Sun En, based on gentry discontents in coastal Kiangsu and around the Po-yang lake, against the Eastern Chin. The rebellion was crushed by the emerging Liu Sung dynasty, but not without leaving a residue of sentiment and substructure, especially in Kiangsi, on which later less-political and more quietistic initiatives could capitalize. Meanwhile, in the north, Taoism briefly acquired political ascendancy in the early days of the Toba Wei under the leadership of K'ou Ch'ien-chih. He revived Chang Tao-ling's title of *T'ien-shih*, Heavenly Master, withdrew from the ambiance of revolution, borrowed monasticism from Buddhism and first used the term *Tao-chiao*, Taoist religion in contrast to *Ju-chia*, Confucianism, and *Fo-chiao*, Buddhism. The ascendancy, however, exercized through Ts'ui Hao, a prime minister who saw himself as the new Chang Liang, the wily councillor to the founder of the Han so vividly portrayed by Ssu-ma Ch'ien, proved ephemeral. Subsequent Toba Wei rulers preferred to patronize Buddhism. But the episode was a precedent for the T'ang sponsorship of Taoism, and the Heavenly Master's sect after various vicissitudes became Taoism's most enduring organization, as a kind of registrar-generalship, down to 1949 when the last Heavenly Master fled to Taiwan with all his spells and talismans.

From the deposits left by the three revolutionary forms of the Taoist religion emerged the *San-tung*, the three arcana, and based on these texts the three lineages: Mao-shan, founded by T'ao Hung-ching (456–536), was most important for doctrine; Ling-pao, emerging in the sixth century, for liturgy and cult; and San-huang for occultism and piety, though its functions here tended to be subsumed in the ongoing Heavenly Master's lineage. Indeed, it is a matter of dispute as to how far sects or lineages should be distinguished.[23] They are best envisaged, as often with Taoism, on a medical analogy, as prestigious teaching colleges with special fields of excellence. With the emergence of the *San-tung*, the Taoist religion abandoned liberation theology for princely establishment. T'ao Hung-ching formed a mutually fruitful alliance with alchemical medicine, both *wai-tan* and *nei-tan*; hitherto a parallel intellectual stream. Imperial physicians such as Sun Shih-mo (581–682) or the more legendary Lu Tung-pin tended to be associated with Taoism and lent lustre to it, though not all Taoists were alchemists nor all alchemists Taoists. Subsequently, indeed, in the Five Dynasties and early Sung periods as Taoism shifted its centre of gravity from court to country or urban populace, patrician monks and consultants were sidelined by more hands-on general practitioners or paramedics. Therapy, with the appearance of the new *T'ien-hsin* (Heavenly Heart) and *Lei-fa* (Thunder Magic) techniques, took increasingly penitential and exorcistic forms with *nei-tan* reinterpreted in more psychological terms.[24] By the Sung, Taoism had reinvented itself in leadership and sociology.

Under the T'ang, however, Taoism's greatest strength in public life lay in its ability to respond to events, or to create them, by the timely discovery of anomalies and wonders and by appropriate liturgies. Taoist spokesmen like Tu Kuang-t'ing became in effect the media managers of successive regimes. This made the Ling-pao lineage, which had emerged in the sixth century, of equal if not greater importance than Mao-shan.[25] From a political point of view Taoism was a religion of opportunism and spin, it read the signs of the times against a background of sacred cosmography and glossed them publicly by interpretive symbolic action. Where Confucianism looked to merit and to a lesser extent to expertise, Taoism looked to resourcefulness and improvization. It lent support to those not bound by rules, those prepared to think the unthinkable, to trouble-shooters, and to emergency plenipotentiaries. It privileged men such as Li Lin-fu, Hsüan-tsung's aristocratic non-examination prime minister; Li Mi, Su-tsung's strategic policy adviser; and Wang Chien, salt smuggler, revolutionary bandit, regional governor and dynastic founder in Szechwan at the turn of the T'ang and Five Dynasties periods. Taoism mastered the moment. If the business of a statesman is, as Olivares said, 'to search out ways in the midst of impossibility', then Taoism signposted these ways.[26] Its advocacy of *wu-wei*, indirect rather than direct action, also resonated in the age of Yang Kuei-fei, with feminine backstairs politics. Hsüan-tsung's two sisters, the Yu-chen and Chin-hsien princesses, were associated with two sumptuous Taoist temples in Ch'ang-an. A statue of the first was located at the Tung-t'ien temple endowed and visited by her, which later became the home of the alchemist Hsueh Chang before providing Tu Kuang-t'ing with refuge during the confusion at the end of the T'ang.[27] Finally, Taoism found acceptance among the Sino-barbarian aristocracy, half Chinese, half Turkish, of which the T'ang dynasty may be regarded as the greatest example. For them it represented an export version of Chinese culture, less ethnically bound than Confucianism, less resolutely cosmopolitan than Buddhism. It was a brandname with whose polyvalency and indeterminacy they, as frontiersmen, could identify. Taoism thus became temporarily under Hsüan-tsung the apex of a flexible and composite establishment.

Both Confucianism and Taoism coexisted with Sinism, what Michel Strickmann (1981) called the nameless religion of the people and others have referred to as the shamanistic substrate of Chinese religion. This second description is contested by Edward Davis as involving a confusion between Shamanism and spirit-possession, though others again have thought the distinction too sharply drawn.[28] However named, this religion, diffused and uncentred, and unlike Hinduism not defined by any set of texts or body of myth, is increasingly recognized by scholars as an entity in its own right. It was more than a residue left when the supposed contributions of Confucianism, Taoism and Buddhism have been subtracted. Its local placement was capable of challenge as well as response to those more literate and better-organized ideologies. It was not ahistoric or unchanging. It was not a mere substrate, but projected itself all the way to the Altar of Heaven at which the emperor officiated at the winter solstice, though its main strength did lie in the villages and their spontaneous organizations. There its two chief constituents were on the one hand prognostication, of favourable times through almanacs and of favourable places through *feng-shui*, and on the other hand paramedicine, exorcism through spirit-possession, a kind of group therapy whereby dissociated complexes were either reinte-grated to the ego or returned to the unconscious by transference to mediums, *wu*, possessed by superior powers.[29] It was with these rural shrinks, often also local landlords and community leaders, that both Confucianism and Taoism had to coexist.

It was a coexistence which mixed conflict, indifference and col-laboration. The Confucian attitude to religion was encapsulated in the saying ascribed to the Sage in the *Analects*: 'Respect the spirits and ghosts (*shen* and *kuei*), but keep your distance from them'. Single in theory, Confucianism's practice was multiple. High-minded indif-ference was not always expedient. In a backward province, a district magistrate might have to confront local customs and religious centres with either rejection or accommodation. If Confucianism dis-tanced itself from Sinism, Taoism engaged with it either negatively or positively, more often the first. Of the three Taoist revolutionary movements, while the Yellow Turbans largely ignored popular reli-gion by remaining within classical parameters, the Five Pecks of Rice actively combated what it called *yin-ssu*: the excessive cult of ver-nacular divinities practised by shamans and thaumaturges under the protection of powerful local families, what it saw as the rival religion of *Po-chia chih tao*.[30] Only Sun En's movement, in its desire to mobilize a maximum of friends against a minimum of enemies, accepted the support of powerful local shrines devoted to python cults around the Po-yang lake, and that with some distaste. Similarly, of the three Taoist scholastic lineages which repudiated revolution for princely establishment, all operated at intellectual levels higher and more complex than that of the popular cults and sought to disengage Taoism from any links with them bequeathed by Sun En's movement. The revived Heavenly Master's sect initially followed this line too, and it was only later that it lent support to the new exorcisms of *T'ien-hsin* and *lei-fa* which revived links with the paramedics of spirit-possession, the *wu*. Taoism only moved gradually and partially from being, under the T'ang, in Michel Strickmann's interpretation of Mao-shan, a reformation from above, a life and death struggle against the spirit mediums, to being, in Kristofer Schipper's phrase, 'the written tradition of Chinese indigenous cults' under the Sung.[31] It was a transition effected under the sponsorship of the Heavenly Master's sect as it was refounded at Lung-hu shan in Kiangsi, in the late T'ang period.

A similar reversal of alliances was effected in the Buddhist community by the relocation of Tantrism, *Mi-chiao*, from court to country in the early Sung, from large imperial monasteries to small private oratories where, as a religion of requiems, it necessarily formed partnerships with local practitioners of folkloric funerary rites.[32] It was one of several means whereby Buddhism sought to survive the diminution of imperial patronage in the Sung counter-revolution.

Back in the Golden T'ang, multiplicity was part of the self-image of Chinese Buddhism. *Pan-chiao*, the division of doctrines, that is the arrangement of *sutras* in order of depth and ultimacy in accordance with the particular school making it, was a common practice of Buddhist scholastics. Opponents' views might, in absolute terms, be false, but all doctrines were relatively true, and their dialectic gave an ever-closer approximation to the truth. Mahayana was syncretic and progressive. From the Four Aryan Truths and the foothills of Hinayana, the pilgrim was led to the nursery slopes of *Prajnaparamita* and the pass represented by the clamorous silence of Vimalakirti by which the questions of Manjusri, the god of wisdom, were brought to an end. Then the trail bifurcated into the alternative pistes of logical

*Madhyamika* and psychological *Vijñānavāda*, to emerge onto the snowblinding uplands of emptiness, *sunyata* before the twin peaks of the *Avatamsaka*, the Buddha's first sermon understood by only one, and the *Saddharmapundarika*, the Buddha's last sermon, intelligible to all. These were the *sutras* of Hua Yen and T'ien-t'ai, the high points of Chinese Buddhist scholasticism, each claiming a greater elevation over the other, as the Everest of the *Tathagata*, *Ju-lai*, He who Comes. Alternatively, for those dismayed by such intellectual rigour, there was the leap of faith, the single invocation of the Buddha, *nien-fo*, which was sufficient to attain the Western Paradise of Amitabha, the Ching-t'u or Pure Land, or the personal flight of Ch'an which went straight to the top across all verbal ravines, or the secret underground route of Tantrism which went not in the light but in the dark, not by knowledge or faith but by magic – *mudras*, *mantras*, *abhishekas*, gestures, formulas and initiations. All this was embraced, by T'ien-t'ai especially, as the Buddha's infinite skill in means, *upayakasaulya*, applicable in every circumstance and condition, a kind of universalization of incarnation, Shakti forever in the embrace of Siva.

If the primary contribution of Buddhism to Chinese thought was the critical turn in metaphysics, the realization through the unpacking of *sunyata* that ontology could be based on cognitional analysis, its second contribution was as a treasury of concepts and images, a repertoire of actions which could be utilized by others than Buddhists. The direct constituency of Buddhism under the T'ang was always limited to a coterie of consort families, imperial women, palace eunuchs, by-appointment merchants and an upper-middle-class monastic élite; but the indirect currency of its coin, through private monastic cells, shrines, requiems, images, pilgrimages and protective invocations was much more extensive. Buddhism became the type of religion in China, as Christianity did in the West, its answers half-remembered even when its questions were three-quarters forgotten.

### Minor league

In addition to its three native products and the naturalization which turned Buddhism in China into Chinese Buddhism, T'ang China was host to five guest religions. Only the latest, Islam, and that only in the long run and with later reinforcements, succeeded in establishing itself as more than marginal. Nevertheless, the presence of these guests, temporary or permanent, contributed to the unique cosmopolitanism of the T'ang and found expression in the exoticism of the imagery available to T'ang writers and iconographers.

First, Zoroastrianism – Mazdaism, the good religion of Ahura Mazda as it was known to its devotees – which had been proclaimed by the prophetic reformer from Balkh, not long before the foundation of the Achaemenid empire. China had been aware of Iran as a land of magicians as far back as the Shang period, but the Zoroastrian reformation was something new.[33] Mazdaism, however, was the least missionary of the great religions. It was what Christianity might have remained without St Martin of Tours, the religion of an ethno-class. Like Judaism, from which it may have borrowed the notion of prophecy, it was directed less to the world than to a community. Nonetheless, if Zoroastrianism was not propagated westward except marginally in Armenia, political and mercantile contacts between the Sassanid empire and China were sufficiently strong and constant as to implant Parsee communities in the Middle Kingdom by both land and sea.[34] These communities, found in most major Chinese cities, were probably Sogdian rather than Farsi in background, except in Canton and Yang-chou. At the beginning of the sixth century, empress-dowager Ling of the Toba Wei was of Iranian ancestry a fact which probably reflects an alliance between the Sassanids and the Wei against the nomads of Inner Asia. It is reported that she performed sacrifices at Mount Sung near Lo-yang to the Hu T'ien-shen, the high god of the Iranians. Zoroastrianism came to be known as the *Hsien-chiao*, the religion of the Divinity, maybe because in East Asia it did not always take the orthodox dualist form. It was also known as the *Erh-yüan chiao*, the Two Principles' religion, and the *pai-huo chiao*, the fire worshippers' religion, names which indicate a fair acquaintance with its tenets and practices.

In the mid-sixth century there was a flurry of Sino-Iranian diplomatic activity. Embassies were sent to both Ch'ang-an and Nanking by the Sassanids and their Central Asian satellites, probably in connection with the rise of Turkish power on the steppe. These embassies established the Sassanids in Chinese eyes as reliable tributaries and something more. Their brilliant secular aristocratic lifestyle, the world of polo, chess, hunting, armchairs and music, was admired and the court of Chosroes II Parviz (590–628) at Ctesiphon became the model for the hard-riding but sophisticated court of T'ai-tsung at Ch'ang-an. In 621 a Mazdaist temple was authorized to the west of the capital. In 638 there was a Sassanid embassy, no doubt appealing for aid against the Muslims. In 674, Peroz (Firuz), son of Yazdgird III, the last Sassanid emperor, who since his father's death in 651 had been conducting guerrilla warfare in Sogdiana with covert Chinese support, withdrew with his government in exile to Ch'ang-an. In 677 he requested the construction of another Mazdaist temple at the capital in addition to the three which already existed and this request was eventually complied with in the revived reign of Chung-tsung during the government of empress Wei. Unlike the Bourbons, the Sassanids never returned from their oriental Koblenz, but contemporaries did not know this and the Sassanid–T'ang alliance, of which the diffusion of Mazdaist temples in China was an expression, must have seemed a hopeful one for both parties, not least intellectually. In the good religion of Ahura Mazda, China was exposed for the first time to what was, despite its dualist scholasticism, a prophetic, world-affirming, ethical monotheism.

Second, Nestorianism. Christianity, present in China from AD86 if recent tombstone evidence is confirmed, was known to the T'ang as the *Ta-ching chiao*, Great Luminous, that is Catholic, religion, or the *Ta-chin chiao*, Great Western, that is Roman, religion.[35] It was the second religion of the Sassanid empire. It might indeed have become the first had it not been bespoken by the Basileus and had the Shahs, who sometimes took Christian wives, been prepared to defy the *mobeds*, the Mazdaist clergy. Nestorianism, the name usually given to the branch of Eastern Christianity brought to Ch'ang-an in 635 by the Syrian monk Abraham and authorized by emperor T'ai-tsung to build a church there, is really a misnomer. Though a number of Syrian and Persian dioceses had refused to endorse the condemnation in 431 by the Council of Ephesus of the conservative, scripturalist, Judaizing Christological heresy of the Syrian Greek patriarch of Constantinople, Nestorius, who denied the single hypostatic union in favour of a bipersonal partnership, and had formed their own ecclesiastical community under the Catholicos of the East, at Ctesiphon, much had happened since. Rome had always had a penchant for the Antiochene school, of which Nestorianism could be regarded as only a deviant expression, and for the prudent Christocentric Marial devotion it fostered.[36] Moreover, since the Council of Chalcedon in 451, where the Fathers endorsed Pope Leo's Christological furmula of two natures in one Person, Monophysitism, the opposite heresy from Nestorianism had been the principle concern for orthodoxy in both East and West. Rome had only reluctantly agreed to the condemnation of three Antiochene theologians at the second Council of Constantinople in 555. By the seventh century, the Antiochene school, as revived by St Maximus the Confessor, was again in the ascendant and the third Council of Constantinople in 681 redressed the balance of the second by its condemnation of the quasi-Monophysite doctrine of Monothelitism. It was not unreasonable then for the church of the East, which traced its origins to St Peter at Antioch, to portray itself as both Catholic and Roman, the church of Pope, Basileus, Shah and, hopefully, the Son of Heaven.

Nestorianism was an urban religion, its first home the caravan cities of the Fertile Crescent. Its mission to China was based on its arch-dioceses of Merv, Herat and Samarkand, already established under Sassanid auspices. Further east, its initial flock would have been among the Sogdian merchant communities along the silk route. But Nestorianism was also a *limes* religion. So long as the Sassanid empire lasted, the mission had a diplomatic aspect as well. Abraham was a Syrian not a Sogdian and was probably dispatched directly by the Catholicos at the instance of Chosrhoes II. In China itself Christianity took on a military character. It was associated with mercenaries from Central Asia, especially in the heavy cavalry which employed the famous large horses from Ferghana so much admired by emperor T'ai-tsung. In 742, there was a Christian community at Ling-wu in the oasis and military base of Ning-hsia on the Upper Yellow river. Ning-hsia became emperor Su-tsung's headquarters at the beginning of the rebellion of An Lu-shan (himself a Sogdian but probably not a Christian) and the famous Sian stele, rediscovered in 1623, which gives the early history of the Nestorian mission in China, was erected in 780 at the instance of a Syrian general in the Loyalist army, part of the text being in Syriac in Estrangelo script. Indeed, it is possible that Kuo Tzu-i himself, the Imperial commander-in-chief, from Hua-chou in Shensi and commandant at Ling-wu at the outset of the rebellion, was a Christian or Christian sympathizer. Certainly there were Christians in his clientela. In the next generation, with the decline of the frontier armies following the abandonment of the T'ang empire in Inner Asia and the increasingly civilian ethos of the Silver T'ang period, this identification of Christianity with the camp may have inhibited further evangelization.

Nevertheless, the Ning-hsia area, under the name Tangut or Onggut, long retained a Christian imprint which was reinforced by fresh mercenary immigration. Christianity later came to be known as the *Shih-tzu chiao* the religion of the cross. Known by its iconography, Christianity perhaps affected that of others. Recent archaeology at what appears to be a Christian church of seventh-century date, attached to a Taoist monastery outside Ch'ang-an, has uncovered a statue of the Virgin. It has been suggested that Marial imagery influenced the evolution of the male or androgynous Boddhisattva Avalokitesvara into the female Kuan-yin, goddess of mercy, which constituted a significant feminization of sensibility in Chinese Buddhist piety.[37] The church of the East might have rejected the definition of Ephesus, but it still conveyed the message of the Christotokos.

Third, at the opposite pole of religious sensibility, there was Manichaeism, another import of the Sino-Iranian connection, though in East Asia its major concentration came to be among the Turkish-speaking Uighurs. Manichaeism was known to the Chinese as the *Ming-chiao*, the Religion of the Light, the particles of which imprisoned in matter were the object of its soteriology. Contrary to earlier views which associated Manichaeism with Zoroastrianism, on account of the dualism which was more central to it than to the Good Religion, it is now understood that Manichaeism, in both form and content, was a version of Christianity.[38] Mani, from Semitic Mesopotamia not Iranian Fars, proclaimed himself the Apostle of Jesus Christ, the promised Paraclete, and the new St Paul, whose missionary journeys and dedication to the Gentiles he imitated. Mani was an ecumenist. Reacting against his own Christian background in an exclusive brethren sect, the Elkesaites, his was the most comprehensive of Christianities. All things to all men, it transcended denominations, even religions, in a dualist higher Catholicism, which was both a speculative theory of everything and practical path of salvation for both laity, auditors and religious *perfecti* asking little of the former, much of the latter. With its loose structure of itinerant bishops, undercover missioners, local cells, back-country safehouses and aristocratic fellow travellers, Manichaeism appealed to expatriates, travellers, social indeterminates, people of mixed descent, those away from home or who had no home. Like all gnosticisms, it was a religion of nostalgia, the yearning of the light particles for the True Light, the Stranger God, the Alien Christ. Secrecy of doctrine was matched by clandestinity of organization. As a higher final revelation, Manichaeism could accommodate itself to lower ones – Catholicism, Mazdaism, Buddhism and Taoism – and could seek safety in their shadow. Manichees, whether professed or auditors were not required to flaunt their beliefs. Unlike the Nestorians, the Manichees, if not their patrons, were on the whole pacifists, who rejected the violence of matter as well as its sex. Consequently, Manichaeism was propagated through merchants or medical men rather than through mercenaries. It was a civilian form of Christianity, not always recognized as heretical because its devotees had taken the orthodox side in the Arian controversy about the Trinity.

Manichaeism was first noted in China in 694 when Iranian missionaries arrived at Lo-yang to minister to a probably already existing congregation and presented empress Wu with a set of their scriptures. In 719, a Manichaean astronomer arrived at Ch'ang-an as part of an embassy from a ruler in Tokharistan, no doubt asking for aid against the Muslims. In 732, emperor Hsüan-tsung signed an edict which authorized foreign Manichees to erect a church in Ch'ang-an. Chinese converts, it may be assumed, were rare, but one of them, it would appear, was Li Mi, national security adviser to emperor Su-tsung in the crisis of 756, an adept of Mao-shan Taoism, for whom Manichaeism would have been a higher form of the way and Mani a Western incarnation of Lao-tzu. It was Li Mi, the Chinese Kissinger, who devised the T'ang–Uighur alliance which gave the first light cavalry for the suppression of An Lu-shan and the second privileged access to Chinese culture. In 763, doubtless in recognition of Li Mi's role as honest broker, Manichaeism became the official religion of the Uighur state, only the second adoption of a sedentary religion by a steppe power and a unique event in the history of a religion which preferred shadow to limelight, homelessness to establishment. The alliance was uneasy. The Uighurs used the threat of defection to the Tibetans to extort more princesses and silk. Kuo Tzu-i maintained it, primarily by his personal prestige as a soldier, but also it may be guessed by common Christian sympathies. In 768 Manichaean churches received the title *Ta-yun kuang-ming ssu*, Temples of the Manifest Light of the Great Cloud, from emperor Tai-tsung, a name perhaps indicative of better understanding of Mani's particular Christology. In 771 the same emperor authorized the construction of further churches in Yang-chou, Shao-hsing and

Nan-ch'ang. These were places where Uighurs were not likely to be, so it was probably at this time that a small but persistent Chinese community was formed. Following the end of the Uighur alliance and the proscription of foreign religions in 845, this community found refuge in the then border province of Fukien. Here, despite involvement in the unsuccessful rebellion of Fang La in the 1120s, they survived and proliferated. Marco Polo, who regarded them as crypto-Christians, believed that there were a million and a half households scattered round south China. Though part of the Ming revolution against the Mongols and their collaborators, and giving it its brand name as the dynasty of light, Manichaeism was repudiated once the dynasty was established, though there may be echoes of it in the Yung-lo emperor's ecumenism. It therefore shrank back into the shadows as a local form of Buddhism or Taoism. A Manichaean church was still in use in Ch'uan-chou, the medieval superport of Zayton, in the 1980s though Mani the Apostle of Jesus Christ had long been transformed into Moni the Buddha of Light.

Fourth, Judaism, like Manichaeism Semitic in speech and in the T'ang period Mesopotamian rather than Palestinian in home location.[39] If the early date of AD86 for the first Christian activity in China is confirmed, it will probably indicate – what might have been suspected anyway, the even earlier presence of Judaism, for the Church generally began by grasping the coattails of the synagogue before turning to the Gentiles. Consequently, the Christianity which will have reached China by AD86 will have been Semitic rather than Greek in language, and may still have adhered to the law. Jewish communities certainly existed in Persia in post-exilic Old Testament times, and from them later Zoroastrianism borrowed the doctrine of a messiah, just as it borrowed a stricter dualism from Manichaeism. These communities were of a pre-Christian Judaic kind: that is, messianic expectation was still high, and rabbinic orthodoxy, tannaitic or amoraitic, was not yet established. It was natural then that Christian missionaries should use them as stepping-stones to China. When such Jewish communities first reached China is not clear. An inscription in the K'ai-feng synagogue dated 1663 claimed that the religion had been in China since Chou, that is preimperial, times before 221BC. This is not impossible, but the tradition recorded by a Jesuit in the seventeenth century that the first community arrived in the reign of Han Ming-ti (58–75) is more probable because it would put the first foundation in relationship with the destruction of the Temple in AD70. Thereafter, until the Sung, evidence about Judaism in China is strangely lacking given the openness of trade routes and the receptivity of the T'ang. No Chinese name for Judaism is found and it was not referred to in the proscription of foreign religions in 845. Yet Jewish communities were strong in Dravidian India, the Khazars were converted to Judaism around 740, the Falashas in Ethiopia and the Tats in the Caucasus possibly date to this period, and Jews served as prime ministers in Ummayad Spain – thus Judaism had not lost its proselytizing capacity elsewhere, so in China either the capacity was not present in sufficient degree or the milieu was more resistant. China has never been tainted by anti-semitism. Possibly Judaism was simply eclipsed in Chinese eyes by another, newer, Semitic monotheism which was more militant.

Fifth, Islam, the Ishmaelite younger brother of Judaism born out of the population displacement and sectarian ferment following the Samaritan and Synagogic revolts in Palestine in the reigns of Justinian and Heraclius and against the background of Byzantine-Sassanid hostility.[40] T'ang officials will have learnt of the Muslim explosion first from the Sassanid court in initial refuge in the Sino-Iranian borderlands and then in China itself. Assistance against rebels was a recognized privilege of tributary status. Some military support was given by the Chinese in the reign of empress Wu, who was then fighting against the Tibetans in the West and feared a Muslim–Tibetan alliance. Like Judaism, Islam received no name in the T'ang period. It was neither authorized nor proscribed. Nevertheless, the Caliphate and the Arabs (*Ta-shih*) were a factor in Chinese politics and the T'ang contributed to the definition of the Islamic frontier in the East, as did the Carolingians and Macedonians in the West. In 651 a Muslim embassy was received at Ch'ang-an, possibly from the Caliph Uthman, more likely from a local commander in Iran. In 713 Hsüan-tsung received a mission from Kutaiba, the Muslim commander-in-chief in Central Asia, demanding his submission to Islam. In the K'ai-yuan era, Hsüan-tsung, despite appeals from the Sogdian princes and the Byzantine emperor Leo III, was slow to respond to the Muslim danger, probably because a third more conciliatory embassy was received in 726 from the Ummayad Caliph Hisham. When in the T'ien-pao era he did respond through his

Korean viceroy Kao Hsien-chih, who, following his successful campaign against Western Tibet across the Pamirs and Hindu Kush wished to protect his communications and consolidate his Sogdian clientela, his intervention was a disaster. Kao Hsien-chih was defeated in July 751 at the battle of the Talas river by Muslim forces of the now Abbasid Caliphate commanded by Ziyad ibn Salih. However, no more than the Ummayads did the Abbasids want a full-scale war with China – the Talas river had been a hard fought battle – and they responded positively to Li Mi's reorientation of Chinese foreign policy. They sent troops to aid the T'ang armies against the Sogdian An Lu-shan, hoping, no doubt, for cooperation against their common enemy, the Tibetans.

It has been supposed that these troops, some of whom remained in China and married Chinese wives, were the origin of the present-day Chinese-speaking Muslim community in Kansu, Ning-hsia, Chinghai and Shensi. If this is so, it was a notable contribution to both Islamic and Chinese history. In Islamdom, the Chinese Muslims, known to themselves as Tungans (*Tung-kan*) and to the Chinese as *Hui* (Uighurs) were unique in being the only Muslims enjoying the advantage of print before the nineteenth century, thereby achieving higher levels of literacy in the Muslim world. In China, the Tungans became the best-organized and most politically-effective minority, capable of mounting formidable rebellions, lending powerful support to the Imperial authorities both at home and in Sinkiang and Tibet, and, between the two, operating a system of regional autonomy in the northwest. It was the only minority with ongoing international ties through the *haj*, the dervish orders and the Muslim universities and the only one affected by cultural currents arising outside China. It was an example of the kind of institutional and intellectual diversification which China denied herself by the proscription of foreign religions after 845 and the subsequent cultural introversion of the Sung counter-revolution. The Tungan community, reinforced several times from outside, remains as fossilized witness to the vibrant pluralism of T'ang China, a unique place in the intellectual world of the second half of the first Christian millennium for the number, sophistication and interpenetration of its mental parameters. Those parameters provided China with a semantic field, a semiotic medium and a synceretic forum unequalled anywhere else.

## Eurasian intellectual comparisons, 500–1000

Chinese intellectual life under the T'ang was both complex and plural, and none of the other Eurasian intellectual worlds reached its level of sophistication. Thus, to schematize, India enjoyed a lesser degree of both complexity and plurality; Islamdom manifested plurality without complexity; Byzantium complexity without pluralism; while Latin Christendom deployed neither to any extent. Since intellectual capacity is a function of both, China enjoyed a global preeminence here, as in the political, economic and social spheres, a preeminence which was not structural and old, but conjunctural and new.

## India

Between 500 and 1000, India, Aryan and Dravidian, was rich through commerce and agriculture, socially sophisticated through the beginning of caste, but politically divided, partly because diffused wealth and social infrastructure allowed it to support a multiplicity of states. India, however, lacked print and it lacked an examination system. In its intellectual spectrum, complexity was less conspicuous than pluralism. In particular, India operated less than China in the syntagmatic and critical register. Buddhism, which brought this register to China through its successive scholasticisms – Madhyamika, Vijñānavāda, T'ien-t'ai and Hua-yen, was in decline in India, buffeted by foreign invasions and subverted by Hindu resurgence. Where it continued under the Palas of Bengal, it took the post-critical form of Tantrism. It is significant that neither the *Mahaprajnaparamitasastra* nor the *Avatamsaka-sutra*, which revolutionized thought in China, had much impact in their native subcontinent. Indian thought was strong in logic, its autopsy, less strong in methodology, its vivisection. Logic may be a step away rather than a step towards critical thinking. Similarly in the critical paradigmatic register, the advances made in grammar by Panini preempted the systematic development of literary criticism as found in China. The good was the enemy of the better. Grammar and logic narrowed the path to critical thinking without completely closing it. Hindu metaphysics, *Vedanta*, unlike Buddhist, was categorical rather than critical as it developed from Sankara's non-duality *advaita* in the eighth century to Ramanuja's qualified non-duality, *visishtadvaita*, in the eleventh and on to Madhva's duality and Vallabha's pure non-duality. Plurality, however, was not impaired in those registers already accessed. In literature, Sanscrit, since the fourth century dominant over Pali and Prakrit, was joined as a literary language by Dravidian counterparts: Tamil from AD 600, Kannara from the mid-eighth century, Malayalam from the tenth century and Telegu in the mid-eleventh. Hinduism diversified itself into Saivite and Vaishnavite branches: the first mystical, extreme, less iconic, less related to the Epics; the second evangelical, inclusive, more iconic, more related to the Epics. Meanwhile, Hinduism remained juxtaposed to its own attempted reformations, Buddhism and Jainism, it gave refuge to Parsees in Bombay, encountered Christianity and Judaism in Kerala, and had to confront the newcomer Islam which converted as well as conquered in the Punjab.

## Islamdom

Like India but more so, intellectual life in the world made by Islam during its first four hundred years was plural rather than complex. The genius of early Islam was extravert, and where introvert mystical. Creativity took precedence over recollection, the categorical over the critical. Islam coexisted with other faiths less by tolerance than by indifference. Conversion was left to Allah and the tax system and both acted slowly. Muslims long remained a minority within the territories they ruled. Early Islamdom therefore was pluralist *ad extra*. *Ad intra* it subdivided itself, earlier than Christianity, over questions of authority as answered by Sunni, Shia, Ismaili and Twelver, and Kharijite theorists. Questions of authority belong to the realm of logic rather than method. The earliest Islamic philosophy, the body of thought known as *kalam*, discussion, divided its field between inductive cosmology and deductive religious science.[41] Neither left much room for critical thinking. In cosmology, the exponents of *kalam*, the *mutakallimum*, produced a range of striking and original theories about space and time. The leading theory was that of the Basrian Mutazilite or rationalist school founded c.780 by Abu al-Hudhayl al Allaf who died in 841, and recapitulated by ibn Mattawayh early in the eleventh century. Its cosmology was atomistic: a system of dimensionless but space and time occupying atoms, minimal, homogeneous particles from which the heterogeneous, dimensive universe was constructed. The antecedents of this system are still debated. It was not necessitated by Islamic doctrine

or by the occasionalist theory of causality favoured by Muslim theologians. It was not derived from Democritean or Epicurean atomism
whose particles were both heterogeneous and dimensive, though part
of its attraction to Muslims may have been in its rejection of the
Platonic orthodoxy of the classical world. Its affinities, it would
appear, lay rather with the cosmology of Buddhist Sarvastavadin
scholasticism, of whose phenomenalist realism Mutazilite *kalam* may
be seen as a more positivistic transposition. Muslims were in touch
with Buddhist cosmology on their eastern frontier in Kashmir, and
the *medrese*, or higher Islamic college, has often been supposed to be
of Buddhist derivation from the Balkh region. Fifth-century Sarvastavadin texts have also been discovered at Merv.[42] Like T'ang China,
early Islamdom borrowed from outside itself, Indian numerals thus
becoming Arabic numerals to the Franks, and Mutazilite *kalam* may
have been a creative loan from the ancient East, just as its successor,
*falasafiya*, the reception of Platonic and Aristotelian texts, was a creative borrowing from the ancient West. Both, by action and reaction,
added to the pluralism of the intellectual world of early Islamdom.

### Byzantium

If the intellectual world of Islamdom between the Ummayads and
the Fatimids may be characterized as pluralism without complexity,
that of Byzantium between Justinian I and Basil II may be characterized as complexity without pluralism. Byzantine thought has often
been described as encyclopaedic but uncreative. It preserved but did
not originate. Byzantinists have rightly rejected this view, but they
have not always described the true situation appropriately. In the
period in question Byzantine thought became more complex in the
sense of deploying a greater number of registers, but this development was not matched by an increase in pluralism within and across
those registers. An increasingly sophisticated mind was exercized on
a diminishingly comprehensive set of themes. Four illustrations may
be given of this situation.

First, the last of the great speculative theologians of the patristic
period was St Maximus the Confessor (580–662), the champion of
Chalcedonian orthodoxy against the Monothelitism favoured by
emperor Constans II. His originality lay less in his Christology than
in his extended Antiochene hermeneutics of the Prophetic word of
the Bible and the Living word of the Incarnate Logos in His Church

and its liturgy. His mystagogics was as much a method as a message. Similarly, St Photius, patriarch of Constantinople under Michael III and Basil I, made advances in philology which anticipated features of the Italian Renaissance, though he was a scholiast content to annotate what had been acquired, rather than a scholastic seeking new insights.[43] Third, a major achievement of Byzantine thought, associated particularly with St Cyril and Methodius, was the rediscovery of the Hellenistic critical principle that any language can be translated into any other language, that there are no semantically privileged languages (a view rejected by Muslims for whom the Koran is not fully translatable from Arabic), and that Christianity need not be confined to the trilingualism of Greek, Latin and Syriac as stand in for Hebrew, the three languages of the Cross. Other literary languages might by used to translate sacred texts, a view not to be confused with Protestant vernacularism. This rediscovery, however, was not much exploited until considerably later. It did not go beyond translation and create new texts in the Slavonic languages mobilized by mission. The pitch was enlarged but the play remained the same. No new games were invented. The result was not lack of creativity, for inevitably tradition repeated became tradition changed, but limitation of variety. Finally, this may be seen from the Hesychast movement, one of whose fountainheads may be found in the writings of Symeon the New Theologian (949–1022). Hesychasm was innovative; while claiming to continue the apophatic spirituality of St Gregory of Nyssa, it shifted its emphasis from passive, infused contemplation to active, acquired meditation. Nevertheless, from its headquarters on Mount Athos, the first of whose monasteries was founded in 963 by Athanasios of Athos with the support of emperor Nicephorus II Phocas, it came in subsequent centuries to dominate the spiritual life of the Eastern Orthodox world, even monopolize it, to the detriment of alternatives. An addition in technique, it became a subtraction in products. The circle was enlarged but it enclosed less.

## Latin Christendom

The intellectual world of what Newman called the Benedictine centuries was characterized by the absence of either complexity or pluralism. As the economy was dominated, whether in Anglo-Danish Northumbria or Dark Age Rome, by the multiple estate; as society was everywhere dominated by aristocratic kinship in a world where social order had been replaced by intersubjectivity; so the intellectual landscape was dominated by a few isolated peaks: St Benedict, St Bede, and John the Scot, also called Eriugena. St Benedict, magnified by the missionary Pope Gregory the Great, was hugely influential, Bede was influential among an élite and Eriugena was only influential, in his own description of the return of diversity to unity, 'through the most secret channels of nature by a most hidden course'.[44] Pluralism was limited and complexity lacking, especially in the critical registers.

The *Rule of St Benedict* was arguably the most influential book written in Latin between 500 and 1000. Composed around 540 at Monte Cassino, it was taken up by the Papacy under Gregory the Great as surcharged by St Martin's evangelicanism, and widely utilized. Eventually, under the guidance of St Benedict of Aniane (750–821) it was imposed as the monastic norm by Louis the Pious in the Capitulation of Aachen in 817. Inculcated east of the Rhine by Rabanus Maurus, abbot of Fulda and *Preceptor Germaniae*, in tenth century England it was restored by the great Wessex triumvirate of Dunstan, Aethelwold and Oswald. Yet the *Rule* was not cut from whole cloth, it was a patchwork taken from other rules, in particular the so-called Rule of the Master, and it did not enunciate the principles of its compilation. Bede was a critical historian who initiated the shift, crucial to the transition from ancient to modern history, from the texts of other historians to the documents of the participants. Yet he taught more by example than precept and did not sufficiently enunciate the role of the historian in history-writing. Consequently, though admired and imitated by writers like Paul the Deacon, his innovations were not fully grasped and Latin historiography fell back into annals and *gesta*. John the Scot – Eriugena, though the appellation may have been a nickname rather than biography – was immensely ambitious in his scope. His *De Divisione Naturae* or *Periphyseon*, inspired by St Maximus the Confessor's cosmogenetic hermeneutics, was a true theory of everything, what is and what is not, perhaps modelled also on Mutazilite *kalam* minus its atomism. Yet the huge work was categorical rather than critical in character. Overinfluenced by the Pseudo-Dionysius at the expense of Maximus, it dealt in essences rather than existence, concept rather than judgements. Though Eriugena, who may have withdrawn to Malmesbury abbey after the death of his patron Charles the Bald, continued to have a subterranean influence which may be traced in Anselm, Bernard and Bonaventure, he had no real successors as a system-builder, till the age of Aquinas.

As the first Christian millennium came to an end, what was most intellectually creative in Latin Christendom was not thought but action: the actions of the liturgy, basilical and monastic, in the Mass and the office, which have remained the foundation of Western Christian worship down to the present. Their long-term effects in weathering the Western mind, drop by drop, week by week, should not be underestimated. For contemporaries, they provided the possibility of contemplation for the religious and a piety of performance for the laity who were being gradually supplied with parish churches by aristocratic munificence.[45] The Benedictine centuries may have inhabited a flat, circumscribed monotonous intellectual world, but it was not without achievements or promise for the future. Nevertheless, the contrast with the complexity and pluralism of T'ang China was stark. In the mind, as in politics, economics and sociology, China was globally preeminent as it never had been in the past. The East had truly risen.

# 6
# Return to the West: Reflux and Prognosis

It is time now to return to Andre Gunder Frank's argument in *Reorient* in favour of the permanent centrality of China in the world order. The preceding chapters, it may be hoped, have demonstrated that China's preeminence, whether it be conceived politically, economically, socially or intellectually, or most reasonably as the conjunction of all four dimensions, was not permanent but acquired, conjunctural not structural. It was acquired through what may be called the Rise of the East in the second half of the first Christian millennium, by a winning combination of exceptional political skill, economic enterprise, social invention and intellectual sophistication. China under the T'ang, and in particular in the reign of emperor Hsüan-tsung, stood where the United States stands today. In every dimension, by all measurements it was the unique superpower. Andre Gunder Frank is not alone in thinking that in the first half of the third Christian millennium China will be restored to that position, if indeed it has ever left it. For, in his argument, China's centrality is only subject to temporary and partial eclipses, occasional abeyances or dormancies. To assess this prognosis one must enquire whether China is likely to recover its old, or discover a new, winning combination. Evidence may be sought in what may be termed the reflux: the return of the balance of advantage from the East to the West in the first half of the second Christian millennium, 1000 to 1500. In particular, attention needs to be focused on Latin Christendom which was eventually to succeed to China's position of preeminence. This period, before the successive rocket propulsions of European take-off in the Great Discoveries, the Reformations, the Enlightenment and the Industrial Revolution, nevertheless saw its foundations put in place, not least through borrowings from China. A Rise of the West rather than a decline of the East, the reflux was not simultaneous or similarly caused in the four dimensions of politics, economics, society and the intellect, which therefore need to be considered separately. The search for the rudiments of the rise of the West may supply clues to the rudiments of a possible, future re-rise of the East.

## Politics, 1000–1500

In the political history of Eurasia in the first half of the second Christian millennium, the central event was what may be called the Inner Asian irruption. By this is meant the preliminary tremors of the little invasions of the Khitan, the Tanguts, the Jurchen and the Kara Khitai; the great invasion of the Mongolian explosion itself; and the aftershocks produced by the Mongol successor states, in particular that of Tamerlane, which only came to an end in the early sixteenth century. The incidence of the irruption was uneven across Eurasia and its effects depended on local conditions and responses, but its degree of presence or absence was a major factor in many subsequent developments, not least in establishing a new geopolitical context for politics, one in which seapower could predominate over landpower.

The origin of the Inner Asian irruption went back to the transition from Golden to Silver T'ang. Then Li Mi had abandoned the T'ang empire in Inner Asia and sought strength in weakness by an alliance with the Uighurs against the rebellion of An Lu-shan. That abandonment and alliance led to a new level of compenetration between the civilized and the barbarian worlds, which was symbolized by the conversion of the Uighurs to Manichaeism in 763 and by the subsequent adoption by other Inner Asian peoples of Judaism, Nestorian Christianity, Islam and Buddhism. Interpenetration gave Inner Asia what it had previously lacked: organization through availability of literate personnel, notably Uighur scribes, and an agenda in relation to the civilized worlds beyond itself. For the Inner Asian irruption was no natural phenomenon, it was not an episode in a timeless war of nomads against sedentarists or a descente *batailleuse* à la Braudel of people evicted from their overpopulated environments by some climatic fluctuation. Nor was it simply a product of some cycle of steppe politics and blood tanistry. Rather, throughout its successive mutations and enlargements of scale, it was the implementation of a political programme based on social restructuring and a new form of state and conducted by leaders with an ideology of conquest, limited or unlimited.

The Inner Asian irruption began with the foundation of the Khitan state in 907 by A-pao-chi.[1] The Khitan state, known in Chinese history as the Liao dynasty (907–1125), was the first rudimentary form of the new politics. It has been designated an *ordo* state from its most conspicuous feature: one or more 'hordes', or encampments of partly detribalized soldiers, closely attached to the ruler or his consort by a personal entourage.[2] The Khitan, former vassals of the Uighurs and rebels against their successors the Kirghiz, began as Mongol-speaking nomadic pastoralists or transhumants in the valleys of the Khingan range in what were to become the Chinese provinces of Chahar and Jehol. Through the effectiveness of their light cavalry and its administrative infrastructure, they extended their rule to the Chinese population of northern Shansi and Hopei, the Korean state of Po-hai in southern Manchuria, the Tungusic-speaking Jurchens of northern Manchuria, and in the west to some of the now sedentarized Uighurs. The Khitan state became a major international player and received embassies from as far distant as Mahmud of Ghazna, the leading powerholder in the Islamic world at the beginning of the eleventh century. For their Chinese subjects in the south the Khitan provided a subordinate Confucian bureaucracy recruited by examination. They were also vigorous patrons of Buddhism, now at a discount in China proper, especially of the Hua-yen school, and in 1075 at the height of their power printed a full edition of the *Tripitaka*, the Buddhist canon. To assert their own élite identity as separate but unequal, the Khitan devised two scripts for their own language: one derived from the Uighur (ultimately Syriac Estrangelo) alphabet, one derived from Chinese characters; a neat expression of the double duality between two aspects of the Khitan and the massive presence of China to the south. For the Sung the Khitan irruption was more than a border problem, it prevented them from attaining the line of the Wall, the optimum defensive position (though the Wall itself did not effectively exist at this time) and forced them into a high degree of costly militarization which had to be imposed on an increasingly civilian society.[3] Empire in Inner Asia had cost the T'ang much, but its absence was to cost the Sung more.

Early in the eleventh century, a second Sino-barbarian border state known to the Chinese as the Hsi Hsia dynasty (1028–1227) was created in parts of Ninghsia, Kansu and Chinghai by the Tanguts. The Tanguts were Turkified Tibetans – their name was derived from the Turkish for Tibet – subsequently sinicized and then reTibetanized. They were not nomadic pastoralists or transhumants, but sedentary pastoralists in the grasslands of the Ordos and Alashan, though they lived for preference in fortified cities. Their state originated in association with the Chinese defence system in the early Silver T'ang period, when Tibet was an expanding and aggressive power. It only reached full autonomy and ascendancy in the northwest, where Chinese, Tibetan, Turkish and Mongol cultures met, under Li Te-ming (1004–1032) and Li Yüan-hao (1032–1048) while the Sung were preoccupied with the Khitan. Unlike the Khitan, the Tanguts, even when at their most powerful they moved westward, did not, however, use the *ordo* system. They were heavy rather than light cavalry men, mailed knights like those of the Iranian world. Moreover, despite the multiethnic character of their state, they did not operate parallel or stratified administrations. Like the Khitan, however, the Tangut were patrons of Buddhism, though of Tantric Tibetan rather than scholastic Chinese provenance. Like the Khitan, the Tanguts devised two scripts for their own language: one based on the Tibetan, ultimately Indian, alphabet, which did not find much use, the other based on Chinese characters, in which there is considerable literature. Particularly in the reign of Jen-tsung (1140–1193), a civilian, Hsi Hsia was an effective and coherent military and commercial state with a world monopoly of the medicinal root rhubarb.[4]

For the Chinese the significance of the Tangut emergence was both military and political. Hsi Hsia lay athwart the main trade routes to Central Asia; the desert route from Ninghsia across Alashan to Barkol, the silk route up the Kansu panhandle to Hami and Turfan, and the Tsaidam route from Sining past Lake Koko-nor to Cherchen. It therefore impeded the import of horses, large and small, essential to Chinese defence against the Khitan and the Tangut themselves. To circumvent this obstacle, the Northern Sung devised a system whereby the import of horses from Chinghai and beyond was linked to the export of tea from Szechwan for which Inner Asians were acquiring a taste.[5] The system, of limited success in promoting Chinese cavalry, had profound consequences internally for the activities of the bureaucracy and ultimately for the profile of the Chinese state. At a time when the state was withdrawing from involvement in the land market, the horse-procurement system involved massive intervention in commerce, in the markets for tea and for salt with which the state purchased it. This intervention continued beyond the Tangut emergency with multiple side-effects. The bureaucracy became divided between interveners and non-interveners, technocrats and guardians, corrupt and pure as Confucian moralists put it. Government fiscality shifted from agriculture to trade and the private finance initiative, *kuan-tu shang-pan* (officials supervise, merchants manage), introduced to the salt monopoly by prime minister Ts'ai Ching early in the twelfth century became the model for bureaucracy/business relations. A hypertrophy of the state was set in motion which absorbed ever higher percentages of gross national product to support a military establishment both huge and high-tech, justified by the increasing threat from Inner Asia.

That threat acquired new dimensions with the third Inner Asian irruption, that of the Jurchen, a Tungus-speaking, mixed agricultural, hunting and fishing people of the forests and rivers of Central Manchuria, the ancestors of the group who founded the last, Manchu or Ch'ing dynasty (1644–1912). The Jurchen, vassals of the Khitan, having overthrown the Khitan state in a revolt between 1117 and 1123, went to war with the Sung over the Khitan possessions in Shansi and Hopei, captured Kaifeng in 1127, and established an empire in north China, Manchuria and parts of Mongolia, known to themselves and to the Chinese as the Chin dynasty (1127–1234). The Jurchen state was on a much larger scale than the previous Inner Asian irruptions. Its territory included what had been the heartland of successive Chinese dynasties and its population of 50 million in 1207 – as much as both Christendoms combined – was overwhelmingly Chinese. Though the Sung survived and even flourished at Hang-chou south of the Yangtze, it was as if the United States had lost all territory east of the Mississippi and had had to reconstitute itself on the basis of Texas and California. China was thrown towards a new ocean, and river and sea power acquired a new importance for the Chinese state.

Like the Khitan, some of whose personnel they absorbed, the Jurchen used an *ordo* system of decimal units for military mobilization. Unlike the Khitan, however, more like the Hsi Hsia, they operated a single ethnically stratified hierarchy rather than parallel administrations. Like the Khitan, the Jurchen devised a script for their language based on Chinese characters, and patronized Chinese schools of Buddhism, though Ch'an or Ching-t'u rather than Hua-yen. Confucian education enjoyed wide prestige and parallel examinations in Jurchen and Chinese supplied the higher and lower levels of the bureaucracy in the integrated but dual system. Taoism put forth its last creative development in the non-Tantric anti-elixir Ch'uan-chen (integrated realization) school founded by Wang Che (1112–1170), 'Crazy Wang', a middle-class intellectual from northeast Shantung. The Jurchen therefore did not threaten Chinese civilization. After a major war in the mid-twelfth century, in which their attack was countered by massive Chinese land and river power, they did not even threaten the Southern Sung state: 'the Yangtze is our new Great Wall', a Sung official said. The second Chin/Sung war in the early thirteenth century was a Sung initiative though it did not turn out well for them. What the Jurchen did do was to further militarize the Chinese state in the south as well as the north, ratcheting up defence costs by adding a new and costly naval dimension. This further divided its bureaucracy between those who accepted the partition of China and those who did not, and exacerbated the social tensions between those who paid the increased fiscality and those who spent it. The Sung, especially the Southern Sung, had contained the Inner Asian irruption, but China – the intelligentsia, the landlords once they too had to pay tax, and the xenophobic populace – was dissatisfied with their achievement and did not recognize its immensity.

The Inner Asian irruption now took a different direction. The overthrow of the Liao by the Jurchen in the 1120s was not the end of the Khitan. A scion of the royal house, Yeh-lü Ta-shih, escaped to the west and on the basis of the *ordo* system, which was in principle transplantable, recreated an empire in Central Asia known to the Chinese as the Hsi or Western Liao dynasty (1125–1218) and to the locals as Kara Khitai or Black Cathay. The empire covered what were to become eastern and western Turkestan, sedentary areas then Iranian-speaking, but its seat of power was to the north in the grasslands of Zungharia and Semirechie. This move extended the Inner Asian irruption from East Asia to Western Asia. The ruler took the title of *gurkhan* or universal khan and his subjects included Buddhists, Manichees, Nestorian Christians and Muslims. In September 1141, Yeh-lü Ta-shih defeated the Seljuk sultan Sanjar at the battle of Qatawan in modern Uzbekistan. Adapting to the Central Asian context the *gurkhan* adopted Christian colouring against his Muslim opponent and gave his son the eschatological name of I-lieh (Elijah). The name signalled a Christian counter-revolution under steppe leadership against Islamdom, a message not misinterpreted by the Cistercian Otto of Freising in his account of Prester John, the great Christian ruler come out of the east. Its eschatology set the stage and sounded the overture chords for the greatest of the Inner Asian irruptions: the Mongolian explosion of Chinggis Khan and his successors for three generations.[6]

So far the effects of the Inner Asian irruption had been largely confined to East Asia. The Mongolian explosion was the first global political event. Inflated by its passage through the territories of the four previous irruptions, it affected East Asia and Western Eurasia directly, Black Africa indirectly and America remotely. In Eurasia the political impact was not uniform. It has been observed that those areas where the Mongols did not penetrate, largely because their light cavalry was met by effectively organized heavy cavalry – Japan, Egypt, Rumelia and Latin Christendom – subsequently became major regional centres of political power, whereas those most penetrated, such as North China, eastern Iran, Iraq and Syria never fully regained that status. *Post hoc*, however, is not *propter hoc*. India, which only suffered marginally from the aftershock of Tamerlane's incursion in 1398–99, did not draw obvious political advantage from the absence of Mongol conquest. China, which did suffer full conquest, first of the Chin by Ögödei, then of the Southern Sung by Khubilai, was not thereby changed radically in its political institutions. The Ming revolution, which restored both Chinese unity and Chinese rule, reacted more against the Southern Sung than against the Mongols. It tried to give the bureaucratic state a different cast, at once more autocratic, populist and physiocratic, but within a century, by the time of the Three Yangs, the cast had reverted to type with emperors reigning and ministers ruling in the interests of cultivated urban oligarchy. Similarly Latin Christendom, spared by the Mongols who were intimidated by the heroic resistance of its knights even in lost battles, continued to evolve along its own lines in city states, ecclesiastical palatinates and territorial principalities before entering a new age of bureaucratic monarchy and imperial agglomeration at the beginning of the sixteenth century. In particular, it pursued its path of constitutionalism: political structures limited in space and agenda by countervailing institutions legally entrenched. Here Latin Christendom may be contrasted with the leading successor state of the Byzantine empire, Muscovy, which, confronted more directly by the Mongols, discarded the embryonic constitutionalism of Kiev and Novgorod in favour of a novel brand of clericalized authoritarianism derived from neither Byzantium nor the Mongols.[7]

It was the Muslim world which was most affected politically by the Mongols. Much of its eastern half came under the rule of Chinggisid dynasties: the Chaghadai khanate in Central Asia, the Golden Horde in Kazakhstan, the Volga valley and the North Caucasus, the Ilkhanate in Persia, Iraq, Azerbaijan, eastern Anatolia and northern Syria. Though converted to Islam, these dynasties retained a Mongol structure of government by militarized clans: what has been called the *inju* ('share') state, a sedentarized army billeted on the edge of cities. In those parts unpenetrated by the Mongols, both the Mamluks and the Ottomans displayed Mongol influence in their institutions. Both were party states, which, in the first case, copied the Mongols to resist them successfully in Syria; in the second, to make conquests from Christendom in the Balkans to form the future base of Rumelia. Muslim India, too, eventually found itself under a Mongol-type regime when the Timurids, the successors of Tamerlane, extruded from Central Asia by the joint though rival pressures of the Uzbeks and the Safavids, transplanted their political machine elsewhere like the Kara Khitai, and reinvented themselves as the Mughals. These regimes, alien in character or alienated from sections of their own societies, were effective enough as power centres, but they lacked the long-term ability to mobilize resources displayed by Christian constitutionalism.

It was the Muslim world, too, which was the scene for the last act of the Inner Asian irruption: the aftershocks in the Mongol successor states initiated by Tamerlane, the greatest figure in Central Asian political history. Illiterate but cultivated, the barbarian with a portable bath, porcelain tea services and a taste for architecture,

Tamerlane was a more deliberate conqueror than Chinggis. He rein-vigorated the divided and crumbling Chaghadai khanate by political and social reforms and used its resources to create an imperial system focused on Samarkand. In the course of his campaigns to this end, which were based on heavy rather than light cavalry, Tamerlane annexed the fragments of the Il-khanate to the west, gravely damaged the Golden Horde to the north so that it succumbed to the princes of Muscovy in the next century, looted the sultanate of Delhi to the south providing its Hindu enemies in Vijayanagar with a breathing space, checked the rise of the Ottomans in the far west giving the Byzantine city state another half century of life, and, to the far east, threatened China with invasion, on which campaign Tamerlane died at Otrar in 1405. It was a threat which Ming China did not take lightly. The Yung-lo emperor responded to it by a flurry of diplomatic activity which eventually arrived at a *modus vivendi* with Tamerlane's successors and, by the great maritime voyages under the Muslim eunuch-admiralissimo Cheng Ho, which sought allies in the Islamic world to the west of Tamerlane, notably at Mecca now controlled by the Mamluks, and possibly beyond Islamdom in the Latin Christendom which had entered Chinese horizons through the Mongols. Cheng Ho's voyages were the first exercise of global seapower uniting the seas of the East Asia, Western Eurasia and Black Africa, perhaps even those of Australia and the far south Pacific. Memories of it were still alive when Vasco da Gama entered the Indian ocean and there are signs that it may have been known to the Catalans even earlier, just as the Portuguese discovery of the Azores was known to Korean cartographers. Global seapower was the ulti-mate answer to the explosion of the Heartland. It was the instrument by which the West, in the form of the constitutional states of Latin Christendom, redressed the balance against the East by annexing the manpower of Black Africa and the treasure – golden, silver and green – of pre-Columbian America. As Braudel put it, though America may not have commanded everything, it allowed Europe to spend beyond its income and invest beyond its savings.

## Economy, 1000–1500

To use global seapower for economic as well as political purposes the West needed to acquire more advanced nautical technology. This it did largely by borrowing from China – in construction, propulsion, navigation and weaponry – through the increased westward flow of information generated by the Inner Asian irruption.

In construction, the first acquisition was the fixed sternpost rudder, present in Canton in the first two centuries AD, but only appearing in Latin Christendom at the end of the twelfth century and then in the northern seas of the Hanseatic league rather than in the Mediterranean of the Italian city states. It was diffused from China, it would seem, by Kara Khitai along the lakes, rivers and porterages of southern Siberia or across Transoxania and the northern Caspian and thence via the Volga route to the Baltic. The sternpost rudder allowed larger ships to be better navigated. Larger ships prompted multiple masts; up to four are recorded in a third century Chinese text, but Europe had to wait until the fifteenth century to see more than two. Size put a premium on safety, if only for insurance reasons, but watertight compartments, though reported by Marco Polo for Chinese ships, were only adopted in the West in the eighteenth century after further experience of them on the Siberian rivers. In propulsion, the Europeans eventually adopted the Chinese preference for sail over oars, though not definitively till after Lepanto in 1571 or even after the Armada in 1588 where the Neapolitan galleases performed well. They also adopted partially, though as a subsidiary element, the Chinese preference for fore and aft over square rig. The Arab dhow utilized the Chinese principle which permitted closer sailing to the wind, and the lateen sail, the Mediterranean version, is depicted first in a Byzantine manuscript of the sermons of St Gregory Nazianzen dated to around 880. In general, Europeans in the age of the Great Discoveries preferred mixed rig – square on the fore and main masts, fore and aft on the mizzen – which combined the lesser crew requirements of the first with the manoeuvrability of the second. Thus they obtained the best of both worlds in wind power. In navigation, Europeans borrowed the magnetic compass in the mid-thirteenth century probably along the southern sea-route, where it had apparently been used by Tamil navigators since the fourth century AD. Finally, the European adoption in the thirteenth century of the T'ang invention of gunpowder plus the application of it to naval gunnery in fourteenth-century China gave Latin Christendom the possibility of projective weaponry at sea. Armour plating, another East Asian invention, only came later.

Meanwhile, as Latin Christendom progressed, Chinese shipping, having already attained a high degree of preindustrial technical perfection, made little further progress. Cheng Ho's voyages, beyond their strategic purposes, aimed to bring private Chinese shipping under greater official control so that its horizons tended to contract to the China seas. Construction of large ships was discouraged lest they fall into the hands of the pirates who emerged when the high-seas fleet was laid up on account of costs, shortage of timber and infighting between eunuchs and regular officials. The rivers and the Grand Canal, now extended to Peking, were more attractive to navigation than the sea, and China's oceanic vocation temporarily fell into abeyance.

Improved nautical technology was only facultative. It opened the way to a new kind of territorial expansion, itself one of the motors of economic growth. Concomitantly, and acting as a multiplier, Latin Christendom was also gaining economic strength from two other motors: technology and taste, both surcharged by further borrowings from the East.

In technology, perhaps the most significant reinforcement was the transfer in the fourteenth century of the technique of iron-casting, the first blast furnaces and foundries appearing in the lower Rhineland and the Alpine region around 1380. The addition of cast iron to wrought iron, virtually a new material, opened a fresh range of products and customers to European smiths: the casting of cannon, the construction of clocks (another fourteenth century innovation possibly influenced by Chinese prototypes), the manufacture of iron pans for brine boiling (salt and iron a typical Chinese alliance) and the improvement of arrow heads (the real secret of English success at Agincourt).[8] Almost equally significant was the transfer, also in the fourteenth century, of water-driven machinery for the primary processes – spinning of wool or reeling of silk – of textile manufacture. Such machines, which required the conversion of rotary to longitudinal motion, were developed in China in the Sung period, first for hemp (before the spread of cotton in the Ming, the most widely used fibre) and then silk. In 1372 a Luccan entrepreneur introduced a similar machine in the silk industry at Bologna and this *molino Bolognese*, though at first inefficient and not widely copied, was the ancestor of improved mills in the Venetian and Piedmontese Alps whence the technology was brought to England by the

Lombe brothers at Derby early in the eighteenth century and subsequently applied with more revolutionary effect to cotton on one side of the Pennines and to wool on the other. It only needed coal, one of the areas of China's technological precocity in the Sung period, remarked on by Marco Polo, to be applied to siderurgy and textiles to make an industrial revolution.

In taste and consumption in the West the impact of the Inner Asian irruption led in opposite but ultimately convergent directions. On the one hand, the *Pax Mongolica* opened the way to the import of Chinese goods on a greater scale. Silks, ceramics and medicinal rhubarb all became more widely available as Central Asian finance houses, the *ortaq*, took charge of the immense fiscality of the Mongol empire and repatriated or exported their profits in the form of commodities. The earliest surviving Muslim porcelain collections, in Mamluk Syria, date from this period. They were the precursors of the great Ottoman and Safavid collections at Topkapi and Ardebil which in turn inspired the first European collectors. The industrial conurbation of Ching-te-chen in Kiangsi, which later came almost to monopolize porcelain production in China, received its first impulse from this export demand. The famous blue and white ware was developed to satisfy it, but it later became fashionable in China itself as an exotic as monochromes gave way to polychromes. Though India, Islamdom and Christendom all now possessed silk industries of their own, the most valued weaves still came from China. Latin Christendom in particular developed a new taste for weaves intermediate between the heavy brocades and light gauzes current in antiquity. Such fabrics received names associated with their points of origin or transit: satin (Zaiton, Ch'uan-chou, the Sung Sinoport in Fukien), organdie and organza (Urgench, the midpoint on the northern land route), taffeta (from a Persian word meaning cloth), scarlet (originally a fabric not a colour, from a luxury cloth produced in Samarkand in Tamerlane's day), and tussore (from the wild silk, *t'u-ssu*, used in manufacture in Shantung). Simultaneously, in both Islamdom and Christendom as they expanded into colder climates with the conversion of the Volga Tartars and the Lithuanians, élites were affected by the Mongol aristocracy's taste for fur and adopted its scale of values with sable first, ermine second and miniver last. Silk and fur pulled in different directions towards a sharper dichotomy between indoor and outdoor clothes. This had implications beyond dress in shelter as another means of thermoregulation: in house construction, room arrangement and the rise of the chimney. Comfort made its first appearance alongside status and display.

On the other hand, the *Pax Mongolica* brought the Black Death. It remains the most convincing explanation if that surge in mortality was indeed, as still seems most likely, an infection of *Yersinia pestis* in both bubonic and pneumonic forms rather than anthrax (too little contagious), a group of diseases, or an unidentified microorganism. Striking a demography which had advanced to the limits of its technological resources, the Black Death reduced the population of Latin Christendom by about a third. It thereby brought about a drastic fall in gross consumption and a prolonged period of economic contraction. But, though gross consumption fell, per capita consumption and productivity rose as the survivors of the successive plague episodes (for the Black Death was not a oncer after it established Western reservoirs) found themselves in possession of more resources for spending or investment. China, less affected by plague though closer to its primary reservoir, did not enjoy this boost to consumerism and saw its population recover much quicker from the losses, real and imagined, occasioned by the Inner Asian irruption.[9] Peasant prudence, encouraged by early Ming puritanism, became more firmly entrenched, whereas in Europe, aristocratic extravagance, for example in the use of fur, spread from masters (and mistresses) to servants, whatever sumptuary laws might enact. Women and children, perhaps more valued in the new world of death, claimed greater freedoms not least in dress, the activities of girls under 12 being particularly deplored by the baffled authorities. The Black Death, therefore, like the opening of the trans-continental trade routes, promoted the growth of consumerism in the West and ultimately the formation of a consumerist society which should imitate that portrayed by Marco Polo in his account of the Southern Sung cities.

The point to which the two tendencies of life and death converged was a significant mutation in the consumer sensibility of Latin Christendom. Hitherto, in long perspective and at a high level of generality, the West in its spending and investing had gone for the eternal, for building rather than dress or food, for initial outlay rather than for subsequent maintenance, while China had gone for the ephemeral, for food and dress rather than building, replaceable rather than permanent materials. Europeans wished to make a Parmenidean universe, Chinese were content to live in a Heraclitean universe. The one built a Durham cathedral in stone, the other erected a Forbidden City in wood. The contrast may be related to a deeper dichotomy of temporal orientation between the continuous, uniform time of the West, *chronos*, whether cyclical, linear or immobile; and the discontinuous, differentiated recreative time of the East, *kairos* or *shih*. It was in the later Middle Ages, with the appearance of the idea of fashion (as opposed to luxury or extravagance), some of whose styles such as the tall headress known as the *hennin* favoured in the Burgundian court originated in T'ang Ch'ang-an, that Latin Christendom began the conquest of the ephemeral with the consequence for economic growth and social flexibility which Gilles Lipovetsky has indicated. No doubt the Christian notion of the sacramentality of matter always contained the potential for the conquest of the ephemeral: for St Augustine time was next to God while space was next to nothing; but it took light from a long dead supernova in the East falling in the anxious, febrile world which followed the Mongolian explosion to actualize it.[10]

Territory, technology and taste, the three motors of economic growth, required management. Here, too, Latin Christendom, less advanced initially than either of the Indias, Southeast Asia or the Muslim world, and so less set in its ways, borrowed from the East to reequip its own endogenous mercantile institutions. Five instances may be given:

- First, not a Chinese invention this time (though a dispute continues about the origin of zero), Arabic, that is Indian, numerals. These were first described outside the subcontinent in 662 by the Syrian Monophy site bishop Severus Sebonkt. In 820 they were more fully described by al-Khwarazmi in his *Kitab al-adad al-hind* (Book of Addition and Subtraction according to the Indian Calculation), later translated into Latin. Through his influence and their evident advantage in calculation fiscal and commercial, by the end of the eleventh century they had come into wide use in the Muslim world. From there, Spain and Sicily in particular, they penetrated Latin Christendom, rather slowly, especially after Fibonacci's *Liber Abacus* in the early thirteenth century. Thus Europe, which supplied itself with scripts and musical notation, borrowed its mature numbers from elsewhere.

- Second, paper: as more mass producible than papyrus or parchment, it was primarily a precondition for modern bureaucracy and business, but secondarily an alternative to glass in windows, useful in packaging, beautiful as wallpaper, an adjunct in cleanliness and hygiene.[11] Paper, the matting or felting of vegetable fibres in a mould to produce a smooth surface, was an invention of the late Han period, traditionally ascribed to an early second-century court eunuch Ts'ai Lun, though probably his real role was its introduction to the bureaucracy. Improved under the T'ang, with production expanded especially in Szechwan based on bamboo, paper technology was transmitted West by Chinese prisoners after the Talas river disaster and became established in the Islamic world; over 12,000 documents from Egypt between 800 and 1388 being preserved in the Archduke Rainer collection in Vienna. Known and manufactured in Latin Christendom since the twelfth century, but less obviously preferable to parchment than its oriental counterparts, the victory of paper was only assured by its superior adaptability to another East Asian import, print.

- Third, printing itself, which unlike paper did not make Islamdom a waystation on its transit to Latin Christendom, except in China itself and marginally in Mamluk Egypt, probably on account of Muslim reluctance to submit the Koran to it and the relatively aniconic character of Muslim shrine and pilgrimage piety. Such piety, along with the need in China for texts for the examinations played a major part in the origin and spread of printing both in its original woodblock form and in its subsequent form, particularly convenient for alphabetical scripts, of moveable type adopted late in the fourteenth century, about the time the last Franciscan missionaries were being withdrawn from China. In China, moveable type which was ascribed by the Confucian polymath Shen Kua to a certain Pi Sheng (990–1031) was always secondary to woodblock printing, the earliest surviving examples of which date from the reign of the empress Wu, whereas those by moveable type, in Uighur script from Tun-huang, are only from 1800. Like paper, print had many customers, but in business, in the form of handbills, notices, patterns and catalogues it laid the foundations in the sixteenth century for that essential adjunct of consumerism and fashion: advertising, the secular counterpart to religious propaganda.

- Next, if one turns from physical to social technology, Didier Gaza-gnadou has traced the transit across Eurasia from China to Islamdom to Christendom of a public postal service by relay horses.[12] Initiated by the T'ang under the auspices of the *Ping-pu*, the board of war, as the *i-chan*, the horse post was expanded to the scale of their world empire by the Mongols as the *yam, ula, wu-la*, and so forth. It was copied by the Mamluk sultan Baybars al-Bunduqdari who had observed it in Syria in the course of his war with the Il-khanate in 1260. It was introduced to Latin Christendom in 1386 by Gian Galeazzo Visconti in Milan with the significant addition that private correspondence as well as official mail was allowed to use it. From Milan it was extended to the Habsburg dominions by the princes of Thurn and Taxis who became hereditary postmasters of the empire. Though China had its private mail firms, the so-called letter *hongs*, the tendency to concentrate on profitable routes, meant the linking of public and private post gave Europe an advantage in the diffusion of information. The postman became the most visible public servant.

- Finally, among the new institutions developed in thirteenth-century Latin Christendom were sophisticated salt monopolies, which served both as fiscal support for the state and as financial regulation for the economy: *kuo-chi min-sheng*, the state's taxes and the people's livelihood, in the classic Chinese definition of the ends of salt administration. From the middle of the thirteenth century, such administrations known as *ordines salis* were successively established by Genoa, Venice, the county of Provence and the kingdom of France. While taxation of salt had existed earlier both in Latin Christendom and in the Byzantine empire to a limited extent, systematic salt administrations had not. Nor were they a feature of the Muslim world where salt sources were too numerous and widespread for such administration to be practicable. Salt administration, however, had been a conspicuous feature of the Chinese institutional scene since Silver T'ang times and it was fully described by Marco Polo as a topic likely to interest his readers. It is difficult therefore not to think that the sudden appearance of *ordines salis* in medieval Europe, in discontinuity with what had gone before, owed something to the Chinese example. Salt administrations were a major boost to business in Latin Christendom, for, unlike China, the private finance initiative they represented worked more to the advantage of the investor than to that of the state. The particular system imposed by the early Ming, known as the *k'ai-chung fa*, injured the formation of capital through stealth taxes, while the Venetian and Genoese systems subsidized it to promote the growth of the economy.[13] What was parasitic in China, in Europe became symbiotic. Salt surcharged business.

## Society, 1000–1500

In the economic sphere, the reflux, the redressment of the balance between East and West, may be accounted for in terms of technological transfers from China to Latin Christendom. This was the thesis maintained by Joseph Needham and it is still defensible. In the social sphere, on the other hand, the emphasis must be on independent development. Between 1000 and 1500 the societies of both China and Latin Christendom became more complex and sophisticated, but the change was greater in the second than in the first and it was on different lines. Attempts to define that difference theoretically can lead to essentialism and logomachy. It is better to proceed less holistically and more institutionally. Margaret Thatcher said that society does not exist; by this she did not mean that social institutions do not exist, but only that the set of them does not itself constitute an institution. In Hayek's terms, society is not a taxis but an intertaxis. By 1500 the social institutions of China and Latin Christendom were beginning to approximate in complexity and sophistication, but their sets were differently composed and arranged. By 1500 European society, by whatever name one gives it, was recognizably itself. Of the new and distinctive components added to Latin Christendom's social portfolio between 1000 and 1500, three were particularly significant in the reflux.

First, there was the European family system of nuclear households based, for both genders, on late, sacramental, permanent and preferably neolocal marriage, with conjugality as its cardinal value. This system, which antedated the Black Death but was extended by it, subordinated filial ties to those of husband and wife, made more use of female intelligence in household strategy and tactics, encouraged capital accumulation to ensure neolocality in each generation, and led to fewer but better-educated and more cherished children. Its demography was less dynamic than that of Ming China, but it was more securely founded. It was an élitist system which made marriage a privilege, not a universal expectation, and it left a residue of unmarried females (whereas in China it was males who were more likely to be unmarried) who had to be provided for in upmarket convents or as maiden-aunt teachers. Second, turning from kinship to association, but related to the first because of its similar emphasis on consent, commitment and contract, were the new religious orders: indeed, the beginning of orders, since the term cannot really be applied to the Benedictines before the expansion of the Cluniac connection. Such orders – Cistercians, Premonstratensians, Carthusians, Templars, Hospitallers, Franciscans, Dominicans, Carmelites, Bridgetines – were remarkable for their variety (eremitic, cenobitic, mixed, military and mendicant), degree of organization (St Stephen Harding's *Carta Caritatis* was the first European written constitution), and mutual acceptance of each other's vocations. Thus St Bernard of Clairvaux, not the founder of the Cistercians but their chief propagandist, was also involved in the foundation of the Templars and the Carthusians, an adviser of Popes but a critic of the Curia, and inspired the feminist piety of the convent of Helfta. Europe's subsequent secular pluralism was thus prefigured in the ecclesiastical sphere. Third, a further step in this direction was taken by the lay confraternities which proliferated across Latin Christendom in the period after 1300, often under mendicant auspices.[14] Confraternities, which mixed devotional, insurance and charitable activities, were less distinctive of Latin Christendom than religious orders since similar institutions inspired by Buddhism, Taoism, Confucianism or the Sinitic religion existed in medieval China, but they were more pervasive in Europe and more formally recognized. In Italy, where the movement started, Florence had six confraternities in 1250, 10 in 1275, 22 in 1300, 42 in 1375, and 52 in 1400. In 1453 Lille already had 40 confraternities, Bordeaux had 50 by 1500, Rouen 150 by 1550, while the rural diocese of Grenoble acquired 90 Holy Spirit confraternities over the same period. In England at the end of the Middle Ages there were around 30,000 confraternities: an average of three per parish, one for every 100 inhabitants, parishioners belonging often to two or three. England was a nation of guild members before it became a nation of shopkeepers; for the confraternities, whose officers had charge of many small investments and sources of income, were schools of management as well as Marial piety. Expressions of multiple sociability, their interactions and cross-memberships began the transformation of *Gemeinschaft* into *Gesellschaft*, civic community into civil society.

Meanwhile in China, meritocracy, as accredited by the examination system, continued its permeation of social institutions despite the Inner Asian irruption and the Ming revolution which for a time threatened it. It was in the Sung period that the examination system became a means of élite legitimation as well as a method of civil-service recruitment. Men now took the examinations who had no intention of making more than a minimal career in the bureaucracy. Aristocracy, however, except in the form of privileged imperial relatives, had ceased to be a factor in society. It was in the middle-Ming period that the examination system was at its most effective in promoting social mobility in the sense of raising new families to the bureaucracy. For the most part, however, though the examinations were fairly administered, its tendency was élitist, given the marginal advantages of family tradition, good education and library availability in conditions of intense competition – 50 or more candidates for every place. True, degree-holding was never the sole determinant of scholar-gentry (*shih*) membership; personal qualities, peer esteem, lineage prestige and wealth all played a part in the constitution of a class as much created by society as the state. In Kiang-nan, degree-holding was becoming so common as not necessarily to confer *shih* status. On the other hand, not all gentry were scholar-gentry in the sense of being subject to the Confucian *paideia*. The rural entrepreneurs, who extended Chinese agriculture in the Yangtze valley by deforestation, drainage and irrigation, sought social prestige and legitimation through association with local Buddhist, Taoist and Sinitic cults, from *ling*, spiritual power as well as from *wen*, cultural polish. Here, in contrast to the differentiation taking place in Latin Christendom, there was, as Edward L. Davis (2001) has shown, a process of hybridization between at the top, Confucian teachers, Buddhist monks and Taoist masters, at the bottom, village mediums (*wu*), and in the middle country technicians in exorcism, *fa-shih*, who mixed Tantric and Taoist rituals.[15] The result was a homogeneous structure both in town and country, capillary rather than articulated in character. Yet even at this level of military and magical subélites, a meritocratic colouring was being imparted as literacy spread, as writing manuals and models circulated, and as family documents were being composed. Confucian China, held together by a written word independent of sound and by the élites and subélites who possessed it, was coming into being both in the components of society and its arrangement.

As meritocracy matured and multiplied in China, in Latin Christendom, behind the triumphant aristocratic façade never more evident than in the fifteenth century, the rudiments of professionalism were beginning to shape arrangement between components. First, clerical professionalism, that technostructure of canonists and curialists which, reinforced by the rise of the universities and the development of scholastic method, provided the core of such bureaucracies as Latin Christendom possessed before 1500. Second, legal professionalism, whether in canon, civil or common law, which gave an adversarial cast to the social nexus of Latin Christendom quite different from the consensual bias in Chinese society. In England where the Inns of Court and Chancery had been emerging since the reign of Edward I, it has been argued, by W.K. Jordan (in his seminar teaching) for example, that lawsuits, generally civil actions over property, were becoming a greater bond in the later Middle Ages than kinship or even clientage. Third, not absent in China though there increasingly subject to mandarin direction, military professionalism which acquired new dimensions with the reception of gunpower and the deployment of nautical technology in oceanic voyaging. As China after Cheng Ho retreated to estuarial defence, Latin Christendom advanced to high-seas attack. Fourth, financial expertise, particularly in public finance and maritime insurance, neither well-developed in China where a strong state disdained loans and business preferred to limit risk rather than provide against it. In Latin Christendom, the Genoese invention of maritime insurance was diffused wherever there was substantial shipping and the Florentine bankers, the Bardi and the Peruzzi, lenders to popes and kings, became known as the pillars of Christendom. State bonds and marine underwriting became the first socially acceptable forms of business and market investment. From this basis in banking and insurance, there could develop the gentleman entrepreneur, a type rare in China until the eighteenth century. Fifth, medical professionalism, again not absent in China and indeed, if Needham is to be believed, pioneered there by medical examinations borrowed by Salerno via

Baghdad, but more prominent in Latin Christendom because of quarantine for plague. This was first developed by the Italian city states and then adopted by coastal principalities such as Provence and Catalonia before being taken up by the major territorial monarchies. Quarantine, though initially instituted in the teeth of received medical opinion, was the first demonstrably successful piece of preventive medicine, a triumph for applied reason and expertise. China, shielded from plague by reduced contact with Inner Asia after 1368 and the specificity of camel fleas, had no such imperative need for quarantine.

Meritocracy and professionalism may appear at first sight to be two sides of the same coin, but though they shared common enemies in kinship, prescription and ignorance and followed a common direction, their paths ultimately diverged. Meritocracy was rooted in a consensus of values and ends. Professionalism was rooted in the diversity of means and choices. Meritocrats were generalists, while professionals were specialists. The opposite of a professional was an amateur, a neutral term, but the opposite of meritocrat was at best someone lacking in merit and at worst a sociopath. Meritocracy swallowed politics, hence the ambiguity of the Chinese word *kuan* (civil servant or senior cadre), while professionalism coexisted with politics. Expertise, of course, existed in China: outstandingly in medicine, military technology, hydraulics, border control, bandit suppression and salt administration; but it was less-institutionalized into professional bodies than in the Latin West. Wang An-shih's attempt to make expertise part of bureaucratic merit was only partially successful and experts were relegated to the role of unofficial advisers or occasional troubleshooters. As Europe laid down the foundations of a technostructure, China consolidated a regime of Enarchs, tempered under the Ming by eunuch security services and occasional terror.

## Intellect, 1000–1500

Between 1000 and 1500, the intellectual spectrum of Latin Christendom widened both in complexity and plurality, while that of China contracted, a contraction not fully compensated for by an increase in depth in some of the areas still cultivated. As for the intellectual spectra of India, the Muslim world and Byzantium, they showed only local change.

In AD1000, the intellectual world of Latin Christendom was neither complex nor plural. The critical registers were largely untenanted while the categorical registers were occupied largely by single Benedictine tenants. This could no longer be said in 1500. Between the horizons of Sylvester II, pope in 1000, and Alexander VI, pope in 1500, a gulf was fixed. In the transit, the intellect had acquired new tools in paper, print and literary vernaculars, Arabic numerals and improved musical notation as well as new fields for their use. Consequently Latin Christendom now enjoyed a wider semantic field, an extended semiotic network, and a more active syncretic forum to reconcile conflicting messages. Development came both from within and without. The chief external influences came from the Muslim world with the exception of one significant loan from East Asia.

In the paradigmatic hemisphere, the European artistic repertoire was greatly extended between 1000 and 1500. In architecture, Romanesque at Vezelay and Durham went beyond late Antique imitation and prepared for the successive stages of Gothic which were then rivalled by the alternative aesthetic of a Great Renaissance standing in the line of a succession of earlier little renaissances. In painting, Roman and Florentine realism and decoration joined but did not supplant Sienese and Venetian illustration and colour. In vernacular literature, the *chansons de geste* were outmoded by the genre of *courtoisie*, which was followed by Dante's revival of the epic, Boccaccio's narrative invention, Petrarch's lyricism and Chaucer's conversational realism and humour. Similarly in music, the successive layers of plainchant, counterpoint and polyphony were being added, while in the pure formalism of mathematics, ancient arithmetic and geometry were, beginning with Adelard of Bath's translation of al-Khwarazmi, to be complemented by algebra. By the time of the Mertonians in the early fourteenth century, mathematics, already applied to both metaphysics and physics by Archbishop Bradwardine, was poised to become the handmaiden of science as the mechanical clock paradigm of reality took hold. Paradigmatic thinking, moreover, had ceased to be purely categorical. Dante's *De Vulgari Eloquentia* was arguably the first work of literary criticism since late antiquity, but Gothic architecture had already prompted a work of aesthetic theory in Abbot Suger's *Libellus de Consecratione Ecclesiae Sancti Dionysii* of 1144. Beauty and its nature had returned to the agenda, not least in the Rome of the restored papacy.

In the syntagmatic hemisphere, Latin Christendom made advances in both the categorical and critical quadrants. In the first, the advances affected both outlines and details. As regards outlines, two new segments were adumbrated. First, there was Aristotelianism, partly garnered from existing Latin works, notably Cicero, but mainly advanced from translations from the Arabic. Particularly through the translation of the commentaries of Averroes (Ibn Rushd), Aristotle was understood as the author of a separate philosophical system and not simply as a specialist in logic subordinate to Plato in metaphysics and to St Augustine in theology. The recognition of Platonism and Aristotelianism as non-isomorphic and incompatible provided Latin Christendom with its basic pluralism as Raphael indicated in his *School of Athens*. Second, as a result of the opening of the transcontinental routes by the Mongolian explosion, there was a further infusion of Chinese alchemy in its *wai-tan* medicinal form, as expressed in the writings of Roger Bacon, some texts ascribed to Albertus Magnus and in the teachings of Arnold of Villanova, all of which culminated in the early sixteenth century in the attempted medical revolution of Paracelsus. Alchemy may have been a delusion as chemotherapy and chemistry, but its advent in fuller form turned the systemic dichotomy of Platonism and Aristotelianism into an unstable trichotomy and helped to break the shell of a too-comprehensive essentialist science into which Aristotelianism threatened to confine the European mind by offering another paradigm.

Of the details, the most significant in the long run was the distinction derived from Avicenna (Ibn Sina) between essence and existence. Ancient philosophy had been essentialist and its preference had been continued by Christendom in the writings of St Augustine and John the Scot. Its focus was the concept, whether *ante rem*, *in re* or *post rem*, not the judgement. Its fundamental polarity was between the transient and the permanent rather than between the contingent and the necessary. The existential reorientation in philosophy which began during the Middle Ages came about through the introduction of Semitic thought forms into the Graeco-Roman inheritance, not as might have been expected via the Christian Bible, but through the more radical Hebraicism of Muslim philosophy, the short-lived successor to *kalam*. The first significant use of the essence/existence distinction was made by St Anselm of Canterbury in the famous ontological argument of his *Proslogion*, written at the end of the eleventh century. Here the distinction was used both to ground the existence of God independently of the character of the cosmos and to assert the uniqueness of God in that, in His case alone, essence implied existence. Anselm's critic, Gaunilo of Marmoutier, accepted the distinction but rejected the argument on the ground that existence was not a predicate, though he did not fully grasp its role as affirmed in judgement. Aquinas, coming after Abelard's *Sic et Non* and Peter Lombard's *Sentences*, did. While he rejected Anselm's argument for the existence of God, he accepted from a more existential standpoint the unique identity of essence and existence in God. Anselm assumed man's knowledge of God's essence and so could affirm His existence. Aquinas denied such knowledge, but argued that His existence could nevertheless be affirmed, not so much from the attributes of the cosmos, its essence, as from its contingency, its participated existence. In his thought, which utilized Aristotelianism while introducing the new Avicennan parameter, existence took precedence over essence, judgement over concept, the evidenced over the assumed. The Thomist world was rational but contingent: one whose quantitative properties, once Aristotelian essentialism had been discarded, could be investigated by science rearmed by mathematics.

The existential reorientation in categorical thinking led to an equally significant initiative in critical thinking.[16] In the philosophical debates in Oxford and Paris in the first half of the fourteenth century, two problems were at issue: epistemological, what was knowable, and, (here the critical element appeared) cognitional, how was it knowable. In cognition, Duns Scotus initiated the critical departure by making a distinction between *cognitio abstractiva* and *cognitio intuitiva*, rather in the manner of Newman's separation of inference and assent. *Cognitio abstractiva* was the Aristotelian process of thinking by abstraction, while *cognitio intuitiva* was its conclusion: not so much intuition in the modern sense as certification by a power of judgement akin to Newman's illative sense. In epistemology Scotus was less existentialist than Aquinas; both the minimum univocal *esse* with which cognition started, and the maximal singular *haecceitas* with which it concluded, belonged to the conceptual or essentialist sphere. Nevertheless, however conservative his intentions, Scotus had initiated a new critical way of doing philosophy which in a plurality of forms was taken up by a succession of thinkers: Peter Auriol, William of Ockham, Walter Chatton, Adam Wodeham, John of Reading, Nicholas of Autrecourt. Ockham's version was particularly innovatory. He stood Scotus on his head and put *cognitio intuitiva* at the beginning of the intellectual process rather than at the end. He made certification empirical rather than conceptual, existential more than essential, negative no less than positive. He thereby opened the way to positivism in science and scholarship and to minimalist consensualism in religion, though he may have seen himself more as providing a critical defence of Thomist existentialism against Scotus. Though later medieval scholasticism was subsequently given a bad name by humanists as logic for logic's sake, it was a first rehearsal of heuristics: the study of the method and unity of the sciences. With its appearance, Latin Christendom finally acquired a full panoply of intellectual registers.

While the intellectual world of Latin Christendom between 1000 and 1500 expanded in both complexity and pluralism, that of China contracted in both respects. Such advances as were made, and they were not inconsiderable, were rather in depth within a more limited compass. Some complexity and pluralism were to return in the six-teenth century with the Confucian critical initiative of Wang Yang-ming and the Buddhist reformation of Te-ch'ing and Chu-hung, but in 1500 such creativity was not conspicuous.

In the paradigmatic heart of Chinese thought, there was, however, a twofold increase in depth. On the one hand, with regard to pure formalisms, the Sung and the Yüan were the culmination point of Chinese algebra. Solutions were found by Chu Shih-chieh (early fourteenth century) for equations with up to four indeterminates, an achievement not matched in Europe until the seventeenth century. On the other hand, in the visual arts, the Sung and the Yüan were the high point of Chinese landscape painting in the work of such masters as Li Ch'eng, Fan K'uan, Kuo Hsi, Ma Yüan, Hsia Kuei and Ni Tsan. These men and their not much inferior successors in the fif-teenth century, created a new aesthetic: the *wen-jen hua*, the literary man's style, an intellectual expressionism which displayed the inner, integrated mind of the scholar through its outer portrayal of nature; whether as objects defining space, as in the so-called northern school, or as space defining objects, in the so-called southern school. This expressionism, supposedly the work of amateurs who despised expertise and professionalism, increasingly represented the main-stream of painting as an academicism without an academy.

Beyond the paradigmatic heartland, stratification replaced pluralism. Although individual Sung emperors such as Chen-tsung and Hui-tsung imitated their T'ang predecessors in being patrons of Taoism, both it and Buddhism, maintained by the Southern Sung gentry, were relegated to inferior rather than parallel places in official esteem as expressed in the examination system. In society, Taoism and Tantric Buddhism remained strongly represented in towns and villages, but in syncretized, unthematized forms. As Buddhist scholasticism fell out of fashion, so the critical metaphysics it had fostered fell into abeyance. The Sung period was the classic age in the formation of the schools of Ch'an Buddhism, which were then imported into Japan, as Zen; but Ch'an was only the intellectual man's anti-intellectualism, less an acquired contemplation than a literary genre of Rortian conversation.[17] The space vacated by Buddhism was not occupied by Confucianism. Neither of the two Sung neo-Confucian philosophical developments, the majoritarian rationalist school of Ch'eng I and Chu Hsi or the minoritarian idealist school of Ch'eng Hao and Lu Chiu-yuan, were critical in being based on cognitional analysis. Both were categorical in character, meta-ethics as much as metaphysics. Unlike scholasticism in Latin Christendom, they were not based on any new method of enquiry, hypothesis, argument, counter argument and judgement, such as Aquinas had perfected. Neo-Confucianism was speculative hermeneutics of a selected portfolio, the Four Books, within the classical canon. It, too, was a *wen-jen hua*, a literary man's philosophy, an expression of the Sung counter-revolution which preferred generalists to specialists, merit to professionalism. Its cosmology was a-systemic and instrumentalist in character: 'of our quality' as the early Jesuits recognized, but alien to the rational contingent and mathematically mediated universe they purveyed.[18]

Stratification was also a factor in the intellectual development of the centres of civilization between China and Latin Christendom. Islamdom expanded in both India and what had been the Byzantine world, so that their cultures had to retreat temporarily into subaltern institutions as ruling institutions modelled on the Mongol *ordo* state were established by the Mamluks and the Ottomans. The widespread disjuncture of politics and society contributed to a loss of intellectual confidence and the adoption of modes of withdrawal particularly in Hindu India and Orthodox Slavdom.

The early modern expansion of Europe is a historical commonplace even if its roots are still regarded as a riddle.[19] The late medieval expansion of the Muslim world following the Inner Asian irruption is less often remarked. The Mongolian explosion was an immense shock to Islamdom. It was a shock, however, which was survived, absorbed, even taken advantage of, by conversion of the conquerors, imitation of their political institutions to reconstruct the old sultanates which had failed to withstand the infidel onslaught, compensation by missionary activity in Black Africa and Southeast Asia, and at the intellectual level by a successful counter-reformation in religious practice. Here existing institutions such as the *haj* (more than a pilgrimage, also a focus of unity, an intellectual exchange and a source of élites) and the dervish orders or Sufi *tariqats* moved centrestage to substitute for the Abbasid caliphate of Baghdad, to add *masifa*, direct experience to *elm*, indirect acquaintance, and to supplement the *ulema* and the *sadr*, the too-lax oligarchy of jurists, mosque officials and local notables, in the leadership of the *umma*, the Islamic community.[20] If the *haj* was one and inimitable, the *tariqats* which were often associated with it as tour organizers and resident tutors at study centres in the Holy Places, were many and diverse. The Naqshbandiyya and Yassawiyya in Central Asia, the Chishtiyya in Muslim India, the Qadiriyya in Iraq, the Mevleviyya and Bektashiyya in the Ottoman empire, the Shadhiliyya in Muslim Egypt, differed in their intellectual outlook. Some, as regards the *sharia* were liberal, others conservative; some, in politics, militant, others quietistic; some learned, others professing ignorance. Their primary thrust, however, was always devotional: the performance of *dhikr* or *zikr*, 'commemoration', that is prayer, sometimes silent, sometimes aloud, often prolonged, supplementary, because more theocentric to *salat*, the regular Muslim fivefold prayer schedule at the mosque. The dervish orders represented a new form of pluralism without complexity. They created a parallel Islam focused on the *mazar*, the saint's tomb or the *zawiya*, the dervish hostel, not opposed to the mosque but an alternative polarity, less vulnerable in bad contexts, more inward in good. Dervishes could join the *ulema*: members of the Shadhiliyya were associated with the Azhar university in Cairo and the Naqshbandiyya supplied personel to the *medrese* of Bokhara;

but the truth at which they aimed, *al-Haqiqah* was esoteric (*batin*) and ineffable, a flight to the absolute, into what was more real than the world.

Comparison might here be made with Hesychasm, the most vital force in Eastern Orthodoxy in the later Middle Ages and with the *Suddhadvaita*, pure or consistent, non-duality movement, promoted in Hindu India by Vallabha in Gujerat and Caitanya in Bengal. They, too, were counter-reformations in the face of adverse circumstances, an appeal from the world to what lay beyond it. Yet the differences are more striking than the similarities. Where dervishism was plural, Hesychasm was one, a single lineage centred on Mount Athos. If one, it was also complex since it was rooted from the fourteenth century in the theology of Palamism, a philosophy of religion more critical than those of ibn al-Arabi and Jalal ad-Din Rumi, the theorists of the two forms of *dhikr*, silent and aloud. Moreover, while ibn al-Arabi saw the dervish flight as an ascent to *al-Haq*, the Truth, a kind of God beyond God, this was explicitly rejected by Palamism which taught that only the energies of God, an inferiorization of His being, were attainable by the contemplative, not His essence, which remained the unknowable Godhead. In this respect the Sufi was closer to the Latin contemplative, such as Ruysbroeck, than the Hesychast. The *Suddhadvaita* movement, on the other hand, was resolutely pantheist. It claimed indeed to be more consistently pantheistic than the other schools of Vedanta, including even that of Sankara. Firmly rooted in a partly critical philosophy of religion, *Suddhadvaita* was also multiple in that its object of devotion, Vishnu or Krishna, was the most protean of the Hindu divinities, at once Arjuna's charioteer and the ultimate Godhead. Hindu thought in the age of Vijayanagar thus retained its character as both complex and pluralistic. Now, however, in 1500 its standard of comparison had to be Latin Christendom rather than Ming China. Nevertheless, measured against this yardstick, it had once more, as in the days of the T'ang, to take second place. The reflux had brought Latin Christendom in matters intellectual to where China had stood at the end of the first millennium, just as it had done in matters social, economic and political. Before the expansion of Europe became conspicuous in territorial acquisistion, institutions, science and industry, the balance of advantage had returned to the West.

## Prognosis

It might appear that at the beginning of the third millennium, China enjoyed a set of advantages similar to those enjoyed by Latin Christendom just prior to its achievement of successive take-offs from the sixteenth century.

First, like Latin Christendom in 1500, China today possesses an idiosyncratic but effective political system which can limit violence both within and without.[21] It is able to make changes in leadership and policy without internal upheaval. With a background ideology which mixes Marxist technocracy and Paretan sociology, it has shown itself capable of working with market forces and globalization. Like Castile, it can be both a land and a seapower. It is in a position to take advantage of geopolitical changes, whether a shift to the Eurasian heartland as envisaged by Halford Mackinder and now promoted by global warming, or the replacement of the Atlantic by the Pacific as the mega-Mediterranean in an ongoing oceanic world order, previously adumbrated by Cheng Ho. Next, like Latin Christendom, the Chinese economy has shown itself capable of importing technology from economies more advanced than its own. This has particularly been so, as has been shown by Thomas G. Moore (2002) in highly competitive fields, very different in themselves, such as textiles and shipbuilding.[22] Here, Chinese producers have been faced by oversupply and a global buyers' market, yet have responded successfully against the bias of political technocracy by deregulation, market coordination and upmarketization of products. Shanghai, where many of these developments have their focus, has some of the features of sixteenth-century Antwerp: not a political capital, but a deltaic metropolis, the junction of two maritime systems, an oceanic terminus. Indeed, more than Antwerp, it is becoming a political power, an essential element in a winning coalition. Third, like Latin Christendom, contemporary Chinese social life, as the political conquest of society by a totalitarian state recedes, displays both strong family solidarities, especially where education is concerned, and multiple urban sociabilities, especially evident in Hong Kong. Together, and interconnected, these have the potential to create a civil society in counterpoise to both state and market. That such a potential has existed from late imperial times has been shown by William T. Rowe (1989) in his study of Hankow, the business quarter of the triple city of Wuhan.[23] Though temporarily submerged by totalitarianism, such familism and sociability may now resurface in more relaxed circumstances, perhaps stimulated by the reabsorption of Hong Kong and closer relations with Singapore. Finally, like Latin Christendom, as Chinese students pour into the world's universities, as Chinese scholars and scientists enter the international republic of letters, and as autochthonous religiosity returns with modern appurtenances in movements such as the *Fa-lun kung*, China's intellectual spectrum may be expected to increase in both complexity and pluralism. Peking could again become what it was in the 1920s: a place of intellectual ferment and Sino-foreign collaboration, a true ideopolis of post-industrial and educational services, such as formerly inspired Teilhard de Chardin in his vision of the convergence of the noosphere.

In all directions, then, as the veteran Kuomintang politician and proponent of a vitalist scientific humanism, Ch'en Li-fu, put it, the storm clouds are clearing over China.[24] What will be revealed will be a new imperial meridian, a second Hsüan-tsung or Ch'ien-lung *redivivus*, as the world order in all its dimensions reorients itself to become once more Sinocentric. Andre Gunder Frank could be justified by the future.

Two caveats may be entered against this hopeful scenario, one minor, one major, preceded by an introductory observation. The observation is that the gap between the People's Republic and the Western world today is probably greater than that between Latin Christendom and Ming China in 1500. Economic measurement is easier than political, social or intellectual assessment, but it is not straightforward, even if statistics are accurate. Different impressions of gross domestic product and per capita income will be given by exchange-rate parity and purchasing-power parity comparisons. Exchange-rate parity comparison, harder but more notional, gives the United States a gross domestic product eight times that of China and a per capita income thirty times. Purchasing-power parity comparison, softer but more real, will divide the disparity by as much as a factor of three, but the gap remains formidable, and the compensation afforded by purchasing-power parity computation will diminish as the two economies become more genuinely comparable in scale. On either estimate, China has a long way to go before achieving equality with the West, let alone dominance in the global economy. Whatever China's rates of growth, the West, too, will continue to grow. Indeed, China's very growth may so stimulate other parts of the global economy, including its current centre in the United States, as to make dominance a mirage and multipolarity progressively a reality. This is a point which will be elaborated in the major caveat.

The minor caveat to the scenario of a new Sinocentric world order based on the same kind of portfolio as that held by Latin Christendom in 1500 lies in consideration of detail in the four dimensions concerned.

First, in the political dimension, the states of Latin Christendom in 1500, whether constitutional or authoritarian in tendency, were highly legalized in character. Inns of court, *parlements*, *audiencias*, schools of canon law, plus an apparatus of charters, contracts and dispensations, were significant institutions. Consequently the lines between Church and state, state and society, the various institutions within society, and even between individuals, the foundational freedoms of modern constitutionalism, were in the course of demarcation. Contract and right, asserted by a powerful legal profession, were already basic, while in contemporary China the bias is still towards consensus, compromise or arbitration, the secret suppression of conflict rather than its open resolution. The People's Republic may be a constitutional state in the minimum sense of providing procedures for the orderly and non-violent transfer of power. It may have ceased being a totalitarian state in that it has withdrawn its power from a number of fields of activity. It may be becoming a post-ideological authoritarianism on the model of early Kuomintang Taiwan, though one may suspect that the ideology once manifest as system remains latent as shibboleth.[25] Nevertheless, China still has a long way to go before becoming a *Rechtstaat*, let alone a constitutional state in the fullest sense. Decision-making remains the result less of the leadership or of due process, than of an obscure and shifting parallelogram of forces generated by a multiplicity of horizontal and vertical connections: a polycratic chaos, albeit of a Mandelbrotian kind. The People's Republic may share idiosyncrasy with the Christian commonwealth of 1500; but it has yet to show that it is as politically effective. Post-Mao China is more suggestive of what Nazi Germany or Fascist Italy might have become had they survived the loss of the Führer and the Duce into an age of Speer and Ciano and to a third and fourth generation of leadership.

Second, in the economic dimension, business in the more developed centres of Latin Christendom in 1500 displayed financial sophistication, especially in the fields of public finance, banking and insurance, still not well-represented in the People's Republic. Even less-developed areas, such as Castile with its wool sales at Medina del Campo, its textile manufacture at Segovia, its marine underwriting at Burgos, or Naples with its active land market for Genoese capital, were more engaged in the world economy than is China today. Shanghai may be like Antwerp, and Hong Kong may be another Genoa, but they abut greater continental inertia, stronger vested interests, a heavier bureaucratic incubus, more risk-aversion, and deeper veins of inhibitory ideology than Flemish and Italian banking cities faced in the empire of Charles V. A stand-off between coastal and interior China, the blue and the yellow, as in the days of the Southern Sung or more briefly in the Warlord era, would seem as likely as the conquest of the second by the first. Such a schism might be unwittingly promoted by what has been called *nomenklatura* capitalism, the linking of political and business interests.[26] China has good traditions of both state action and small businesses, what has been less satisfactory is the *kuan-tu shang-pan* tradition of state/merchant partnership, of which *nomenklatura* capitalism could be regarded as a new form.

Third, in the social dimension, while China today has ongoing traditions of strong family bonds and multiple associative sociability, in two respects its society differs markedly from that of Latin Christendom in 1500; one negative, one positive. The element which would appear to be absent, or present in a lesser degree, is that of gender parity. In 1500, it might be argued whether Confucian dowagerism or Christian conjugalism made better use of female intelligence and initiative. The emergence of foot-binding under the Sung, however distasteful, does not seem to have curtailed women's activities as much as was once thought. The Yüan inherited a steppe tradition of political activity by princesses especially during interregna, and the wife of the their court painter Chao Meng-fu, Kuan Tao-sheng, herself a notable painter and poet, played a full part in the intellectual life of the time. Similarly, the House of Burgundy had established a tradition of politically active princesses such as Charles V's aunt Margaret of Austria, while in Italy aristocratic women such as Santa Francesca Romana and St Catherine of Genoa played a full part at least in new religious initiatives. In 2000, however, it can be scarcely doubted that feminism in some sense, the lineal descendent of the medieval *beatas* and mixed-gender confraternities, is the key to unlocking the full utilization of human capacity at every level of society. In contemporary China gender parity has still a long way to go in terms of party committees, boardroom appointments, faculty membership or senior clinical posts. The feminism championed in Mao's early writings which might have been forwarded by a Chiang Ch'ing regime, has yet to be fulfilled. If China lacks something Latin Christendom was already acquiring, it possesses something Latin Christendom lacked, a Communist party of 60 million, with their dependents, a fifth of the population, an élite with a less-positive function than their nearest analogues in Latin Christendom, the clergy and the nobility. Though successful societies can carry residuary classes, their parasitic presence can impede that success. The party today is neither a meritocracy nor a professional body, while its costs are considerable. Its euthanasia as a social institution through the decomposition of its functions should be a priority of a future leadership.[28] As Mao dimly perceived, the last revolution must be against the party itself.

Finally, in the intellectual dimension, while it may be hoped that China is on the threshold of a new and more profound May 4 movement, it is difficult to see in any of its registers, paradigmatic or syntagmatic, categorical or critical, performance or promise comparable to that of Latin Christendom in 1500. Then the Renaissance provided new paradigms in painting, sculpture and music, while Humanism provided in philology a sytagmatic advance which, because it was both empirical and falsifiable, may for the first time be called truly scientific. The two categorical developments in turn prompted critical reflection on how they had been achieved. China has yet to exhibit its Botticelli, Valla, Erasmus or Vasari. No pre-reformation seems in sight.

To the minor caveat of the non-equivalence, on closer inspection of Latin Christendom in 1500 with China in 2000, must now be added a major caveat to any prognosis of China's early return to centrality in the world order. The argument outlined above for a Chinese take-off assumed a single winning portfolio for rises to centrality on the part of a civilization or specific region of the world. More seriously, moreover, it assumed an ongoing position of centrality or hegemony which may be occupied by a succession of locations. It ignored the possibility that the Rise of the West in the second half of the second Christian millennium may have so changed not only the balance but the seesaw itself as to make these two assumptions unwarranted and enquiry based on them no longer in point.

That such a possibility is indeed the case would take another book to argue. Here, in conclusion, it can only be suggested that globalization has, to vary the metaphor, irreversibly altered the pitch and rules of the game as well as the relative strengths of the players. Globalization, in the sense of an interlocking set of institutions going beyond a world market, was begun by the Mongolian explosion, but was carried forward by the subsequent expansion of Latin Christendom. As a traditional Chinese historian might have put it, what was started by the barbarians of the steppe was continued by the barbarians of the sea. Initially the new world order was centred, at least economically, and successive capitals of the world market may be traced in Antwerp, Seville, Amsterdam and New York. Today the United States is the unique superpower in more than just a military or financial sense. Nevertheless, there are indications that globalization is entering a post-centric phase, the kind of non-hegemonistic system which has been ascribed to the Islamic world in the later Middle Ages.[27] The system of which the United States is the centre is one which seeks for partners, for others, for union rather than unity. It is programmed towards polycentricity, even pancentricity and ultimately a-centricity. As this term is approached, questions of rise and fall, hegemon and clients, centre and periphery will lose significance. Globalization is producing an Einsteinian universe in which there are no absolute places and times, but we have lived so long in a gravity-ridden solar system of power relations that we feel weightless and adrift in a galaxy of multiple suns with only an empty centre of their coexistence. In this sense, the rise of the West may never be reversed. No doubt new supernovae will appear in its firmament of which it may be hoped that a post-Communist China will be among the most brilliant, but Western institutions will continue to be copied, the values of the West cherished, and its English language, possibly with an Indian accent, universalized. Then civilizations will be extinguished by Civilization in a Teilhardian cosmopolis whose centre is everywhere and whose circumference is nowhere.

# Notes

## 1 Polemic: Before the Rise of the East

1 Luigi Luca Cavalli-Sforza, *Genes, Peoples, and Languages*, North Point Press, New York, 2000.
2 Andre Gunder Frank, *Reorient: Global Economy in the Asian Age*, University of California, Berkeley, 1998, p. 326.
3 *Ibid.*, p. 28.
4 *Ibid.*, p. 37.
5 *Ibid.*, p. 70.
6 *Ibid.*, p. 329.
7 *Ibid.*, pp. 338–9.
8 Jack A. Goldstein, *Revolutions and Rebellions in the Early Modern World*, University of California, Berkeley, 1991.
9 Frank, *op. cit.*, p. 169.
10 Richard Von Glahn, *Fountain of Fortune. Money and Monetary Policy in China 1,000–1,700*, University of California, Berkeley, 1996.
11 Frank, *op. cit.*, p. 153.
12 Immanuel Wallerstein, *The Modern World-System: Capitalist Agriculture and the Origins of the European World-Economy in the Sixteenth Century*, Academic Press, New York, 1974.
13 Frank, *op. cit.*, pp. 111–12.
14 *Ibid.*, p. 140.
15 *Ibid.*, pp. 141–2.
16 *Ibid.*, p. 117.
17 *Ibid.*, p. 127.
18 *Ibid.*, p. 157.
19 *Ibid.*, pp. 163–4.
20 *Ibid.*, p. 177.
21 *Ibid.*, p. 333.
22 *Ibid.*, p. 64.
23 *Ibid.*, p. 115.
24 *Ibid.*, p. 343.
25 *Ibid.*, p. 347.
26 *Ibid.*, p. 351.
27 Chris Patten, *East and West, The Last Governor of Hong Kong on Power, Freedom and the Future*, Macmillan, London, 1998, p. 130.
28 Cavalli-Sforza, *op. cit.*, p. 79.
29 Georgina Ferry, 'Finger Prints and Family Ties', *Oxford Today*, Michaelmas Issue, 2000, pp. 24–5.
30 *op. cit.*, p. 82.

31  Pierre Chaunu, *Seville et L'Atlantique* (1506–1650), Tome VIII (1), *Structures*, SEVPEN, Paris, 1959; Frédéric Mauro, *Le Portugal et L'Atlantique au XVII siècle (1570–1670)*, SEVPEN, Paris, 1960; Anthony Read, *Southeast Asia in the Age of Commerce 1450–1690*, Vol. I, *The Lands Below the Wind*, Yale University Press New Haven, 1988; Robert Delort, *Le Commerce des Fourrures en Occident à la fin du Moyen Age*, 2 vols, École Française de Rome, Rome, 1978.

32  Richard von Glahn, *Fountain of Fortune*, *op. cit.*, pp. 60, 272.

33  Philip C.C. Huang, *The Peasant Family and Rural Development in the Yangzi Delta 1350–1988*, Stanford University Press, Stanford, 1990.

34  Janet Abu-Lughod, *Before European Hegemony: The World System AD 1250–1350*, Oxford University Press, New York, 1989.

35  Jean-Louis Escudier, 'Kondratieff et L'Histoire Économique Française ou La Recherche Inachevée', *Annales, Économics Sociétés, Civilisations*, 48 (2), March–April 1993, pp. 359–83; Joseph Alois Schumpeter, *Business Cycles*, McGraw Hill, New York, 1939.

36  Roger Penrose, *The Emperor's New Mind*, Vintage, London, 1990, pp. 197–9.

37  G. Tchalenko, *Villages antiques de la Syrie du Nord*, 3 vols., Bibl. archéologique et historique, 50, Paris, 1953–58; Roger S. Bagnall, *Egypt in Late Antiquity*, Princeton University Press, Princeton, New Jersey, 1993; John Wacher, *Roman Britain*, Wren Park, London, 2000.

38  Paul Veyne, *Le Pain et Le Cirque. Sociologie Historique d'une Pluralisme Politique*, Seuil, Paris, 1976; Jean Durliat, *De La Ville Antique à la ville Byzantine: Le Probleme Des Subsistences*, École Française de Rome, Rome, 1990.

39  Edward E. Cohen, *Athenian Economy and Society: A Banking Perspective*, Princeton University Press, Princeton. New Jersey, 1992. Seleucid Antioch was essentially an Athenian colony.

40  Elizabeth Wayland Barber, *The Mummies of Ürümchi*, Norton, New York, 1999, pp. 201–2.

## 2  Politics: The Genius of T'ang

1  Omeljan Pritsak, *The Origins of Rus*, Vol. I, *Old Scandinavian Sources other than the Sagas*, Harvard University Press, Cambridge, Mass., 1981.

2  Holmes H. Welch and Anna Seidel (eds), *Facets of Taoism, Essays in Chinese Religion*, Yale University Press, New Haven and London, 1929; Richard B. Mather, 'K'ou Ch'ien-chih and the Taoist Theocracy at the Northern Wei Court, 425–451', pp. 103–22.

3  T.H. Barrett, *Taoism under the T'ang: Religion and Empire during the Golden Age of Chinese History*, Wellsweep, London, 1996.

4  John K. Fairbank (ed.), *The Chinese World Order*, Harvard University Press, Cambridge. Mass., 1968.

5  Richard Guisso, *Wu Tse-t'ien and the Politics of Legitimation*, University of California Press, Berkeley, 1978; Antonino Forte, *Political Propaganda and*

*Ideology in China at the End of the Seventh Century*, Columbia University Press, New York, 1976.

6   Kenneth S. Ch'en, *Buddhism in China, A Historical Survey*, Princeton University Press, Princeton, New Jersey, 1964.

7   Lin Lu-tche, translated and completed by R. des Rotours, *Le Règne de L'Empereur Hiuan-tsong (713–756)*, Collège de France, Paris, 1981; Edward H. Schafer, *The Golden Peaches of Samarkand*, University of Californnia Press, Berkeley and Los Angeles, 1963.

8   Lin, *op. cit.*, pp. 135–9.

9   Lin, *ibid.*, p. xlvi.

10  Lin, *ibid.*, pp. 331–4, 418–56, 475–6.

11  D.C. Twitchett, *Financial Administration Under the T'ang Dynasty*, Cambridge University Press, Cambridge, 1963.

12  Wang Gung-wu, *The Structure of Power in North China During the Five Dynasties*, Stanford University Press, Stanford, 1967.

13  Paul J Smith, *Taxing Heaven's Storehouse: Horses, Bureaucrats and the Destruction of the Sichuan Tea Industry 1074–1224*, Harvard University Press, Cambridge, Mass., 1991.

14  John Keay, *India, a History*, HarperCollins, London, 2000.

15  Daniel Pipes, *Slave Soldiers in Islam: The Genesis of a Military System*, Yale University Press, New Haven, 1981.

16  P. Crone and M. Cook, *Hagarism: The Making of the Islamic World*, Cambridge University Press, Cambridge, 1977.

17  Richard W. Bulliet, *The Camel and the Wheel*, Harvard University Press, Cambridge, Mass., 1975.

18  Patricia Crone, 'Islam, Judeo-Christianity and Byzantine Iconoclasm', *Jerusalem Studies in Arabic and Islam*, Vol. 2, 1980, pp. 59–75.

19  Patricia Crone and Martin Hinds, *God's Caliph, Religious Authority in the First Centuries of Islam*, Cambridge University Press, Cambridge, 1986.

20  Almoor Dhanani, *The Physical Theory of Kalam: Atoms, Space and the Void in Basrian Mutazili Cosmology*, E.J. Brill, Leiden, 1994; Crone and Hinds, *op. cit.*

21  Patricia Crone, *Slaves on Horses, The Evolution of Islamic Polity*, Cambridge University Press, Cambridge, 1980; Daniel Pipes, *op. cit.*

22  Dimitri Obolensky, *The Byzantine Commonwealth*, Weidenfeld & Nicolson, London, 1971.

23  Jean-Marie Martin, *La Pouille de VIᵉ au XIIᵉ siècle*, École Française de Rome, Rome, 1993.

24  Raymond Van Dam, *Leadership and Community in Late Antique Gaul*, University of California Press, Berkeley, 1985; Richard Fletcher, *The Barbarian Conversion: From Paganism to Christianity*, Henry Holt, New York, 1997.

25  Luce Pietri, *La Ville de Tours du IVᵉ au VIᵉ siècle*, École Française de Rome, Rome, 1983, pp. 157–69, 768–86.

26  Colloques Internationales du Centre National de la Recherche Scientifique, *Jean Scot Erigène et L'Histoire de la Philosophie*, ECNKS, Paris, 1977.

27 André Vauchez (ed.), *Lieux Sacrés, Lieux de Culte, Sanctuaires*, École Française de Rome, Rome, 2000.
28 Pierre Toubert, *Les Structures de Latium Medieval*, École Française de Rome, Rome, 1973.
29 Richard Fletcher, *The Quest for El Cid*, Oxford University Press, Oxford, 1991; Henry Chadwick, *Priscillian of Avila: The Occult and the Charismatic in the Early Church*, Oxford University Press, Oxford, 1976, pp. s232–3.

## 3 Economy: China takes Centre-Stage

1 Jean-Noel Biraben, *Les Hommes et La Peste*, Mouton, The Hague, 1975.
2 William H. McNeill, *Plagues and People*, Anchor, New York, 1998; Daniel Panzac, *La Peste dans L'Empire Ottoman 1700–1850*, Peeter, Louvain, 1985.
3 Mary Kilbourne Matossian, *Poisons of the Past: Moulds, Epidemics and History*, Yale University Press, New Haven, Conn., 1987.
4 Pierre Darmon, *La Grande Traque de la Variole*, Perrin, Paris, 1986; Joseph Needham. *Science and Civilisation in China, Vol. 6 Biology and Biological Technology, Part VI, Medicine*, Cambridge University Press, Cambridge, 2000, pp. 124–7.
5 Needham, *op. cit.*, p. 150; Richard W. Bulliet, *The Camel and the Wheel*, Harvard University Press, Cambridge, Mass., 1975.
6 Graham Twigg, *The Black Death: A Biological Reappraisal*, Batsford, London, 1984.
7 Edward H. Schafer, *The Vermilion Bird: T'ang Images of the South*, University of California, Berkeley, 1967.
8 John McNeill, 'Chinese Environmental History in World Perspective', unpublished paper, July 1994.
9 Jurgen Kovacs and Paul U. Unschuld (eds), *Essential Subtleties on the Silver Sea: The Yin-hai jing-wei, A Chinese Classic on Ophthalmology*, University of California Press, Berkeley, 1998, pp. 43–8.
10 Charlotte Furth, *A Flourishing Yin: Gender in China's Medical History, 960–1665*, University of California, Berkeley, 1999.
11 Nigel Lawson, *The View from No.11: Memoirs of a Tory Radical*, Bantam, London, 1992, p. 424.
12 Michel Cartier, 'Aux origines de l'agriculture intensive du Bas Yangzi', *Annales, Économies, Sociétés, Civilisations*, 46(5), Sept.–Oct. 1991, pp. 1009–19.
13 Yoshida Tora, *Salt Production Techniques in Ancient China*, Brill, Leiden, 1993.
14 Philip C.C. Huang, *op. cit.*, pp. 21–43.
15 Richard von Glahn, *The Country of Streams and Grottoes: Expansion, Settlement and the Civilizing of the Sichuan Frontier in Song Times*, Harvard University Press, Cambridge, Mass., 1987.
16 Paul J. Smith, *op. cit.*
17 Harriet J. Zurndorfer, *Change and Continuity in Chinese Local History: The Development of Hui-chou Prefecture, 800–1800*, Brill, Leiden, 1989.

18  E.B. Vermeer (ed.), *Development and Decline of Fukien Province in the 17th and 18th centuries*, Brill, Leiden, 1990.

19  Joseph Needham, *The Development of Iron and Steel Technology in China*, Newcomen Society, London, 1958; *Science and Civilisation in China*, Volume 5, *Chemistry and Chemical Technology*, Part VII, *Military Technology: The Gunpowder Epic*, Cambridge University Press, Cambridge, 1986.

20  Robert Finley, 'The Pilgrim Art: The Culture of Porcelain in World History', unpublished paper, Arkansas, 1996.

21  Joseph Needham, *Science and Civilisation in China*, Volume 5, *Chemistry and Chemical Technology*, Part I, *Paper and Printing*, by Tsien Tsuen-Hsuin, Cambridge University Press, Cambridge, 1985; Joseph Needham, L. Wang and D.J. de S. Price, *Heavenly Clockwork*, Cambridge University Press, Cambridge, 1960; Elizabeth L. Eisenstein, *The Printing Press as an Agent of Change: Communications and Cultural Transformations in Early Modern Europe*, 2 vols, Cambridge University Press, Cambridge, 1979; David S. Landes, *Revolution in Time: Clocks and the Making of the Modern World*, Harvard University Press, Cambridge, Mass., 1983.

22  Catharine Jami and Hubert Delahaye (eds), *L'Europe en Chine: Interactions Scientifiques, Religieuses et Culturelles au XVII et XVIII siècles*, College de France, Paris, 1993.

23  Karl A. Wittfogel and Feng Chia-sheng, *History of Chinese Society. Liao (907–1125)*, American Philosophical Society, Philadelphia, 1949.

24  Needham, *Science and Civilisation in China*, Volume 5, Part VI, *op. cit.*, pp. 111–13.

25  Sucheta Mazumdar, *A History of the Sugar Industry in China: The Political Economy of a Cash Crop in Guangdong. 1644–1886*, UMI, Ann Arbor, Michigan, 1994.

26  For the signiffance of the *lou*, which is also found in New Guinea the original home of sugar, and in pre-Columbian America where it was used in salt production, I am indebted to conversations with Mr Patrick Hase of Hong Kong in July 2001.

27  Jacques Gernet. *Les Aspects Économiques du Bouddhisme dans la Société Chinoise de $V^e$ au $X^e$ siècle*, École Française d'Extrème Orient, Saigon, 1956.

28  Gilles Lipovetsky *L'Empire de l'Éphémère, La Mode et son Destin dans les Sociétés Modernes*, Gallimard, Paris, 1987, p. 154.

29  *Ibid.*, p. 13.

30  *Ibid.*, p. 79.

31  *Ibid.*, p. 38.

32  Didior Gazagnadou, *La Poste à Relais: La Diffusion d'une Technique de Pouvoir à travers l'Eurasie – Chine, Islam, Europe*, Editions Kimé, Paris, 1994, pp. 28–38.

33  Hill Gates, *China's Motor: A Thousand Years of Petty Capitalism*, Cornell University Press, Ithaca, 1996.

34  Janice E. Stockard, *Daughters of the Canton Delta: Marriage Patterns and*

*Economic Strategies in South China, 1860–1930*, Stanford University Press, Stanford, California, 1989, pp. 170–1.

35  Paul J. Smith, *op. cit.*, pp. 305–17.

36  David Herlihy, *The Black Death and the Transformation of the West*, Harvard University Press. Cambridge, Mass., 1997; Norman F. Cantor, *In the Wake of the Plague: The Black Death and the World it made*, Simon & Schuster, New York, 2001.

37  Warren Treadgold, *A Concise History of Byzantium*, Palgrave Macmillan, Basingstoke, 2001.

38  Roger Collins, *Early Medieval Europe 300–1000*, Palgrave Macmillan, Basingstoke, 1999.

39  Matossian, 1987, *op. cit.*

40  Hubert van Zeller, *The Benedictine Idea*, Burns Oates, London, 1959, p. 45.

## 4  Society: A Multiple China

1  Gérard Delille. *Famille et Propriété dans Le Royaume de Naples (XV$^e$–XIX$^e$ Siècle)*, École Française de Rome, Rome, 1985.

2  Delille, *op. cit.*, p. 382.

3  Francis Fukuyama, *The End of History and the Last Man*, Hamish Hamilton, London, 1992. pp. 235–44; *Trust: The Social Virtues and the Creation of Prosperity*, Hamish Hamilton, London, 1995, pp. 61–146, 416.

4  Tony Saich, *Governance and Politics of China*, Palgrave Macmillan, Basingstoke, 2001, pp. 241–71.

5  James Hayes, *South China Village Culture*, Oxford University Press, Oxford, 2001, pp. 29–31.

6  Lin, *op. cit.*, pp. 452–6.

7  Richard von Glahn, *The Country of Streams and Grottoes, op. cit.*, pp. 37–67; F. von Richthofen, *Baron Richthofen's Letters 1870–1872*, North China Herald, Shanghai, 1903, pp. 164–5.

8  Arthur P. Wolf and Chieh-shan Huang, *Marriage and Adoption in China 1845–1945*, Stanford University Press, Stanford, 1980.

9  Stockard, *op. cit.*, pp. 170–5.

10  Richard von Glahn, *op. cit.*, *The Country of Streams and Grottoes*, p. 161.

11  Wolf and Huang, *op. cit.*, pp. 89–90.

13  Howard S. Levy, *The Lotus Lovers: The Complete History of the Curious Erotic Custom of Footbinding in China*, Prometheus, Buffalo, 1966.

14  Fukuyama, *Trust, op. cit.*, pp. 130–1, 92.

15  Alain Huetz de Lemps and Jean-Robert Pitte (eds), *Les Restaurants dans le monde et à travers les âges*, Editions Glenat, Grenoble, 1990, pp. 67–77.

16  Lin, *op. cit.*, pp x, 175.

17  Peter Ackroyd, *London: The Biography*, Vintage, London, 2001, p. 188.

18  Denys Lombard, *Le Carrefour Javanais: Essai d'Histoire Globale*, 3 vols, École des Hautes Etudes en Sciences Sociales, Paris, 1990, II, pp. 131–208.

19  Eve Levin, *Sex and Society in the World of the Orthodox Slavs 900–1700*, Cornell University Press, Ithaca, 1989, p. 135.

20  Jack Goody, *The Development of the Family and Marriage in Europe*, Cambridge University Press, Cambridge, 1984, pp. 31–48, 101–5, 197–8.

21  Victor Saxer, *Sainte-Marie-Majeure: Une basilique de Rome dans L'histoire de la ville et son église*, École Française de Rome, Rome, 2001, pp. 101–6.

22  Levin, *op. cit.*, p. 20.

23  Evelyne Patlagean, *Pauvreté Économique et Pauvreté Sociale à Byzance 4ᵉ–7ᵉ siècles*, Mouron, Paris, 1977.

24  G. Dagron. *Constantinople Imaginaire*, PUF, Paris, 1984.

25  Bernard J.F. Lonergan, *Insight: A Study of Human Understanding*, Philosphical Library, New York, 1970, p. 212.

26  Richard Fletcher, *The Barbarian Conversion: From Paganism to Christianity*, Holt, New York, 1998, p. 155.

27  Martin, *op. cit.*, pp. 171–3, 532–62.

28  Étienne Hubert, *Espace Urbain et Habitat à Rome, Du Xᵉ siècle à la fin du XIIIe siècle*, École Française de Rome, Rome, 1990, pp. 64–70, 134–8.

29  Sharon Farmer, *Communities of Saint Martin: Legend and Ritual in Medieval Tours*, Cornell University Press, Ithaca, 1991.

30  Richard Fletcher, *Bloodfeud, Murder and Revenge in Anglo-Saxon England*, Penguin, London, 2002.

## 5  Intellect: China's Complex Pluralism

1  Charles Morazé, *Les Bourgeois Conquérants (XIXᵉ siècle)*, Armand Colin, Paris, 1959.

2  Claude Lévi-Strauss, *Mythologiques IV, L'Homme Nu*, Plon, Paris, 1971, pp. 575–86.

3  Chow Kai-wing, *The Rise of Confucian Ritualism in Late Imperial China: Ethics, Classics and Lineage Discourse*, Stanford University Press, Stanford, California, 1994.

4  Charles Hartman, *Han Yü and the T'ang Search for Unity*, Princeton University Press, Princeton, New Jersey, 1986.

5  Holmes H. Welch, *The Parting of the Way: Lao Tzu and the Taoist Movement*, Beacon Press, Boston, 1957; Holmes H. Welch and Anna Seidel (eds), *Facets of Taoism*, 1929, *op. cit.*; Michel Strickmann, *Le Taoisme de Mao Chan: Chronique d'une révélation*, Institut des Hautes Études Chinoises, Paris, 1981; Nathan Sivin, editor and introduction by Joseph Needham, *Science and Civilisation in China*, Vol. 6, *Biology and Biological Technology*, Part VI, *Medicine*, Cambridge University Press, Cambridge, 2000.

6  Welch and Seidel, *op. cit.*, p. 166.

7  Edward L. Davis, *Society and the Supernatural in Song China*, University of Hawaii Press, Honolulu, 2001.

8  Nathan Sivin (ed.), *Science and Technology in East Asia: Selection fron Isis*, Science History Publications, New York, 1977.

9  N.J. Girardot, *Myth and Meaning in Early Taoism*, Faber, London, 1983.

10  Isabelle Robinet, *Méditation Taoiste*, PUF, Paris, 1979.

11  Franciscus Verellen, *Du Guangting (850–933): Taoiste de Cour à la fin de la Chine Médiévale*, College de France, Paris, 1989; Suzanne E. Cahill, *Transcendence and Divine Passion: The Queen Mother of the West in Medieval China*, Stanford University Press, Stanford, 1993.

12  Cahill, *op. cit.*, p. 244.

13  L.S. Cousins, 'The Dating of the Historical Buddha: a Review Article', *Journal of the Royal Asiatic Society'*, vol. 6, part I, April 1996, pp. 57–63.

14  Richard H. Robinson, *Early Madhyamika in India and China*, Madison, Milwaukee and London, 1967.

15  Étienne Lamotte (ed.), *Le Traité de la Grande Vertu de Nagarjuna (Mahaprajnaparamitasastra)*, 4 vols, Louvain, 1944, 1949, 1970, 1978; K. Venkata Ramanam, *Nagarjuna's Philosophy as presented in the Mahaprajnaparamitasastra*, Rutland, Vermont and Tokyo, 1966.

16  Robinson, *op. cit.*, p. 27.

17  Fung Yu-lan, *A History of Chinese Philosophy*, Vol. II, Princeton University Press, Princeton, New Jersey, 1953, p. 377.

18  Thomas Cleary (ed.), *The Flower Ornament Scripture, A Translation of the Avatamsaka Sutra*, 3 vols, Shambhala, Boulder and London, 1984.

19  *Ibid.*, Vol. I, p. 190.

20  *Ibid.*, Vol. III, p. 365.

21  Lin, *op. cit.*, pp. 87–94.

22  Davis, *op. cit.*, pp. 294–8.

23  *Ibid.*, pp. 245–6.

24  *Ibid.*, pp. 21–4.

25  John Langerwey, *Wu-shang pi-yao: Somme Taoiste de VI$^e$ siècle*, École Française d'Extrême Orient, Paris, 1981.

26  J.H. Elliot, *The Count – Duke of Olivares: The Statesman in an Age of Decline*, Yale University Press, New Haven and London, 1986, p. 561.

27  Verellen, *op. cit.*, pp. 129–32.

28  Davis, *op. cit.*, pp. 2–9.

29  Richard J. Smith, *Fortune-Tellers and Philosphers: Divinition in Traditional Chinese Society*, Westview Press, Boulder, 1991, pp. 13–48, 49–91, 131–72; Davis, *op. cit.*, pp. 87–114, 156–70.

30  Welch and Seidel, *op. cit.*, pp. 53–82.

31  Davis, *op. cit.*, pp. 9–10, 88

32  *Ibid.*, pp. 115–52.

33  Barber, *op. cit.*, pp. 189–205.

34  Richard C. Foltz, *Religions of the Silk Road: Overland Trade and Cultural Exchange from Antiquity to the Fifteenth Century*, St Martin's Press, New York, 1999.

35  *The Times*, London, 3 August 2002.

36  Saxer, *op. cit.*, pp. 54–5.

37  *The Times*, London, 23 February 2001.

38  Samuel Lieu, *Manichaeism in the Later Roman Empire and Medieval China*, Manchester University Press, Manchester, 1985; *Manichaeism in Mesopotamia and the Roman East*, Brill, Leiden, 1994.

39  Donald D. Leslie, *The Survival of the Chinese Jews*, Brill, Leiden, 1972; Michael Pollack, *Mandarins, Jews and Missionaries*, Jewish Publication Society, Philadelphia, 1980.

40  Patricia Crone, 'Islam, Judeo-Christianity and Byzantine Conoclasm', *op. cit.*

41  Dahnani, *op. cit.*

42  Foltz, *op. cit.*, p. 48.

43  Nigel Wilson, *Scholars of Byzantium*, University of London, London, 1983.

44  John O'Meara (ed.), *Eriugena: Periphyseon (The Division of Nature)*, Dumbarton Oaks, Washington, 1987, p. 244.

45  Fletcher, *Bloodfeud, op. cit.*, pp. 119–20.

## 6   Return to the West: Reflux and Prognosis

1  Herbert Franke and Denis Twitchett (eds), *The Cambridge History of China: Volume 6 Alien Regimes and Border States, 907–1368*, Cambridge University Press, Cambridge, 1994; F.W. Mote, *Imperial China 900–1800*, Harvard University Press, Cambridge, Mass., 1999.

2  Karl A. Wittfogel and Feng Chia-sheng, *op. cit.*

3  Arthur Waldron, *The Great Wall of China, From History to Myth*, Cambridge University Press, Cambridge, 1990.

4  Clifford M. Foust, *Rhubarb: The Wondrous Drug*, Princeton University Press, Princeton, New Jersey, 1992.

5  Paul J. Smith, *op. cit.*

6  L.N. Gumilev, *Searches for an Imaginary Kingdom: The Legend of the Kingdom of Prester John*, Cambridge University Press, Cambridge, 1987.

7  John Fennel, *The Crisis of Medieval Russia 1200–1304*, Longmans, London, 1983; Charles J. Halpern, *Russia and the Golden Horde: The Mongol Impact on Medieval Russian History*, Indiana University Press, Bloomington, 1985.

8  Joseph Needham, L. Wang and D.J. de S. Price; Landes; Anne Curry (ed.), *Agincourt 1415: Henry V, Sir Thomas Erpingham and the Triumph of the English Archers*, Tempus, Stroud, 2000.

9  Mote, *op. cit.*, pp. 743–50.

10  Jean Delumeau, *La Peur en Occident (XIVᵉ–XVIIIᵉ siècle)*, Fayard, Paris, 1978.

11  Joseph Needham, *Science and Civilisation in China*, Vol. 5, *Chemistry and Chemical Technology, Part I: Paper and Printing, op. cit.*

12  Gazagnadou, *La Poste à Relais.*

13  Jean-Claude Hocquet, *Le Sel et La Fortune de Venise*, Vol. 2, *Voiliers et Commerce en Mediterranée 1200–1650*, Presses Universitaire de Lille, Lille, 1979.

14  Jonathan Barry, 'Identité urbaine et classes moyennes dans L'Angleterre Moderne', *Annales, Économies, Sociétés, Civilisations*, July–August 1993, pp. 853–83; Gervase Rosser, 'Les fraternités urbaines anglaises à la fin du Moyen Age'; *Annales, Économies, Sociétés, Civilisations*, 48(5), September–October 1993, pp. 1127–43; Jean Delumeau, *Rassurer et Protéger: Le Sentiment de Securité dans l'Occident d'autrefois*, Fayard, Paris, 1989, pp.

250–60, 385–94; Eamon Duffy, *The Stripping of the Altars: Traditional Religion in England 1400–1580*, Yale University Press, New Haven and London, 1992, pp. 142–54.

15  Davis, *op. cit.*, pp. 211–21; Timothy Brook, 'Gentry Dominance in Chinese Society. Monasteries and Lineages in the Structuring of Local Society, 1500–1700', PhD dissertation, Harvard University, 1984.

16  Katherine M. Tachau, *Vision and Certitude in the Age of Ockham: Optics, Epistemology and the Foundations of Semantics 1250–1340*, Brill, Leiden, 1988.

17  Bernard Faure, *Chan Insights and Oversights: An Epistemological Critique of the Chan Tradition*, Princeton Iniversity Press, Princeton, New Jersey, 1993.

18  Jean-Claude Martzloff, 'Espace et Temps dans les textes Chinois d'Astronomie et technique Mathématique astronomique aux XVIIe et XVIIIe siécles', in Catherine Jami and Hubert Delahaye (eds), *L'Europe en Chine: Interactions Scientifiques, Religieuses et Culturelles aux XVII et XVIII siècles*, College de France, Paris, 1993, pp. 217–30, p. 228; Antonella Romano, *La Contre-Réforme Mathématique: constitution et diffusion d'une culture jesuite mathématique à la Renaissance (1540–1640)*, École Française de Rome, 1999.

19  Alan Macfarlane, *The Riddle of the Modern World: Of Liberty, Wealth and Equality*, Palgrave Macmillan, Basingstoke, 2000.

20  Soraya Faroqhi, *Pilgrims and Sultans: The Hajj under the Ottomans 1517–1683*, I.B. Tauris, London, 1994; Michael Gilsenan, *Saint and Sufi in Modern Egypt: An Essay in the Sociology of Religion*, Clarendon, Oxford, 1973; A. Popovic and G. Veinstein (eds), *Les Ordres Mystique dans L'Islam: Cheminements et Orientations actuelles*, École des Haute Etudes en Sciences Sociales, Paris, 1986.

21  Saich, *op. cit.*

22  Thomas G. Moore, *China in the World Market: Chinese Industry and International Sources of Reform in the Post-Mao Era*, Cambridge University Press, Cambridge, 2002.

23  William T. Rowe, *Hankow, Conflict and Community in a Chinese City 1796–1895*, Stanford University Press, Stanford, 1989.

24  Ch'en Li-fu, *The Storm Clouds Clear over China*, Hoover Institution Press, California, 1994.

25  Andrew Nathan and Bruce Gilley, 'China's New Rulers, What they want', *New York Review of Books*, vol. xlx, no. 5, 10 October 2002, pp. 28–32.

26  Saich, *op. cit.*, p. 105.

27  Abu-Lughod, *op. cit.*

28  David Zweig, *Internationalizing China, Domestic Interests and Global Linkages*, Columbia University Press, Ithaca, 2002.

# Bibliography

Abu-Lughod, J. (1989) *Before European Hegemony: The World System AD 1250–1350*. Oxford: Oxford University Press.

Ackroyd, P. (2001) *London: The Autobiography*. London: Vintage.

Bagnall, R.S. (1993) *Egypt in Late Antiquity*. Princeton, New Jersey: Princeton University Press.

Barber, E.W. (1999) *The Mummies of Ürümchi*. New York: Norton.

Barrett, T.H. (1996) *Taoism under the T'ang: Religion and Empire during the Golden Age of Chinese History*. London: Wellsweep.

Barry, J. (1993) 'Identité urbaine et classes moyennes dans L'Angleterre Moderne', *Annales, Économies, Sociétés, Civilisations*, 48: 4, July–August, pp. 853–83.

Biraben, J.-N. (1975) *Les Hommes et La Peste*. The Hague: Mouton.

Bobbitt, P. (2002) *The Shield of Achilles*. London: Penguin.

Brandel, F. (1974) *Capitalism and Material Life 1400–1800*. London: Collins Fontana.

Brook, T. (1984) '*Gentry Dominance in Chinese Society: Monasteries and Lineages in the Structuring of Local Society, 1500–1700*', PhD dissertation, Harvard University.

Bulliet, R.W. (1975) *The Camel and the Wheel*. Cambridge, Mass.: Harvard University Press.

Cahill, S.E. (1993) *Transcendence and Divine Passion: The Queen Mother of the West in Medieval China*. Stanford: Stanford University Press.

Cantor, N.F. (2001) *In the Wake of the Plague: The Black Death and the World it made*. New York: Simon & Schuster.

Cartier, M. (1991) '*Aux origines de l'agriculture intensive du Bas Yangzi*', *Annales, Économies, Sociétés, Civilisations*, 46: 5, September–October, pp. 1009–19.

Cavalli-Sforza, L.L. (2000) *Genes, Peoples and Languages*. New York: North Point Press.

Chadwick, H. (1976) *Priscillian of Avila: The Occult and the Charismatic in the Early Church*. Oxford: Oxford University Press.

Chaunu, P. (1959) *Séville et Atlantique (1506–1650)*. Tome VIII (1), Structures, S.E.V.P.E.N., Paris.

Ch'en, K.S. (1964) *Buddhism in China, A Historical Survey*. Princeton, New Jersey: Princeton University Press.

Ch'en, Li-fu (1994) *The Storm Clouds Clear Over China*. California: Hoover Institution Press.

Chow, Kai-wing (1994) *The Rise of Confucian Ritualism in Late Imperial China: Ethics, Classics and Lineage Discourse*. Stanford, California: Stanford University Press.

Cleary, T. (ed.) (1984) *The Flower Ornament Scripture: A Translation of the Avatamsaka Sutra*. Boulder and London: Shambhala.

Cohen, E.E. (1992) *Athenian Economy and Society: A Banking Perspective*. Princeton, New Jersey: Princeton University Press.

Collins, R. (2001) *Early Medieval Europe 300–1000*. Basingstoke: Palgrave Macmillan.

Colloques Internationales du Centre National de la Recherche Scientifique (1977) *Jean Scot Érigène et L'Histoire de la Philosophie*. Paris: ECNRS.

Cousins, L.S. (1996) 'The Dating of the Historical Buddha: A Review Article', *Journal of the Royal Asiatic Society*, vol. 6, part I, April, pp. 57–63.

Crone, P. (1980) *Slaves on Horses, The Evolution of Islamic Polity*. Cambridge: Cambridge University Press.

Crone, P. (1980) 'Islam, Judeo-Christianity and Byzantine Iconoclasm', *Jerusalem Studies in Arabic and Islam*, vol. 2, pp. 59–75.

Crone, P. and Cook, M. (1977) *Hagarism: The Making of the Islamic World*. Cambridge: Cambridge University Press.

Crone, P. and Hinds, M. (1986) *God's Caliph, Religious Authoriiity in the First Centuries of Islam*. Cambridge: Cambridge University Press.

Curry, A. (ed.) (2001) *Agincourt 1415: Henry V, Sir Thomas Erpingham and the triumph of the English Archers*. Stroud: Tempus.

Dagron, G. (1984) *Constantinople Imaginaire*. Paris: PUF.

Darmon, P. (1986) *La Grande Traque de la Variole*. Paris: Perrin.

Davis, E.L. (2001) *Society and the Supernatural in Song China*. Honolulu: University of Hawaii Press.

De La Vaissière (2002) *Histoire des Marchands Sogdiens*. Paris: Collège de France.

Delille, G. (1985) *Famille et Propriété dans Le Royaume de Naples (XV$^e$–XIX$^e$ siècle)*. Rome: École Française de Rome.

Delort, R. (1978) *Le Commerce des Fourrures en Occident à la fin du Moyen Age*. 2 vols., Rome: École Française de Rome.

Delumeau, J. (1978) *La Peur en Occident (XIV$^e$–XVIII$^e$ siècle)*. Paris: Fayard.

Delumeau, J. (1989) *Rassurer et Proteger: Le Sentiment de Securité dans l'Occident d'autrefois*. Paris: Fayard.

Dhanani, A. (1994) *The Physical Theory of Kalam: Atoms, Space and the Void in Basrian Mutazili Cosmology*. Leiden: E.J. Brill.

Duffy, E. (1992) *The Stripping of the Altars: Traditional Religion in England 1400–1580*. New Haven and London: Yale University Press.

Durliat, J. (1990) *De la Ville Antique à la Ville Byzantine: Le Problème des Subsistences*. Rome: École Française de Rome.

Eisenstein, E.L. (1979) *The Printing Press as an Agent of Change: Communications and Cultural Transformations in Early Modern Europe*, 2 vols. Cambridge: Cambridge University Press.

Elliott, J.H. (1986) *The Count-Duke of Olivares: The Statesman in an Age of Decline*. New Haven and London: Yale University Press.

Escudier, J.-L. (1993) 'Kondratieff et L'Histoire Économique Francaise ou la Recherche Inachevée'. *Annales Économies, Sociétés, Civilisations*, 48: 2, March–April, pp. 359–83.

Fairbank, J.K. (ed.) (1968) *The Chinese World Order*. Cambridge, Mass.: Harvard University Press.

Farmer, S. (1991) *Communities of Saint Martin: Legend and Ritual in Medieval Tours*. Ithaca: Cornell University Press.

Faroqhi, S. (1994) *Pilgrims and Sultans: The Hajj under the Ottomans 1517–1683*. London: I.B. Tauris.

Faure, B. (1993) *Chan Insights and Oversights: An Epistemological Critique of the Chan Tradition*. Princeton, New Jersey: Princeton University Press.

Fennel, J. (1983) *The Crisis of Medieval Russia 1200–1304*. London: Longman.

Ferry, G. (2000) 'Finger Prints and Family Ties', *Oxford Today*, Michaelmas Issue, pp. 24–25.

Finley, R. (1996) *'The Pilgrim Art: The Culture of Porcelain in World History'*. Arkansas: unpublished paper.

Fletcher, R. (1991) *The Quest for El Cid*. Oxford: Oxford University Press.

Fletcher, R. (1997) *The Barbarian Conversion: From Paganism to Christianity*. New York: Henry Holt.

Fletcher, R. (2002) *Bloodfeud, Murder and Revenge in Anglo-Saxon England*. London: Penguin.

Foltz, R.C. (1990) *Religions of the Silk Road: Overland Trade and Cultural Exchange from Antiquity to the Fifteenth Century*. New York: St Martin's Press.

Forte, A. (1976) *Political Propaganda and Ideology in China at the End of the Seventh Century*. New York: Columbia University Press.

Foust, C.M. (1992) *Rhubarb: The Wondrous Drug*. Princeton, New Jersey: Princeton University Press.

Frank, A.G. (1998) *ReOrient, Global Economy in the Asian Age*. Berkeley: University of California.

Franke, H. and Twitchett, D. (eds) (1994) *The Cambridge History of China*, Volume 6, *Alien Regimes and Border States 907–1368*. Cambridge: Cambridge University Press.

Fukuyama, F. (1992) *The End of History and the Last Man*. London: Hamish Hamilton.

Fukuyama, F. (1995) *Trust: The Social Virtues and the Creation of Prosperity*. London: Hamish Hamilton.

Fung, Yu-lan (1953) *A History of Chinese Philosophy*, vol. II, Princeton, New Jersey: Princeton University Press.

Furth, C. (1999) *A Flourishing Yin: Gender in China's Medical History 960–1665*. Berkeley: University of California.

Gates, H. (1996) *China's Motor: A Thousand Years of Petty Capitalism*. Ithaca: Cornell University Press.

Gazagnadou, D. (1994) *La Poste à Relais: La Diffusion d'une technique de Pouvoir à travers l'Eurasie – Chine, Islam, Europe*. Paris: Editions Kine.

Gernet, J. (1956) *Les Aspects Économiques du Boudhisme dans la Société Chinoise de Vᵉ au Xᵉ siècle*. Saigon: École Française d'Extrême Orient.

Gilsenan, M. (1973) *Saint and Sufi in Modern Egypt: An Essay in the Sociology of Religion*. Oxford: Clarendon.

Girardot, N.J. (1983) *Myth and Meaning in Early Taoism*. London: Faber.

Glahn, R. von, (1987) *The Country of Streams and Grottoes: Expansion, Settlement and the Civilizing of the Sichuan Frontier in Song Times*. Cambridge, Mass.: Harvard University Press.

Glahn, R. von, (1996) *Fountain of Fortune, Money and Monetary Policy in China 1000–1700*. Berkeley: University of California Press.

Goldstein, J.A. (1991) *Revolutions and Rebellions in the Early Modern World*. Berkeley: University of California.

Goody, J. (1984) *The Development of the Family and Marriage in Europe*. Cambridge: Cambridge University Press.

Guisso, R. (1978) *Wu Tse-t'ien and the Politics of Legitimation*. Berkeley: University of California Press.

Gumilev, L.N. (1987) *Searches for an Imaginary Kingdom: The Legend of the Kingdom of Prester John*. Cambridge: Cambridge University Press.

Halpern, C.J. (1985) *Russia and the Golden Horde: The Mongol Impact on Medieval Russian History*. Bloomington: Indiana University Press.

Hartman, C. (1986) *Han Yü and the T'ang Search for Unity*. Princeton, New Jersey: Princeton University Press.

Hayes, J. (2001) *South China Village Culture*. Oxford: Oxford University Press.

Herlihy, D. (1997) *The Black Death and the Transformation of the West*. Cambridge, Mass.: Harvard University Press.

Hocquet, J.-C. (1979) *Le Sel et la Fortune de Venise, vol. 2, Voiliers et Commerce en Méditerranée 1200–1650*. Lille: Presses Universitaires de Lille.

Huang, P.C.C. (1990) *The Peasant Family and Rural Development in the Yangzi Delta 1350–1988*. Stanford: Stanford University Press.

Hubert, É. (1990) *Éspace Urbain et Habitat de Rome, Du $x^e$ siècle à la fin du $xiii^e$ siècle*. Rome: École Française de Rome.

Huetz de T.A. and Pitte, J.-R. (eds) (1990) *Les Restaurants dans le monde et à travers les âges*. Grenoble: Editions Glenat.

Jami, C. and Delahaye, H. (eds) (1993) *L'Europe en Chine: Interactions Scientifiques, Religieuses et Culturelles au $xvii^e$ et $xviii^e$ siècles*. Paris: College de France.

Keay, J. (2000) *India, a History*. London: HarperCollins.

Kovacs, J. and Unschuld, P.U. (eds.) (1998) *Essential Subtleties on the Silver Sea: The Yin-hai jing-wei, A Chinese Classic on Ophthalmology*. Berkeley: University of California.

Lamotte, E. (ed.) (1944, 1949, 1970, 1978) *Le Traité de la Grande Vertu de Nagarjuna (Mahaprajnaparamitasastra)*, 4 vols, Louvain.

Landes, D.S. (1983) *Revolution in Time: Clocks and the Making of the Modern World*. Cambridge, Mass.: Harvard University Press.

Langerwey, J. (1981) *Wu-shang pi-yao: Somme Taoiste de $vi^e$ siècle*. Paris: École Française d'Extrême Orient.

Lawson, N. (1992) *The View from No. 11: Memoirs of a Tory Radical*. London: Bantam.

Leslie, D.D. (1972) *The Survival of the Chinese Jews*. Leiden: Brill.

Lévi-Strauss, C. (1971) *Mythologiques IV, L'Homme Nu*. Paris: Plon.

Levin, E. (1989) *Sex and Society in the World of the Orthodox Slavs 900–1700*. Ithaca: Cornell University Press.

Levy, H.S. (1966) *The Lotus Lovers: The Complete History of the Curious Erotic Custom of Footbinding in China*. Buffalo: Prometheus.

Lieu, S. (1985) *Manichaeism in the Later Roman Empire and Medieval China*. Manchester: Manchester University Press.

Lieu, S. (1994) *Manichaeism in Mesopotamia and the Roman East*. Leiden: Brill.

Lin, Lu-tche, translated and completed by R. des Rotours, (1981) *Le Règne de L'Empereur Hiuan-tsong (713–756)*. Paris: College de France.

Lipovetsky, G. (1987) *L'Empire de l'Éphémère, La Mode et son Destin dans les Sociétés Modernes*. Paris: Gallimard.

Lombard, D. (1990) *Le Carrefour Javanais: Essai d'Histoire Globale*, 3 vols. Paris: École des Hautes Etudes en Sciences Sociales.

Lonergan, B.J.F. (1970) *Insight: A Study of Human Understanding*. New York: Philosophical Library.

Macfarlane, A. (2001) *The Riddle of the Modern World: Of Liberty, Wealth and Equality*. Basingstoke: Palgrave Macmillan.

Martin, J.-M. (1993) *La Pouille de vi$^e$ au xii$^e$ siècle*. Rome: École Française de Rome.

Martzloff, J.-C. (1993) 'Éspace et Temps dans les textes Chinois d'Astronomie et technique mathématique astronomique au xvii$^e$ et xviii$^e$ siècles', in C. Jumi and H. Delahaye (eds), *L'Europe en Chine: Interactions Scientifiques, Religieuses et Culturelles au xvii$^e$ et xviii$^e$ siècles*. Paris: Collège de France.

Mather, R.B. (1981) 'K'ou Chien-chih and the Taoist Theocracy at the Northern Wei Court, 425–451', in H. Welch and A. Seidel (eds), *Facets of Taoism, Essays in Chinese Religion*. New Haven and London: Yale University Press.

Matossian, M.K. (1989) *Poisons of the Past: Moulds, Epidemics and History*. New Haven and London: Yale University Press.

Mauro, F. (1960) *Le Portugal et L'Atlantique au xvii$^e$ siècle (1570–1670)*. Paris: SEVPEN.

Mazumdar, S. (1994) *A History of the Sugar Industry in China: The Political Economy of a Cash Crop in Guangdong, 1644–1836*. Michigan: UMI Ann Arbor.

McNeill, J. (1994) 'Chinese Environmental History in World Perspective', unpublished paper, July.

McNeill, W.H. (1998) *Plagues and People*. New York: Anchor.

Moore, T.G. (2002) *China in the World Market: Chinese Industry and International Sources of Reform in the Post-Mao era*. Cambridge: Cambridge University Press.

Morazé, C. (1959) *Les Bourgeois Conquérants (xix$^e$ siècle)*. Paris: Armand Colin.

Mote, F.W. (1999) *Imperial China 900–1800*. Cambridge, Mass.: Harvard University Press.

Musil, R. (1979) *The Man without Qualities*, 3 vols, London: Picador.

Nathan, A. and Gilley, B. (2002) 'China's New Rulers: What They Want', *New York Review of Books*, vol xlix, no. 5, 10 October, pp. 28–32.

Needham, J. (1958) *The Development of Iron and Steel Technology in China*. London: Newcomen Society.

Needham, J. (1985) *Science and Civilisation in China*, vol. 5, *Chemistry and Chemical Technology*, part I, *Paper and Printing* by Tsien Tsuen-Hsuin. Cambridge: Cambridge University Press.

Needham, J. (1986) *Science and Civilisation in China*, vol. 5, *Chemistry and Chemical Technology*, part VII, *Military Technology: The Gunpowder Epic*. Cambridge: Cambridge University Press.

Needham, J. (2000) *Science and Civilisation in China*, vol. 6, *Biology and Biological Technology*, part VI, *Medicine*. Cambridge: Cambridge University Press.

Needham, J., Wang, L. and Price, D.J. de S. (1960) *Heavenly Clockwork*. Cambridge: Cambridge University Press.

Obolensky, D. (1971) *The Byzantine Commonwealth*. London: Weidenfeld & Nicolson.

O'Meara, J. (ed.) (1987) *Eriugena: Periphyseon (The Division of Nature)* Washington: Dumbarton Oaks.

Panzac, D. (1985) *La Peste dans L'Empire Ottoman 1700–1850*. Louvain: Peeter.

Patlagean, E. (1977) *Pauvreté Économique et Pauvreté Sociale à Byzance 4ᵉ–7ᵉ siècles*. Paris: Mouton.

Patten, C. (1998) *East and West, The Last Governor of Hong Kong on Power, Freedom and the Future*. London: Macmillan.

Penrose, R. (1990) *The Emperor's New Mind*. London: Vintage.

Pietri, L. (1983) *La Ville de Tours du IVᵉ au VIᵉ siècle*. Rome: École Française de Rome.

Pipes, D. (1981) *Slave Soldiers in Islam: The Genesis of a Military System*. New Haven: Yale University Press.

Pollock, M. (1980) *Mandarins, Jews and Missionaries*. Philadelphia: Jewish Publication Society.

Popovic, A.G. Veinstein, (eds) (1986) *Les Ordres Mystiques dans L'Islam: Cheminements et Orientations actuelles*. Paris: École des Hautes Etudes en Sciences Sociales.

Pritsak, O. (1981) *The Origins of Rus*, vol. I, *Old Scandinavian Sources other than the Sagas*. Cambridge, Mass.: Harvard University Press.

Ramanan, K.V. (1966) *Nagarjuna's Philosophy as presented in the Mahaprajnaparamitasastra*. Vermont and Tokyo: Rutland.

Reid, A. (1988) *Southeast Asia in the Age of Commerce 1450–1690*, vol. I, *The Lands Below the Wind*. New Haven: Yale University Press.

Richthofen, F. von, (1903) *Baron Richthofen's Letters 1870–1872*. Shanghai: North China Herald.

Robinet, I. (1979) *Méditation Taoiste*. Paris: PUF.

Robinson, R.H. (1967) *Early Madhyamika in India and China*. Milwaukee and London: Madison.

Romano, A. (1999) *La Contre-Réforme Mathématique: constitution et diffusion d'une culture Jesuite mathématique à la Renaissance (1540–1640)*. Rome: École Française de Rome.

Rosser, G. (1993) 'Les Fraternités urbaines anglaises à la fin du Moyen Age', *Annales, Économies, Sociétés, Civilisations*, 48: 5, September–October, pp. 1127–43.

Rowe, W.T. (1989) *Hankow, Conflict and Community in a Chinese City 1796–1895.* Stanford: Stanford University Press.

Saich, T. (2001) *Governance and Politics of China.* Basingstoke: Palgrave Macmillan.

Saxer, V. (2001) *Sainte-Marie-Majeure: Une basilique de Rome dans L'histoire de la Ville et son église.* Rome: École Française de Rome.

Schafer, E.H. (1963) *The Golden Peaches of Samarkand.* Berkeley and Los Angeles: University of California Press.

Schafer, E.H. (1967) *The Vermilion Bird: T'ang Images of the South.* Berkeley: University of California Press.

Schumpeter, J.A. (1939) *Business Cycles.* New York: McGraw-Hill.

Sivin, N. (ed.) (1977) *Science and Technology in East Asia: Selections from Isis.* New York: Science History Publications.

Sivin, N. (2000) editor and introduction by J. Needham, *Science and Civilisation in China,* vol. 6, *Biology and Biological Technology,* part VI, *Medicine.* Cambridge: Cambridge University Press.

Skidelsky, R. (1992) *John Meynard Keynes. The Economist as Saviour 1920–37.* London: Macmillan.

Smith, P.J. (1991) *Taxing Heaven's Storehouse: Horses, Bureaucrats and the Destruction of the Sichuan Tea Industry 1074–1224.* Cambridge, Mass.: Harvard University Press.

Smith, R.J. (1991) *Fortune-Tellers and Philosophers: Divination in Traditional Chinese Society.* Boulder: Westview Press.

Stockard, J.E. (1989) *Daughters of the Canton Delta: Marriage Patterns and Economic Strategies in South China, 1860–1930.* Stanford, California: Stanford University Press.

Strickman, M. (1981) *Le Taoisme de Mao Chan: Chronique d'une révélation.* Paris: Institut des Hautes Études Chinoises.

Tachau, K.M. (1988) *Vision and Certitude in the Age of Ockham: Optics, epistemology and the foundations of semantics 1250–1340.* Leiden: Brill.

Tchalenko G. (1953–58) *Villages antiques de la Syrie du Nord,* 3 vols., Bibl. archéologique et historique, 50, Paris.

*The Times* (2001) London, 23 February.

Toubert, P. (1973) *Les Structures de Latium Médiéval.* Rome: École Française de Rome.

Treadgold, W. (2001) *A Concise History of Byzantium.* Basingstoke: Palgrave Macmillan.

Twigg, G. (1984) *The Black Death: A Biological Reappraisal.* London: Batsford.

Twitchett, D. (1963) *Financial Administration under the T'ang Dynasty.* Cambridge: Cambridge University Press.

Van Dam, R. (1985) *Leadership and Community in Late Antique Gaul.* Berkeley: University of California Press.

Vauchez, A. (ed.) (2000) *Lieux Sacrés, Lieux de Culte, Sanctuaires.* Rome: École Française de Rome.

Verellen, F. (1989) *Du Guangting (850–933): Taoiste de Cour à la fin de la Chine Médiéval.* Paris: Collège de France.

Vermeer, E.B. (ed.) (1990) *Development and Decline of Fukien Province in the 17th and 18th Centuries*. Leiden: Brill.

Veyne, P. (1976) *Le Pain et le Cirque, Sociologie Historique d'une Pluralisme Politique*. Paris: Seuil.

Wacher, J. (2000) *Roman Britain*. London: Wren Park.

Waldron, A. (1990) *The Great Wall of China, from History to Myth*. Cambridge: Cambridge University Press.

Wallerstein, I. (1974) *The Modern World-System: Capitalist Agriculture and the Origins of the European World-Economy in the Sixteenth Century*. New York: Academic Press.

Wang, Gung-Wu (1967) *The Structure of Power in North China During the Five Dynasties*. Stanford: Stanford University Press.

Welch, H.H. (1957) *The Parting of the Way: Lao Tzu and the Taoist Movement*. Boston: Beacon Press.

Welch, H. and Seidel, A. (eds) (1979) *Facets of Taoism, Essays in Chinese Religion*. New Haven and London: Yale University Press.

Wilson, N. (1983) *Scholars of Byzantium*. London: University of London.

Wittfogel, K.A. and Chia-sheng, Feng (1949) *History of Chinese Society: Liao (907–1125)*. Philadelphia: American Philosophical Society.

Wolf, A.P. and Chieh-shan, Huang (1980) *Marriage and Adoption in China 1845–1945*. Stanford: Stanford University Press.

Yang, L.S. (1965) *Essays in Sinology*. Cambridge, Mass.: Harvard University Press.

Yoshida, T. (1993) *Salt Production Techniques in Ancient China*. Leiden: Brill.

Zeller, H. van, (1959) *The Benedictine Idea*. London: Burns Oates.

Zurndorfer, H.J. (1989) *Change and Continuity in Chinese Local History: The Development of Hui-chou Prefecture, 800–1800*. Leiden: Brill.

Zweig, D. (2002) *Internationalizing China: Domestic Interests and Global Linkages*. New York: Columbia University Press.

# Index

Printed in the United States
113464LV00002B/29/A